SOUTHERN TIMBERMAN

Archer H. Mayor

SOUTHERN TIMBERMAN

The Legacy of William Buchanan

The University of Georgia Press / Athens & London

Athens, Georgia 30602

Designed by Richard Hendel
Set in Linotron Plantin
The paper in this book meets the guidelines for permanence and durability of the Committee on Production Guidelines for Book Longevity of the Council on Library Resources.

Printed in the United States of America

92 91 90 89 88 5 4 3 2 1

Library of Congress Cataloging in Publication Data
Mayor, Archer H.
Southern timberman: the legacy of William Buchanan / Archer H. Mayor.
p. cm.
Bibliography: p.
Includes index.
ISBN 0-8203-0999-0 (alk. paper)
1. Buchanan, William, 1849–1923. 2. Businessmen—Southern States—Biography. 3. Lumber trade—Southern States—History. 4. Family corporations—Southern States—History. 5. Company towns—Southern States—History. I. Title.
HD9760.B83M39 1988
338.7′63498′0975—dc19 87-22897
CIP

British Library Cataloging in Publication Data available

In memory of James Heldt,

a dear friend to many in this book.

Contents

Illustrations

Acknowledgments

William Buchanan and the people who followed in his footsteps were remarkably private individuals. My standard historian's dream of uncovering "the" diary or the batch of revealing letters was therefore remote before I started, two years ago, to trace this lumber company's evolution.

As things turned out, at least concerning the years from 1849 to 1946, "remote" was an understatement. Not only were letters and diaries out of the question, but so were business correspondence, company files, financial ledgers, and even, to a large extent, newspaper articles. What remained, and what forms the backbone of this study, were the company minute books, the personal tax rolls, periodical and technical literature of the time, and, most important, the reminiscences of people ranging from 32 to 106 years old.

Traditionally, historical methodology prefers that writers spend their initial research time digging through the basic background texts—newspapers, history books, magazines, and whatever. Thus armed with all the signposts of the times, they can approach the human survivors of the era under scrutiny with a certain amount of specialized intelligence. Less time is wasted asking the informant common-knowledge questions, and there is a higher likelihood that the questioner will be able to truly probe the depths of the subject's memories.

I could ill afford this organized approach. By the time I came upon William Buchanan's one-hundred-year-plus legacy, most of the major characters had already died. In many instances, their children or the people who had worked for them survived, but just barely. Time was pressing, and did not allow me to do my homework before setting out on the road, tape recorder in hand.

As a result, I'm sure many of the people I interviewed were

impressed by my ignorance. I knew little of their world, even less of their particular activities, and was sometimes totally oblivious to major characters that figured in the overall story. It is with deep appreciation that I thank them all here for their patience and for the hours they spent leading me through their lives. It is also with great sadness that I must reveal that my backward strategy was well planned. Already at this date, many of the people who helped me extensively are no longer alive.

Below is a list of almost everyone who shared their time and knowledge with me, often adding scrapbooks, photographs, articles, and maps—so many, in fact, that I could only include a small percentage in the following pages. While risking a cliché, I must stress that without these people, this book could never have been written.

Joe Ahearn
Mac Anderson
A. William Asmuth
Mrs. Douglas Bemis
Lynn Blackman
Walter Blount
Bennett Boskey
Don Brennan
Addys Brown
Robert A. Brown
Thomas R. Brown
Henry G. Buchanan
Willard Buchanan
Charles L. Cabe
Horace Cabe
Charles Carlton
Paul Carnahan
Henry Clepper
A. G. Cockerham
Burton Combes
John Connor
Mildred Cabe Cook
Claude Albritton
Mildred Andrews
Searcy Atkinson
Viola Bird
Lloyd Blackwell
Robert Bolton
Vernon Bremberg
Joe Brennan
Almah Buchanan Brown
T. Richard Brown
William C. Brown
Robert Buchanan
Hugh Burnham
Harold Cabe
Thomas Campbell
John Carnahan
Katy Caver
Mrs. Warren Clohisy
Mr. and Mrs. Truman Collins
A. L. Connor
Mary Connor
Mr. and Mrs. Alred Cross

Allen Crowell
Richard L. Crowell
William Davis
Dan Dennington
Aubrey Drake
Mrs. George Easley
William Farrar
G. L. Frye
John Geilfuss
Shirley Hamm
Wade Hanson
Richard Harrington
James Heldt
Whit Holman
Emmett Jaques
Robert Johnston
Mr. and Mrs. Robert Kasten
Graydon Kitchens
Mr. and Mrs. Arthur Kroos
William Kyle
Zelle Whitmarsh Letts
Fred Madison
Betty Marcus
Robert Maxwell
Billie Jean McCain
Felton O. McDonald
R. D. McMurrough
Alice Pack Melly
Jesse Miller
Josh Morriss
Mr. and Mrs. Carl Muenzner
W. T. Murphy
Harrison Nesby
Leland Nichols
Mary O'Boyle
Robert O'Boyle
William O'Boyle
R. D. Crowell III
Hannah Seeger Davis
Ellis Dawson
Mr. and Mrs. Frank Doughty
Mike Driscoll
Lloyd Ewing
Carlton Frazier
William Fuller
F. R. Goyens
Gene Hanes
Tim Harrington
Florida Harris
Jean Hoff
Mary Ellen Horter
Clara Johnson
Willie Jones
Volley Kees
Mr. and Mrs. Theodore Klein
Mrs. B. S. Krouse
Oscar Lee
Louise Lherisson
J. Q. Mahaffey
Herbert Marshall
Michael Mayor
Ray McCann
Arlo McKinnon
Mrs. Fleet Magee
James Melvin
William Morris
Mrs. J. O. Moore
Roger Mulvihill
Harry Nelson
Mrs. Harry Nichols
Randy Nixon
Nancy O'Boyle
Thomas O'Boyle
Robert O'Connor

Rachel Palmer
D. W. Payne
Floyd Perritt
Bernard Poland
June Ponder
W. Read Porter
Dorothy Portier
Henry Reuss
Richard Rice
Cleveland Riser
David Rode
Polly Pack Rowley
Alex Sanderson
Sophie Schroeder
Robert Schuyler
Elsie Seals
Eugene Searles
Steve Sexton
Jean Skinner
Charles Skinners
Hugh Slugg
Robert Smith
Wilbur Smith
William Stark
Mrs. R. W. Stephenson
W. Harold Sturgis
Mrs. Briner Thomas
Walton Thomas
Herman Uihlein
John Uihlein
Betty Ann Waldheim
Carrie Walker
Ed Walker
Laurence Walker
Lena Walker
Robert Waltz
C. O. Wanvig
Glen Ward
Henry Ward
Temple Webber
William Webster
James Westbrook
George Weyerhaeuser
James Whelan
T. J. Wilbanks
Bryan Williams
Tom Wilson
Jeanette Winters

Undoubtedly some names have been omitted. If this is the case, I offer my regrets and my thanks to those unmentioned few. In addition to the above, there were many others whose names I didn't catch but whose aid was invaluable. They for the most part were employed by organizations as diverse as the Library of Congress and the mayor's office of Minden, Louisiana. I wish I could list all the courthouses, state archives, universities, colleges, local newspaper offices, libraries, and historical societies and commissions that gave me help, but the list would be both too long and incomplete. I extend to them all my gratitude.

Finally, there is a small handful of people whose support and hours of labor on my behalf deserve special mention. Without their help, this book would have been a lesser thing indeed. My thanks to Ana and Brantz Mayor, Ponnie Derby, Dorothy Olson, Nancy Fischer, and most of all Mary O'Boyle II.

Archer H. Mayor
May 1985

Note to Readers

This book is filled with quotes. From the outset, I wanted it to be a volume in which as many people as possible were allowed their own voices. During the interview process, however, I encountered many who were willing to share their memories, but only anonymously. Rather than have some speakers identified and others not, I have decided to leave all of them nameless.

This decision, of course, leaves no one accountable for the contents of the quoted passages except myself. That is as it should be. If anyone takes exception to what follows, whether it be in my words or someone else's, I stand alone as the one to blame.

The Buchanan Family Tree
(The Company-Related Branches)

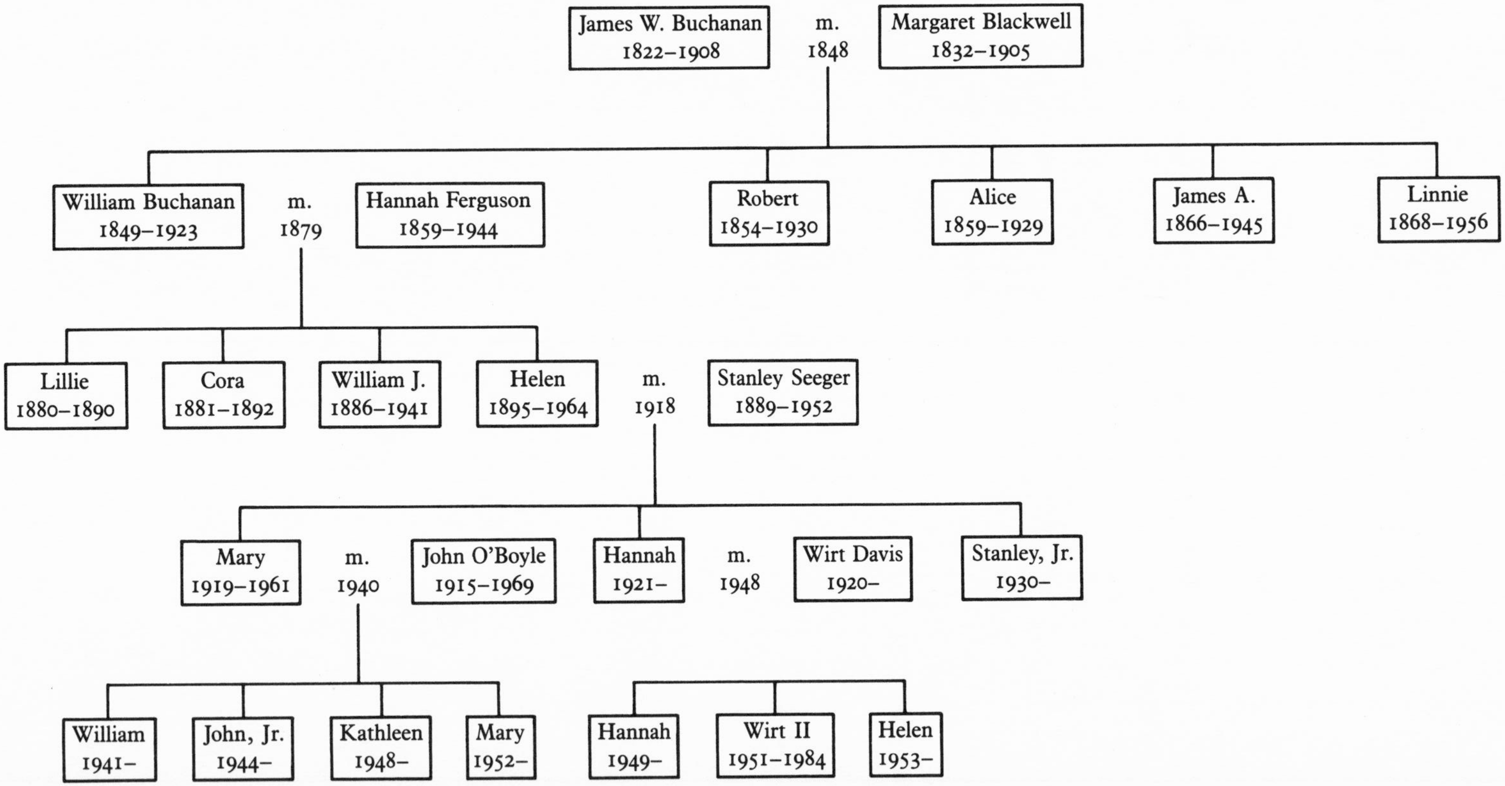

SOUTHERN TIMBERMAN

Prologue

The Civil War reduced the South to rubble. Of a population of 5.5 million whites and 3.5 million blacks, 258,000 white men lost their lives and 200,000 more were wounded. Cities were gutted, farms burned, and livestock butchered. Bridges were gone, ferries destroyed, and railroads torn up. Inflation cut into the Confederate dollar so badly that by March 1865 it took sixty-five dollars to buy one dollar in gold. Banks, industries, and insurance companies by the dozen were forced to close their doors.

Contemporary reports from battle-scarred areas like the Tennessee River valley remarked on mile after mile of total desolation—a former countryside of farms, trees, and villages was swept clean except for an occasional fire-blackened chimney standing gaunt and abandoned.

Technically and historically, an agriculturally backed society should recover economically from such abuse within a couple of growing seasons. But such was not the case. On top of the loss of lives and property, the South was suddenly confronted with an additional deprivation: free labor. Blacks and whites, abruptly on a new footing with one another, succumbed to great mutual suspicion. Former slaves in vast numbers took to the road, indulging in their freedom to do so. White farmers, largely ignorant of the wage system and too impoverished to practice it in any case, angrily watched their fields lie idle in the unrelenting sun.

For that was the final irony of this blighted picture—nature itself conspired with hard times and delivered drought after drought until 1868. Poverty, disease, and starvation began spreading in large patches across the map. Smallpox, tuberculosis, typhoid, and malaria swept the region, hitting blacks the hardest and among them children under five. In some of the more crowded cities, mortality rates reached one-fourth and one-third of the black population.

On the fringes of this wasteland, adding to the fear and hostility, bands of cutthroats and thieves, ex-guerrillas and deserters—both black and white—took advantage of the chaos and preyed upon those who were struggling to regain an economic foothold. Racist organizations—the KKK, the White League, and others born of this social upheaval to reestablish law and order—soon debased their charters to simple, frustrated revenge. Founded to restore a previous way of life, the Klan so quickly became a furious, violent outlet of indiscriminate hatred that even its leader soon urged its demise.

It was a time of muddled, conflicting philosophies and actions. Beginning with a fundamental difference of opinion between the president and the Congress about the goals of Reconstruction, the decade following the enactment in 1867 of the Reconstruction Act turned a formerly structured Southern political system into a free-for-all. "Scalawag" and "carpetbagger" became terms of revilement, although most Southerners-turned-Republican and Northerners-gone-south wrestled altruistically to put the region back on its feet.

The social and political trauma attending this time of upheaval was psychologically severe and long-reaching—indeed, Reconstruction is unjustifiably regarded as one of America's darkest periods—and the financial toll on state governments was sometimes extraordinary. In Louisiana, the state tax went from $.45 per $100 in 1861 to $2.15 per $100 in 1872, while the state debt climbed from $11,000,000 in 1865 to $50,597,000 ten years later. This was due not so much to corrupt Republican leadership—although later views of Reconstruction would look at little else—but rather to the excessive granting of bonds to subsidize railroads, to the repair bills following the wreckage of war, and to the introduction of previously unavailable social services. As a result, property values, which should have been responding to the region's slowly recovering agricultural prosperity, remained flat.

And yet a change was taking place. Always isolated from the country's North and West, the South had traditionally looked to itself for solutions to its problems. Spiritually, this time was no different. The blacks began to return to the farmlands, the whites, for the most part, welcomed them back, both as day laborers and, in what became a sidestep from slavery, as sharecroppers. In many respects, relations between the two were reminiscent of antebellum days—the rabid discrimination of the Jim Crow laws was not to appear until the end of the nineteenth century.

Beginning in 1869, a short spurt of record-crop years blessedly flushed the entire South with a wave of Northern capital. Small farms popped up like desert blooms after rain, splitting up the old plantations and helping distribute the wealth. Catering to this new market, retail stores appeared in towns and villages, drummers hit the roads to sell their wares, and railroads expanded to meet the growing demand for shipping and transportation. In the face of increasing economic might, the days of instability in state government were numbered. Not only were Southerners reasserting their will to self-govern, but Northern capitalists weren't about to let an obviously burgeoning opportunity be wrecked by a few artificially supported, incompetent politicians. These were the days of Boss Tweed and the Crédit Mobilier, when vast numbers of officeholders marched to the jingle of other people's money. Business would have its way, and with the end of Reconstruction in 1877, it did.

So from the ashes rose the phoenix. The battered South, fueled both by a wounded regional pride and an ever-increasing flood of Northern capital, rebuilt itself, economically at least, along more nationally conventional lines. Old orders fell, old alignments were rearranged, and people, inspired once more with feelings of optimism and self-confidence, pulled up stakes and left generational homesteads for new opportunities in the Southwest.

Texas, Louisiana, and Arkansas represented for most of the South a semi-exclusive regional version of the untamed Wild West. It pulled at thousands of Southerners hungry for cheap land, fertile soil, and a less tradition-strangled society. Among those who joined in the general migration was William Buchanan.

1 / The Beginning

William Buchanan left south-central Tennessee around 1869 at age twenty, the six-foot, red-haired, eldest son of a tannery worker. He had been born near Shelbyville, in Bedford County, in the heart of the state's famous rolling bluegrass hills. Shelbyville, however, was already a part of his past—a homestead turned to memories by the passage of arms.

Tennessee, behind Virginia, had been the most brutalized region of the Civil War. Chickamauga, Chattanooga, Lookout Mountain, Missionary Ridge, Shiloh, and an astounding 1,457 other "military events"[1] were all bloody stopping points in an endless sweep of armies that had dominated the state for three years. Early in 1862, the first Federal reconnaissance came through Shelbyville, and thereafter the whole area became a constant crossroads for troops on the march. James Wortham Buchanan, by then a forty-year-old bookkeeper, decided to leave.[2] With his wife, Margaret, twenty-nine, and his children William, thirteen, Robert, eight, and Alice, three, he headed southeast, ending up by the time of the armistice in southern Georgia, quite possibly living in or near his wife's ancestral home.

They were all back in Tennessee in 1866, however, in time for the birth of Margaret's third son, James A. Now they lived near Decherd, a small town a few miles northeast of Winchester—where James W.'s father had been postmaster from 1849 to 1855—in Franklin County. A jack-of-all-trades—he had also once been a merchant, as well as a bookkeeper and a tanner—J. W. Buchanan did well for himself. By the time of his eldest son's departure, he was comfortably nestled in the middle class, with a small spread of land and a live-in mulatto house servant.[3]

What prompted William's joining the migration west is not specifically known, except that his entire life was to be influenced by prevailing social winds.[4] Some of his characteristics, observed by people later in his life, indicated an impulsiveness driven by a good deal of ambition. He was an independent, fiercely private man whose approach to business was to cut through red tape and opposition quickly and effectively by maintaining maximum control. A born leader not born into leadership, his frustration in early life consisted of convincing the world that he deserved an opportunity to command. It could only have increased his impatience as a youth to be located in an area where the most apparent avenues to success had been closed by people preceding him. One interesting statistic that bears this hypothesis out is that he had, by the time he was fifty-three, either participated in or single-handedly brought about the creation of ten separate villages, towns, and cities.[5]

Whatever his motivations for leaving home, when he took to the road in 1869, he was equipped with a small portable sawmill, a tool better suited to the wooded hills of Arkansas and Louisiana than to the fields of central Tennessee.

His destination, if not his goal, was Forrest City, Arkansas, a small settlement about 270 miles due west named after an illustrious fellow Tennessean, General Nathan Bedford Forrest, who until recently had been leader of the KKK.

William's stay in Forrest City, which was incorporated in 1871, lasted approximately two years, during which he was exposed, as obscurely described in a later obituary, to "many difficulties and . . . unhealthy conditions."[6] Surviving whatever these hardships were, he continued southwest, sawmill in tow, and in 1873 he came at last to Texarkana, which was also just incorporating.

Texarkana owed its origin to the arrival of the Texas and Pacific Railroad on the Texas-Arkansas border. It was little more than a clearing in the woods when William got there; in fact, he opened the town's second sawmill to process the trees cleared away to make streets. Another mill operator was Joseph Ferguson, a wealthy sixty-year-old native Virginian who had moved to the area in 1832 and had gradually purchased several thousand acres in both Texas and Arkansas. William's encounter with this man, and especially with two of his children, was most probably the decisive factor in stopping his westward migration.

6

William Buchanan

Part of Joseph Ferguson's land lay some fifteen miles southwest of Texarkana alongside the Texas and Pacific Railroad, three miles from the Sulphur River. It was here, after Texarkana's streets had been cleared, that William established the first permanent sawmill of his fledgling career.

The years and William's apparent aversion to keeping records have obscured what financial arrangement was made between the two men—any number of options was possible. Nor is it known whether the mill, modest as it was, was built by Ferguson or started from scratch by William. The only photograph of it is undated, but was probably taken during the somewhat more prosperous 1880s. In fact, the only hard evidence from this period of William's life suggests that money had never been so unavailable.

Contributing to his penury was what came to be known as the Panic of '73, begun in September of that year. Months earlier, in an effort to avoid growing threats of inflation, Congress had passed the Coinage Act, removing the silver dollar from the nation's coinage. As a result of this move, the sole backing of U.S. currency became the amount of gold bullion held by the government—a happy situation as long as that amount remained stable or increased. Unfortunately, it did not.

The reason it didn't is based largely on corruption. The postwar whiplash of immorality that had tainted Southern governments hadn't originated there. All across the country, from the federal government to the smallest businesses, the industrial revolution, the growth of railroads, and the exploitation of new natural resources—not the least of which was timber—had poured money into the hands of people who were ill-equipped to handle the responsibilities of wealth and power. As examples not of corruption but of the tremendous expansion of this period, the A&P grocery-store chain, Standard Oil Company of Ohio, Montgomery Ward and Company, Bethlehem Steel Company, P. T. Barnum's "Greatest Show on Earth," and scores of less famous enterprises were all born in the three years from 1870 to 1873.

This sudden wealth led to reckless speculation and political degeneracy, weakening the nation's sound financial footing. In addition, an unfavorable balance of trade with Europe had cre-

The water well in the center of Texarkana in 1874, the year William Buchanan arrived and helped push back the forest to make room for the town

ated a deficit that was climbing into the hundreds of millions of dollars. This was further aggravated when the Europeans called in their American loans to relieve their own widespread economic depression. Overextended credit, inflated currency, and the revolving greenbacks-versus-gold-versus-silver dispute finally precipitated a collapse of the entire system.

Major banks failed, businesses foundered, the New York stock exchange closed for ten days. Over half the railroads in the nation defaulted on their bonds. One eventual reaction to all this careless greed and class-conscious favoritism was the rise of political movements like the agrarians, the Free Silverites, the Greenbackers, and the labor unions.

The resultant depression of 1873, which lasted six years, hit Southern farmers hard. With the drop in the price of gold, and the money it backed, loans became scarce and prices fell along with people's incomes. It was during this time that William often turned his fitful profits into groceries for himself and his small crew. Family legend has it that he was once reduced to cutting strips of leather from his boots to sew a broken drive belt back together and so keep the sawmill running.

The economy's intemperance was not his only problem. In these early days of Southern lumbering, major rail lines, mostly

Northern-owned, were still primarily serving their own bailiwick—the Civil War had bred a self-serving prejudice that was slow to come around. As a result of this particular transportation shortage, Southern lumbermen relied on rivers to move their timber from the forests to the mills. William Buchanan was no exception.

He recalled years later how he had strung a boom across the Sulphur River to catch timber his crew was floating downstream, and had secured the far end of it to a sturdy sapling on the opposite shore. Under normal circumstances, this process creates a temporary holding area for the logs from which mule or ox teams can retrieve them for hauling to the mill. In rainy weather, of course, this plan usually gives way to gluey mud and general inertia—a good reason to keep one's eye on the clouds.

Bad timing and worse luck combined to deliver both heavy rain and a "raft" of logs during the same week. William sat on the river's slippery bank, day after day, and watched that distant and no longer so sturdy sapling fight against the strain of the rising water and the weight of the logs. The rain finally stopped, the water ebbed, and William got his timber to the mill, but the economic fragility of his position was obviously not lost on him.

Whatever his thoughts were then, he had to have reflected on the era he inhabited. The South was like a field slowly recovering from a brushfire. Under its charred surface, new growth was at last pushing up, beginning again an ancient struggle for dominance. The ruling patriarchal plantation class of old was thinned out to a small group, fighting for the power it still barely maintained. Opposition parties of all stripes competed for legislative control. Paradoxically, the weapon most often reached for in this battle was Northern capital. And Northern capital was receptive. With the war over and the Thirteenth, Fourteenth, and Fifteenth Amendments passed, the Northern Republicans, once wavers of the abolitionist flag, now turned their affections to capitalism. The attraction of the South's economic potential, out of reach since 1861, was mighty indeed by the end of Reconstruction in 1877.

The end result of this pragmatic mutual yearning was a kind of cooperative cold war. Politically, the South remained estranged and hostile until 1933; economically, she became far less rebellious. The rising Southern middle class, of which William Buchanan was now a part, began to mimic its Northern counterpart in its insatiable appetite for a piece of the pie. One sign of the South's naïvete, however, was that despite the apparent harmony between capital and resource, the truly powerful money remained firmly in Northern hands.

So, typically striving to be at the forefront of the crowd, William by 1877 had sent for his family, and by the next year, leaving his father in charge of the mill, he left for Fort Worth, Texas, with dreams of larger profits.

There, he joined E. P. Cowen, a local wheeler-dealer who already was running a lumberyard on the south side of town, and together they formed Cowen and Buchanan. How well this operation did is not clear; what is apparent, however, is that by the time the year was up, William had impulsively joined the rush to Leadville, Colorado—continually hopeful, no doubt, that this time he would hit it big.

This was not Leadville's first time at bat. Some eighteen years earlier, gold had been discovered in the area and had sustained a modest rush for about two years. This time around it was silver, and the stampede to extract it from the mountains was anything but modest. Incorporated in 1878, the town had a population of forty thousand by 1880. In an example of perfect timing, 1878 also saw Congress pass the Bland-Allison Act, requiring the Treasury to purchase monthly amounts of silver bullion for coinage.

Leadville's silver, however, was not William's primary reason for going there. His brother Robert, now twenty-four and a bit of a wanderer himself, had preceded him. Upon their reunion, however, William immediately assumed the dominant role, a concession that was to become standard family behavior from then on. On April 16, 1879, Buchanan and Company purchased two town lots for three hundred dollars on which a lumber mill was soon erected—Robert was listed as clerk.

The venture as planned, unfortunately, was not to be. William soon contracted "mountain fever," was nursed back to strength by Robert, and ıeturned to the Texarkana area by mid-June. On the nineteenth, he married Joseph Ferguson's daughter Hannah; she was nineteen, he was twenty-nine. There is evidence suggesting this was not a whirlwind romance: throughout his travels, William frequently returned home, despite the hardships that entailed. Presumably, his reasons for doing so went beyond checking up on the family business.

Actually, there was little to keep him in Leadville. Family lore has it that Leadville was the venture that sent William to riches and success. The evidence suggests otherwise. On June 7—roughly the time of William's departure—the *Leadville Daily Chronicle* pointed out that of the thirty-one sawmills operating in the silver town in May, only seventeen were still around one month later. The overabundance of mills was also responsible for pushing lumber prices down to cutthroat levels. In fact, business was so bad that Robert sold the two lots just one year after purchase, at a 66 percent loss.

Still, the Fort Worth–Leadville digression did have its benefits. As William sat watching the water rise in the Sulphur River, the Bowie County, Texas, personal tax rolls had reported his worth at between $76 and $210. In 1880, nine months and already one baby after his marriage, he was credited with $1,380 in total assets (or just over $11,000 in 1984 terms).[7]

According to the rolls, this was his high point until 1890. Nonetheless, life achieved a steady normalcy for a few years. The mill continued operating, slowly denuding the surrounding acreage, a second daughter was born to William and Hannah in 1881, and a son named Will followed five years later.[8]

Other members of the extended family also began to establish roots. William's younger brother and sister, James and Linnie, began attending Professor Hayes's school in Texarkana. And their father, J.W., who had started in the area as a clerk in his son's lumber mill, struck out on his own in 1883 and formed the First National Bank with a partner, absorbing Texarkana's first bank, "Hake's," at the same time.

The location of William's mill had now become a community of sorts, and in June 1882 the official post office of Buchanan, Texas, was opened by the federal government, with William's brother-in-law Joseph G. Ferguson as postmaster.

More intriguing to William, however, were the activities of his eldest brother-in-law, William Thomas Ferguson, who was two years his senior and a resident of Miller County, Arkansas. A Confederate veteran and a successful farmer at the time of Buchanan's arrival near the Sulphur River, W. T. Ferguson, by 1881, was already a widower and the father of five children when he decided to start a small sawmill of his own in partnership with E. W. Frost. Unlike Buchanan, and aided considerably by an income that placed him among the eight richest people in the county, W.T. quickly escalated his business. By 1887, Ferguson and Frost had already acquired two other mills and were studying the possibilities of a fourth located in Stamps, Arkansas.

Their timing couldn't have been better. The depression of 1873 had ended in 1879, and by the next year, the South, economically at least, was firmly settled on its feet and ready to go. In many respects, it had nowhere to head but up. Indeed, to exploitive Northern eyes, the South was one huge resource-rich, labor-cheap cornucopia, and the largest of those resources was timber.

The progression of the American lumber industry across the northern half of the country had been as indomitable as an invasion of army ants on the march. It had also left a comparable swath of destruction in its wake. Content to stay largely in Maine until the 1850s, restricted by antiquated techniques, limited transportation, and a fairly steady market, it was suddenly induced by the nation's increasing growth, and the Civil War, to expand. Rapaciously it moved westward, first to New York, then to Pennsylvania in the 1860s, and finally, in 1870, to the Great Lakes region as far as Wisconsin. This migration was accompanied by technological advances that quickly broke down nature's passive resistance. New saws, new harvesting techniques, and the use of logging railroads all combined to create a furiously effective industry. Twenty years after reaching the area, Great Lakes lumbermen were already running out of trees. The more prescient among them had begun to focus on the pine-rich South.

America's timber resources in those days were viewed like coal or ore—something to be mined rather than cultivated. Wherever lumbermen looked, there stretched an ocean of tall trees; it was,

What is believed to be William Buchanan's mill in Buchanan, Texas, probably in the 1880s

as far as they could see, inexhaustible. Also, early common knowledge had it that a tree took one hundred years or more to grow to maturity—who could afford to wait that long, or want to? This last attitude echoed a truism in American agriculture: when a field played out or was damaged by weather, a replacement always lay ready just a few steps into the wilderness. Conservation and artificial regeneration were not only arcane and expensive; they were believed to border on the imbecilic. Besides, until well after the Civil War, the United States was an agricultural society—trees were a nuisance and their removal cleared the way for farming, which was seen as the nation's road to prosperity.

Eventually, any such pattern spells its own contradictory doom. In time, too many fields were thus produced, and dwindling forests were at a premium. But in 1870 only a handful sensed this pessimistic possibility, and for the most part they were ignored.

And so the Great Lakes lumbermen looked to the South. In 1876, the Southern Homestead Act was repealed, opening millions of federal acres up for private transactions. In 1866, the vengeful Republican party had passed the act through Congress, controlling the sale of well over 47 million acres in the five public-land states of the South: Alabama, Arkansas, Florida, Louisiana, and Mississippi. The provisions of the bill made these lands available in eighty-acre lots to homesteaders; the catch was that none of the homesteaders could be ex-Confederates, and none of the sales could be in cash. The idea was to encourage black freedmen and Federal army veterans to settle and to discourage the growth of monopoly and speculation. The no-cash provision, it was hoped, would insure that all applicants, rich or poor, would have the same opportunity to buy. It was also supposed to bolster the banking business through the resultant wave of mortgage loans.

Ten years after the bill's passage, a mere four thousand settlers had taken advantage of the offer. In contrast, pressure had intensified to undo the restrictions. Both Northern capitalists and Southern "Redeemers"—so called because they were "redeeming" the South from the sins of Reconstruction—united in their desire to exploit this almost 50-million-acre gold mine. The bill was repealed, and a flood of investors, mostly Northern or foreign—many bound together in syndicates—bought up vast tracts of land for as little as forty-five cents per acre. By 1888, when alarmed non-Redeemer legislators finally reimposed some restrictions, 5.5 million acres of Southern federal land had been sold, among them the very cream of the timber crop.

Federal land was not the only fruit on the vine. When the railroads joined the fray, enthusiastic Southern legislatures offered state land and low tax deals by the bunch. From 1880 to 1890, railroad trackage in Texas, Arkansas, and Louisiana increased 211.4 percent; twenty-three thousand miles of track were added to the South overall, as compared to five thousand miles during the previous ten years.

The attractions of bargain land, vast forests, and willing local governments were heightened by an extra bonus for those outsiders wishing to set up business. The per capita income in the South in 1880 was $376; in the Northeast it was $1,353. The entire South, now peppered with small farms largely worked by indebted tenant farmers, offered a cheap labor supply too good to resist.

A few Southerners were clear-eyed enough to see the threat on their doorstep, but the interparty bickering to which most Southern politics had been reduced by this time was so total that any attempt to take a unified stance was preordained to fail. As long as the businessmen dealt directly with the receptive local political "rings" in power, they could usually count on success.

William Buchanan had no doubt carefully watched his brother-in-law navigate these waters. In fact, indications are he went beyond detached interest in 1884 and invested eight hundred dollars in some of W.T.'s activities. Judging from the lifelong relationship these two men developed, it is reasonable to imagine they consulted a great deal with one another during this period.

Supporting this presumption is the company W. T. Ferguson kept and into which he invited William. Along with Frost, names like G. W. Bottoms and C. T. Crowell pop up, both of whom were doing quite well for themselves. In fact, it was Crowell who initially purchased the Bodcaw Lumber Company in Stamps, Arkansas, in 1887.

But Crowell was tiring of the lumber business and was on the threshold of a whole new career in Los Angeles real estate. The year he established Bodcaw,[9] the tax rolls rated the operation at seventy-one hundred dollars, mentioning at the time of assessment that no lumber had yet been produced. Over the next two years, that overall value, now including lumber, never reached more than eleven thousand dollars. It was obviously not an operation with lots of get-up-and-go.

But it was attractive, especially to William, who in 1888 had finally exhausted all his timber reserves on the Sulphur River and had moved to Texarkana to open a lumber sales office with a man named Moore. What William was lacking was cash. What he had were contacts, and it was these he gathered together to help him out.

Unfortunately, the details of how this happened are missing. Buchanan, always a private man, left virtually nothing behind of a personal nature. It well might be that somewhere there is a document outlining the financial specifics of William's acquisition of the Bodcaw Lumber Company, but as yet it has not surfaced.

What is known is that he was living among men both friendly and wealthy, including by now his own father. J. W. Buchanan had done very nicely in the banking business, having accumulated by 1884 a worth of $13,220 on the tax rolls ($152,000 in 1984 terms).[10]

And there were others: E. P. Cowen, his one-year partner in Fort Worth, presumably having grown with the times, sent one of his representatives, A. H. Whitmarsh, to join Buchanan the moment the Bodcaw deal went through, a sure sign of prior interest. W. R. Grim, a newcomer in Texarkana in 1889 and a cashier at the newly organized Texarkana National Bank, also became a close associate, and one worth his weight in gold—in 1902, he became president of the bank; three years later, Buchanan became a major stockholder.

Finding backers, therefore, didn't seem to be a problem.[11] That in itself is a credit to William's personality. Throughout his long life, despite his often autocratic methods and a reserved demeanor, he seems to have infected people with an irrepressible enthusiasm. In exchange for their support, either through their money or their expertise, he shared with them his fast-moving, quick-thinking business style and showed them a rare loyalty in an age of unscrupulous conduct.

The opening moves of William's acquisition of Bodcaw first appeared on paper on January 14, 1889. That day, Crowell, having owned Bodcaw for several years already, suddenly incorporated. Announcing a capital worth of forty-five thousand dollars, he brought in Ferguson, Frost, and Bottoms to divide the stock. But then, almost immediately, a series of stock transfers took place that bring to mind the wild orderliness of a spirited square dance.

Starting out with the four incorporators, the transfers went like this: Bottoms gave to William; Crowell gave to Bottoms. Frost gave to Bottoms; Bottoms gave to Ferguson. Crowell gave to William; Crowell and Bottoms dropped out. Ferguson gave to William; Frost gave to T. A. Brown. Then Frost bowed out and William gave to his brother James A. and to W. C. Brown. And that, a year later, was that.

Once the dust had settled, the company was owned by William, Ferguson, J. A. Buchanan—twenty-three years old and fresh from a course in business—and the Brown brothers, Thomas and William.

What actually went on here is anyone's guess. Again, there are no records detailing whether shares were handed over at par or above, for cash or on credit, or even why the whole complex maneuver was held in the first place. What is clear is that William was in control by the end of that year. Curiously, it was his brother who was the initial majority stockholder, with William having only forty shares worth a total of one thousand dollars—a situation quickly remedied, but which remains another mystery.

None of this was entirely altruistic. Although Ferguson had obviously done a great favor for his brother-in-law, he also came away from the deal with a little under twice the shares he had started out with. Also, his former partners reappeared later, picking up stock both in Bodcaw and in other Buchanan interests. What had transpired in 1889 was to everyone's benefit, as no doubt William had convinced them all it would be. Future repetitions of that success quickly furthered Buchanan's credibility. William Buchanan was becoming a name with which to be associated.

W. C., T. A., and J. R. Brown were not financial backers; they were highly qualified lumbermen. Originally from North Carolina, they had settled in Queen City, Texas, just down the road from Buchanan's Sulphur River outfit. As usual for this early period, it is unclear how William induced them to throw in their lot with his own, besides offering them stock and the glimpse of a dream. But his parallel successes in finding both financiers and professional lumbermen stand well as examples of what might have been his one truly outstanding ability: that of selecting the right people for the job.

So, at the beginning of 1890, at the age of forty, William Buchanan was on the threshold of the life he'd been seeking.

2 / The Buildup

The passage of time has done away with the personal tax rolls covering the Bodcaw Lumber Company for 1890, the first full year it was under William's management. The records for 1891, however, reveal that the company's worth increased 350 percent to $40,500 (a 1984 equivalent of $465,750). More interesting, in part for what it says about the veracity of tax rolls, is the company's own assessment of its worth: $148,819.18 (in 1984 terms, $1,711,420.50). The most visible cause for this increase was a drastic decision: William destroyed Crowell's mill and had it replaced with a more modern one capable of producing 75,000 board feet each day.

The company minutes reveal an immediate flurry of timber, land, and equipment purchases, general construction, and stock sales, many to relatives and key employees, as well as to backers. Early in 1891, the capital stock was increased by $105,000, and a few days later a dividend of 105 percent was paid, presumably to keep some of these people happy. By February 1893, yearly profits exceeded $100,000 (over 1 million 1984 dollars), and in 1895 a double band saw was added that increased the mill's capacity to 350,000 board feet a day, making it one of the largest operations in the entire South. From that point until it closed operations, the company never looked back.

The main reason for this rapid success, besides the ability of the men involved, was again timing. Up to now, the truly vast timberlands that stretched south of Stamps, Arkansas, and covered 85 percent of Louisiana had been commercially unharvestable because of a lack of adequate transportation. Suddenly, that was changing.

One of the great advantages William Buchanan saw in Bodcaw was its location. Attached to Texarkana by the recently built Cotton Belt Railroad, and via Texarkana to the rest of the country, Stamps represented a possible commercial funnel for millions of board feet coming out of Louisiana. Also, the building of a twenty-five-mile spur north of Stamps to Hope, Arkansas, would connect with the Missouri-Pacific Railroad and create a second commercial outlet. In Bodcaw's rickety four-mile-long log railroad, William saw a potential fortune within grasp.

Log railroads were nothing new. They had been in use in the Great Lakes region for years and were designed for quick and temporary access. Occasionally made of wooden rails laid flat upon the ground, they sometimes wouldn't last a year before disintegrating—just long enough to carry the timber from the woods.

In the South, the situation wasn't much different. Standing in the forest, following two gleaming parallel strips of rail with their eyes, observers commented on how odd the sight was. Prejudiced as they were by the conventional appearance of properly built railroads, these people were amazed at the wobbly track laid down upon the forest floor. It dipped and swerved and tilted from side to side, making small loops and slight curves to avoid obstacles as trifling as tree trunks. The object of the exercise was to get the wood out—not to build expensive monuments to man's prowess over nature.

But William Buchanan was not so limited. While he felt that temporary dead-end spurs were fine as collection points for timber felled within a certain radius, he did not feel the same about the main line to the mill.

When he looked at a map of the Louisiana that stretched south of him, he saw a geographical left-leaning V formed by the juncture of the Red River from the northwest and the Ouachita and Black rivers from the north, meeting slightly east of Alexandria. Stamps was located inside the top left-hand corner of that V. He realized that if he could run a railroad down to the bottom of the V, he could virtually control all the area contained within it. Also, having achieved that, it would be a simple matter to send out branches west to Shreveport, east to the Mississippi River, and perhaps even link up to one of the railroads leading south to New Orleans.

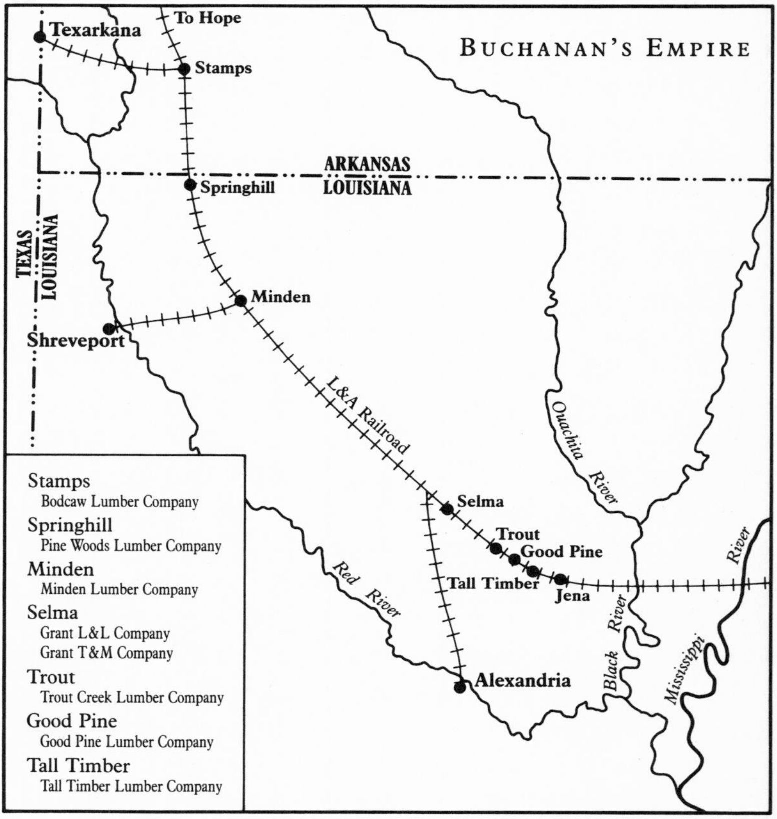

This geographical view of a potential geographical empire was dictated by certain physical realities. When he had approached what was to become Texarkana in late 1873, Buchanan had been obliged to leave his portable sawmill on the east bank of the Red River until he could locate a means sturdy enough to ferry it across. There were no bridges. The lesson was not lost on him. While rivers were an enormous aid in getting a product to mill or market, they could, if they blocked the way or divided a given territory, be an equally enormous barrier. And this was not a problem that time and free-spending legislation could be counted on to cure. Louisiana was notoriously tightfisted when it came to allocating funds that might benefit its rural areas. In 1928, when Huey Long became governor, there were only three major bridges in the entire state.

There was another reason for pushing a railroad to Alexandria, and from there reaching New Orleans. In 1882, Collis P. Huntington's Southern Pacific had reached the latter city, thereby linking it with San Francisco. The mere possibility of plugging into that system was enough to make the capitalist heart beat faster.

With Bodcaw growing steadily, William by the mid-1890s began pushing the railroad toward the Louisiana border, scouting all the while for suitable timberland to buy. As logging superintendent and point man for some of the land and timber deals, he ended up using his brother Robert after one of the Brown brothers was fatally injured on the job. Robert, having left Leadville in 1886,[1] had been operating his own lumber mill in Thornton, Arkansas, for about ten years. But in 1896 the mill burned, and he was ready to return to the family fold.

He proved a good choice for the job. Just five years William's junior, he was the roughest-edged of the three brothers, generally uneducated, uncommunicative, and somewhat bullheaded in his opinions. He mixed well with the country people he met on his lonely excursions into the woods. His lack of pretentions and his propensity for hard work left a favorable impression on people whose sole ambition, frequently, was merely to stay alive.

Times had not been kind to Louisiana farmers. With the carving up of the old plantations, the number of small farms had skyrocketed, but not the number of landowners. The countryside was now filled with people who rented their fields in exchange for a large percentage of the crop raised on it; additionally, they bought their feed, fertilizer, equipment, and staples from local merchants who demanded a similar payment. So long as the weather, the crops, and the market were good, this system limped along. But when all three began to suffer in the mid-1880s, the delicate balance between solvency and debt went askew. Prices fell, so both landlords and merchants demanded more payment in crops; the weather went bad, and the farmer, frequently a black man, found himself in much the same situation he'd been in as a slave, only without the slim protection even that system had afforded.[2] A law was even passed prohibiting a farmer from moving until his accounts were settled.

Robert Buchanan

There was an added wrinkle to this already dismal picture. Since the farmer, for all intents and purposes, no longer owned what he grew, the people he was indebted to demanded that he turn his attention to a crop that yielded the highest price—usually cotton. As a short-range solution, this had some merit, until supply-and-demand principles intervened. As more and more farmers were forced to produce cotton, the excess supply pushed down the market price. More ominous in the long run, the soil began to suffer both from the lack of diversity and a general lack of care. Erosion began picking up where the economy left off.

The result of all this was that by 1889, 70 percent of Louisiana's white farmers were in debt, as were 100 percent of the blacks. By the turn of the century, because of the crop-lien system and other destructive agricultural practices (including cut-and-run timber cutting), 300 million acres of the United States were seriously eroded, a third of that irreparably. The Mississippi River became "Old Muddy" with the washed-away soil of hundreds of thousands of mismanaged acres.

Things would get worse. Beginning in 1893, a depression staggered the United States. Reminiscent of the Panic of '73, it featured many of the same causes and effects, but greatly magnified. Once again, the trouble centered on the supplies of gold held by the Treasury. In 1890, European investors had begun to react to their own financial woes by unloading American securities and demanding payment in gold. Taken alone, this was merely destabilizing. Combined with later events, it marked the start of an avalanche.

The United States had been purchasing a limited amount of silver since late 1878 under the requirements of the Bland-Allison Act. This act, the result of a compromise between silver-producing western states and the gold-standard East, was an irritant to both parties. The metal was coined into silver dollars, stored in the Treasury, and generally silver certificates were issued.

The more pro-silver Sherman Silver Purchase Act of 1890, also the result of a compromise in which the westerners yielded more power, went further. The monthly amount that Treasury had to buy went up significantly, and legal-tender notes, nicknamed Sherman notes, were issued in exchange for the metal. The crucial and fateful provision was that the notes could be redeemed in either silver or gold. As a result of all this political maneuvering, in 1893 the Treasury was sitting on 380 million silver dollars and 157 million ounces of bullion. As this mountain of silver grew, its value began to deteriorate. People started taking advantage of the gold option on the notes, first bit by bit, and then in a rush. In the first five months of 1893, the Treasury paid out nearly $60 million in gold (that's $690 million in 1984 terms).

Abetting this financial unrest were several simultaneous developments. As they had prior to the Panic of '73, the railroads and industries had gone back to issuing stock for pure speculative gain. The timing was inappropriate. Tired of chronic governmen-

What is believed to be one of the later, large Bodcaw mills in Stamps, Arkansas, dated March 1902

tal ineptitude and capitalist venality, industrial workers across the United States were beginning to protest. The year 1890 saw the largest number of industrial strikes in any one year of the nineteenth century. Three years later, with this trend continuing and the marketplace in a stall, business began to falter. Profits fell off, shipments were cut back, and the railroads lost money. They started collapsing like the proverbial house of cards. By the end of the year, 491 banks had closed, most of them in the South, and fifteen thousand businesses had failed. By 1895, one-fourth of all the railroad capitalization in the country was in the bankruptcy courts.

Another major contributor to the panic was the largess of Congress, which over the past several years had been spending more and more money on political debts like pension grants to veterans. These became so lavish under Benjamin Harrison's administration that the Treasury's surplus in 1890 had become a $70 million deficit in 1894.

In August of 1893, Grover Cleveland, just installed in his second term of office, attempted to stop the drain of gold by repealing the Bland-Allison Act. It was the most violent political battle of his career, and all it did was heighten the anger and frustration of those who were in dire need of more circulating currency. For the next three years, by the sides of roads and rail embankments, the nights flickered with the camp fires of men without jobs or homes. In their eyes, government had never been so hostile, nor democracy so close to failure. A deep and seething anger was beginning to stir in people long used to hardship, and the political repercussions of this would not be long in coming.

That was the country Robert Buchanan traveled in search of timber. While the heyday of inexpensive vast tracts of land was over, small farmers were now desperate to sell the wood off their land so they could transform it into cotton-producing fields. The extent of their poverty and despair was enormous. Habitually spending nights at people's homes along his way, Robert once woke to find a farmer's starving dogs had devoured the leather harness to his wagon.

And yet, through it all, William Buchanan flourished. In one of the paradoxes that highlight troubled financial periods in history, the lumber industry improved right on through the Panic of '93. Since 1880, lumber production in the United States had increased 94 percent, an upward trend that would continue annually until 1907. Hedging his bets, Buchanan also made sure that his marketplace was not the chronically depressed South, but rather those states west of the Mississippi that had just recently become members of the Union.

In 1894, William's men reached a small cluster of poor farmers in a town named Barefoot, Louisiana, just twenty-five miles south of Stamps, and began to buy land. Two years later, a fifty-man sawmill and a small company store were established. A few days before that Christmas, J. F. Giles, a Buchanan executive, pulled the sign marked "Barefoot" off the store's front door, wrote "Springhill" on the reverse side, and nailed it back up. The company had come to stay.

The railroad pushed into town early the next year, and the sawmill officially became the Pine Woods Lumber Company, with J. F. Giles as general manager. The mill employed about four hundred men and could turn out 125,000 board feet a day. The renamed town of Springhill was never the same again.

Nor was Stamps, and that raises an interesting point: in all cases except one, William established his mills either on previous

Some of the black workers of the Tall Timber Lumber Company who caused so much resentment in nearby Jena, Louisiana

mill sites or in isolated forest locations. He built the mills, the log ponds, the employee housing, the commissaries, the churches, the doctor's offices, the recreation halls, the railroad depots, the barber shops, and, in a couple of instances, the tennis courts. The expense of all this was impressive, but so was the resulting control he held over his workers.

This was not a unique approach. From the mill towns of New England and the Deep South to the mining towns of Colorado and Alaska, this capitalist principle of absolute control was a favorite strategy, usually enacted to the employees' distinct disadvantage. But in the rural South, it had particularly paternal overtones. These vast and sparsely populated areas had rarely known anything different. Plantations had ruled the economy for untold decades before the Civil War, primarily Northern absentee owners had then taken over the same acreage or more, and now companies like Buchanan's were slowly buying out the landlords. In each case, the local residents looked to someone above them for many of the major decisions in their lives—to move or not to move; to work or to be idle; to be free or to be a slave.

This time, in Springhill, the option was employment offered against a backdrop of destitution. Few people quibbled with the loss of local democracy.

They did show resistance to something else. With the establishing of the Pine Woods Lumber Company, William set a trend he was to carry on wherever he set up business: he imported many of his own black start-up workers.[3] His reasons for doing this are simple to see. The area was sparsely populated and the blacks he brought in were trained, cheap, loyal, and hardworking.

Whites, apart from being slightly less cheap, were all of the above, and were brought along too, albeit in much smaller numbers. They were usually restricted to experts in certain areas of the operation. But the whites had the psychological advantage of being free in their own society.

Ever since Reconstruction, an odd metamorphosis had been taking place in the relationship between Southern whites and blacks. It is often assumed that the repressive Jim Crow laws segregating the races were enacted in the immediate wake of Reconstruction's departure. In fact, the first such law was not passed until 1887 in Florida, and Louisiana didn't follow suit until 1896.

This all had to do with who was in power. The scalawags and the carpetbaggers had been largely replaced in government by the Redeemers, a hybrid political group made up of the pre–Civil War plantation class and members of the affluent middle class. These men attempted to ride a fence between maintaining traditional antebellum Southern values and inviting Northern capital to develop the South's industrial potential. They tended to be paternally disposed toward the blacks and were certainly used to working in close proximity to them. More practically, they also saw that by favoring the blacks to a limited extent, they deprived the lower-class rabble from securing the black vote.

But they were few in number and out of touch. As they marched toward the 1890s, their credibility was dislodged by a growing sense that the North was only interested in exploiting the region, not developing it. A powerful resentment grew among the huge working class the Redeemers had chosen to ignore. As usual, the blacks became the symbol of this growing chasm.

The results were predictable. With the decline of the Redeemers, the poor and the rising working middle-class whites saw the blacks as an obvious barrier to more general white employment and as a potential voting-bloc threat. This limited perception, coupled with a long-standing resentment, gave birth to Jim Crow.

Buchanan, however indirectly, must have realized this. By importing his own black workers into rural areas where blacks were a minority, he was bonding them to him as he might his own soldiers in enemy territory. Once they were settled in his company towns, there was little chance they would leave.

Next down the line in Buchanan's progression through Louisiana was Minden, which he reached in 1901 with the purchase of a small local railroad that he attached to his own. About thirty miles south of Springhill, Minden was already an established little town with several small businesses, all of which were soon dwarfed by the Minden Lumber Company. The lumber mill, constructed that same year, eventually produced 250,000 board feet a day and employed up to three hundred people.

The effect of this sudden industrial invasion of the town was well captured by a local resident named Sarah Killen, writing to a relative in Georgia:

> [April 1, 1901] "Our town is still booming. . . . The Big Mill is going doing a big work. I can't begin to tell. It is just one mile from us. It wakes us up just at half past 4 o'clock. I feel like I am just cut off from the town. . . . 2 or 3 engines all the time up there switching about, the Compress blowing & puffing & we haven't got a horse but what is afraid to go through there. When I go I will have Father to go with me. I can't trust to go with the Children."

She does add with unreserved pride that electricity, supplied by the mill's generators, lights "the streets & store houses & Church houses," and that telephones are "in nearly every house." Even an ice factory is planned. A final, rather telling dichotomy does exist, however: "I do believe all this worldly prosperity is injurious to the Christian religion."[4]

This troubled view of "progress" as a noisy, dangerous, smoke-belching lumber mill was by no means unique to Mrs. Killen. Traditional Southern mores had been hard pressed getting used to the grating jangle of the "New South"; lumber mills and the

The Minden Lumber Company in Minden, Louisiana

men who ran them had in the past been relegated to the heap of white trash. Now they were not only running the town, they were helping insure its future. That took some readjusting—on both sides.

The erstwhile logging road, incorporated in 1901 as the Louisiana and Arkansas Railway Company (or the L&A) soon left Minden behind. By the next year, it had reached Winnfield, seventy miles away, the outer limits of the land of the shortleaf and loblolly pine. This was now the northernmost border of a solid swath of longleaf pine that cut across most of the Deep South, ending up in East Texas. It represented, for a Southern lumberman, the Mother Lode.

These virgin longleaf timberlands were cathedral in appearance. Each tree, as straight as an arrow and up to five feet in diameter, leaped up from a pristine, parklike forest floor, going thirty to forty feet before extending its first branches, bursting out into foliage at the top of a hundred-foot crown. The majestic serenity, dappled by the sun and orchestrated by small animals and the occasional moan of the wind, had the peacefulness of a heaven on earth. Sadly, this tranquility was threatened by the very nature of the tree—virgin longleaf pine was renowned commercially for being heavy, strong, straight, and knot-free.

William certainly displayed added zest when he reached this part of the country. In 1904 he broke ground a few miles west of

A virgin stand of yellow pine, typical of the forests that fell before the saws of William Buchanan and his peers

Jena and incorporated the Trout Creek Lumber Company, and the year after that he purchased the Grant Lumber Company in Selma, Louisiana, some thirty-five miles north of Alexandria. Finally, in 1906, he opened another mill right next to Trout Creek and named it the Good Pine Lumber Company.

At this point he paused, as well he might. In sixteen years, he had created six major lumber mills,[5] the least of which turned out 125,000 board feet a day. He had started a railroad admired by all who knew of it as one of the best small roads in the country, and he was shipping over 221 million feet of lumber in 1906 alone.

It would be nice to study his books and discover exactly how he accomplished this, but that, unfortunately, is impossible. All that remains of his entire operation are the minute books of the separate companies, some of which are comically vague.

An example are the minutes of the Pine Woods Lumber Company in Springhill. Laboring over an unusually appalling specimen of poor penmanship, one gets from these records the impression of meetings held and motions deliberated with all due consideration. Closer scrutiny reveals that in fact there was only one man in the room: J. F. Giles. Armed with proxies in one hand and orders from the Texarkana head office in the other, Giles for years sat alone, or sometimes with one other person, and acted out on paper the solemn deliberations of an invisible board of directors. Even he must have tired of the routine—from 1901 through 1906, the pages are titled and dated, but otherwise blank.

Nonetheless, a vague sense of procedure emerges. Each company, except Grant, was begun with a small initial group of investors, all designated as directors. William was always there, was always named president, and ultimately ended up with about twice as many shares as the next man in line. It was clear from the start that there was to be but one boss of bosses. Also, as such, he remained physically removed, working out of sales offices in a Texarkana bank building.[6]

Below him came names of people who resurfaced throughout his life: relatives like the Fergusons and his own brother. J.A., and loyal members of the entourage like the banker Grim and old friend Marshall Northcott. The only exceptions to this rule appeared for obvious financial reasons. Examples are George, Charles, Randolph, and Arthur Pack, who were among those who took advantage of the Southern Homestead Act repeal and who frequently took partial payment in stock for their hundreds of thousands of acres. Another was E. E. Fitzgerald, an agent of Edward Alis, subsequently famous as part of Alis-Chalmers, which installed some of the machinery in the Bodcaw mill. Fitzgerald was a highly regarded sawmill engineer and was enticed to switch allegiances for a hefty percentage in the Minden Lumber Company.

The subsequent list of common shareholders in each company followed the same pattern. Except for names that were exclusively associated with one particular mill, like a planing-mill foreman or a general manager, the shareholders of all the Buchanan companies were essentially the same. In fact, as the years parade past in these books, family lines of inheritance appear—man, widow, children, grandchildren. In many cases, this inheritance was made possible only by William's permission. That he gave it so freely was another sign of his paternal instincts, and his sensitive feel for public relations.

In fact, he encouraged white-collar employee ownership of

stock. While reminiscences of him often also attribute this characteristic to fatherly benevolence, it is far more likely that the motivation was more practically based. It was difficult to keep a top man working in the boondocks of Louisiana without cutting him in for a part of the profits. But whether through kindness or pragmatism, the results were the same: Buchanan's workers were a faithful lot.

Financially, they were well advised to be so. While their pay was typical for the area and the industry, the dividend payments they received as shareholders were comforting indeed, especially considering that much of their day-to-day overhead was reduced by living in a company town. The only catch was they often had to wait awhile for those dividends to start rolling in.

The Bodcaw mill was the exception, possibly because it was the fountainhead of the entire operation. In its first year, 1890, it paid out 10 percent; the next year, 105 percent; thereafter it settled down to a happily predictable pattern, interrupted only by certain periods of expensive growth, as from 1893 to 1898:

Year	Dividends
1892	20%
1893	20%
1898	100%
1899	73⅓%
1900	66⅔%
1901	20%
1904	166⅔%
1905	145%
1906	226⅔%
1907	180%
1909	90%
1910	12%
1911	200%
1912	375%
1913	340%

The list goes on, and, admittedly, the amounts continue to fluctuate with the fortunes of the company, the mood of the market, and the attitude of the federal government toward uninhibited trade. An example of the latter occurs after 1913, when dividends dropped for the duration of World War I: the government had decided the lumber industry was getting excessively wealthy from the plight of the Europeans. With the above figures as evidence, one could hardly fault their findings. However, in 1920, with those restrictions lifted, dividend yields totaled 450 percent, and in 1923, 600 percent.

Of course, the Bodcaw mill, the first and the largest of the family, was the most lucrative of the lot. Other members of the clan were not so immediately profitable. Pine Woods paid its first dividend twenty-three years into its history, but did handsomely thereafter, and Grant took eight years to get started.

The 1905 acquisition of the Grant Lumber Company marked an expensive departure in the above-mentioned pattern. In 1901, a month before the Minden Lumber Company was incorporated further north, a group of experienced St. Louis–based lumbermen purchased an eleven-mile railroad in Grant Parish and ten thousand acres of "one of the finest areas of yellow pine timber owned by any corporate company."[7]

Capitalized for $75,000, in two years' time its stock increased to $900,000. Its total worth in 1905, now including fifty-three thousand acres, was $1,205,000 (or $13,857,500 in 1984). It was hardly a bargain.

And yet Buchanan helped increase that value. Late in 1903, his L&A Railroad, building a branch road that would eventually connect with the Mississippi River at Vidalia, linked up with the Grant Lumber Company's small railway, immediately putting that company in commercial contact with the outside world.

At that time, the L&A continued on, quickly reaching the Jena area for the groundbreaking of the Trout Creek Lumber Company in 1904. But presumably some deal had been struck with the Grant people, for in February 1905 they formally assessed their worth, and by March William Buchanan had taken over.

He did so in two bites, creating the Grant Timber and Manufacturing Company to control the timberlands, and the Grant Land and Lumber Company to run the mill. Interestingly, officers and financial backers of the old Grant Lumber Company appeared as major stockholders in both these new outfits, and the initial price of shares was set at two and a half times above par, a first for Buchanan. Immediately, there were signs of economic constraints: calls on the shareholders to quickly pay up on their subscriptions; indications that $100,000 worth of stock had gone unsold; massive loans accepted from people like the Packs and Peter Kuntz, an Ohio-based lumber dealer; a lease covering three thousand acres to a turpentine company in exchange for cash and 80 percent of that company's stock. Also, in 1907, the capital value was increased from $500,000 to $672,000, although, as time would tell, to no avail—shares still went begging.

All together, especially in the context of William's prior fiscal patterns, these events take on a strained financial look. As a further indication of this, William's personal stock, by mid-1906, was no longer in control. Arthur Pack (age six—presumably Charles Pack arranged this), Peter Kuntz, and one of the former officers of the old Grant company all owned more shares than Buchanan. Even more telling is a notation in 1911 that A. H. Gates, again one of Grant's previous officer-owners, canceled a long-range timber purchase deal that William had set up—an unheard of reversal in any of the other Buchanan companies.

Money was tight generally throughout the Buchanan empire at this time, and the extra burden of the two Grant companies can't have helped; nor did the burning, in 1906, of the two-year-old Trout Creek mill. Reportedly (and this fits with the scratching for money described above) Trout Creek was to be the last of the Buchanan enterprises, at least for the time being.

Taxes were to dictate otherwise. The tax setup in Louisiana was not particularly enlightened. The levies placed on land were, within guidelines set by the 1879 state constitution, at the discretion of the individual parish police juries, the Louisiana equivalent of county governments. For the most part, these taxes were very low. Nevertheless, when the lumber companies moved in, the police juries were quick to take as much of their share as they were allowed. They did so on an *ad valorem* basis: an annual assessment of the worth of the property and all that was on it. As a result, land with standing timber had a higher value than miles of empty fields, and it was taxed again and again, year after year.

The lumbermen's solution to this economic drain was quick,

direct, and equally single-minded: they stripped the land, and sometimes with a vengeance. Clear-cutting in the early twentieth century was less total than it is in the 1980s. Trees of six inches in diameter and less were too small to be milled and were often left standing, inadvertently developing into seed trees for future generations. But small or not, they could still be taxed, especially if the local police jury held a grudge against the timber owner. Again, the solution was immediate: many such lumbermen simply burned the land—debris, grass, saplings, and all.

In William Buchanan's case, this was obviously not the solution—he had barely begun to cut. Testimony has it that Buchanan envisioned keeping Trout Creek in operation for seventy to eighty years, but when the police jury assessment of his land was delivered in 1905, he realized the only way he could stay solvent was to remove as many trees as quickly as he could.[8] The Good Pine mill was built the next year, and Trout Creek was rebuilt within months of its burning. In late 1912, when the market began to soar again, a third mill, the Tall Timber Lumber Company, was added right across the L&A tracks from Good Pine.

This does not mean that Buchanan was a thwarted reforester whose virtue was derailed by the narrow-minded greed of local politicians. The mere fact that he estimated Trout Creek's lifetime as being seventy to eighty years indicates that reforestation never crossed his mind. With all three Jena-area mills operating simultaneously, it wasn't until 1941 that the last one closed shop. Obviously, using exactly the same destructive cutting practices, Trout Creek all by itself would have taken a lot longer to do the same job—maybe even seventy to eighty years.

On the other hand, it is also difficult to condemn the police juries. They had become aware, along with the rest of the South, that something odd was happening with this economic marriage to Northern capital. At the time of the courtship, in the late 1870s, the South had been led to believe that Northern-style wealth was heading her way. Instead, some thirty years later, the South had been turned into a vast natural resource for Northern industry; raw materials were pouring out of the old Confederacy at a steady rate, but the finished products made from them were still being produced by the same old industrial centers above the Mason-Dixon line.

The frustration was tangible. Buchanan and his peers were cutting as fast as they could; the police juries and their brethren were taxing for all they were worth; and both of them were working against a Northern-held ecological time bomb—in 1910, 62 percent of all the workers in the South were engaged in the extractive industries. It is unhappy to think what might have resulted from all this fratricide had the Great Depression not come along to stop all of them dead in their tracks.

In any case, with the completion of Tall Timber, William Buchanan's empire building essentially came to an end. And even Tall Timber was a bit of a fluke, owing its birth to an improving market and its survival to Europe's decision to tear itself to shreds. It was one last example of William's ambitious drive dovetailing very neatly with his extraordinary good luck in timing.

It also marked the leadership debut of William's troubled bachelor son, Will, who was given a stock majority and the presidency of the new mill at age twenty-six, albeit under careful supervision. It was an interesting demonstration of William's lack of trust in his son that he surrounded him with an executive structure made up entirely of the tried and true old-timers, all equipped with just one share apiece.

William, at the opening of the Tall Timber Lumber Company, was sixty-three years old. His seven mills produced in excess of 1.5 million board feet a day and were on the verge of a three-year annual shipping average of over 300 million board feet. His railroad, a commercial success carrying both passenger and freight trains, covered some three hundred miles, and he employed over five thousand people. At the time, this represented a real fortune. Figures resulting from the Sixteenth Amendment (the 1913 income tax law) reveal that in the entire South, just seventeen people made over $150,000 a year. William, in all probability, was one of them.

3 / Day-to-Day Operations

Unlike the famed lumberjacks of the northernmost regions of the country, loggers in the South were an unremarkable lot. On the average, they were white, illiterate, local family men given to overalls and floppy, broad-brimmed hats. While probably no purer of mind than their rowdy Northern counterparts, they were generally more constrained by the society they inhabited, at least when they weren't in the woods.

In the Buchanan mills, these men mostly lived at home in company housing with their wives and children, commuting to and from the forest on the logging trains. In some instances, when cutting operations had pushed too far into the woods to make this daily trip reasonable, temporary camps were erected. This was true of Bodcaw, Pine Woods, and Grant.

Reflecting the latitude that William gave his individual mill managers, these camps came in all varieties. Some were made of crude housing that had to be demolished each time a move so dictated; others consisted of prefabricated cabins that could be picked up by crane and brought along on flatcars, furniture and all.

But routinely, the men came home every night. The one major problem with this arrangement was that travel time to and from the job site was not paid for by the company—the men had to be in place when the whistle blew at 7:00 A.M. Children in the mill towns at the time remember their sleep routinely punctuated by the clanking and rumbling of the logging trains pulling out into the predawn darkness, carrying the men off to their work. By the same token, the payroll office and the commissary had to stay open to accommodate the loggers returning well after nightfall. This was true six days out of the week.

That morning trip to the woods could be long. Each of the

mills usually had one major, well-built logging road that went out to the heart of its timberlands, sometimes reaching thirty-five miles in length. Off of this central road were several short spurs up to five miles long, laid in the rough fashion described earlier. Considering the slowness of the locomotives, built for brawn over speed, it sometimes took the loggers a couple of hours to get to where they were going.[1]

The locomotives were truncated, squat-looking things; the cream of this crop were Shays. The Shay, designed in the late 1870s by a Northern lumberman of that name, was short, flexible, and distributed power to more of its wheels than was standard. The result was a locomotive that could negotiate both the primitively laid track and the frequently rainy or freezing weather that would have stopped conventional machines. Unfortunately for its passengers, the trade-off was a snail-like pace.

The loggers were all part of a series of specialized, interworking teams, some of which, to promote productivity, were designed to be directly competitive with one another. This situation, coupled with the long hours, the hard work, the general discomforts, and an age-old Southern proclivity for violence often led to tense moments:

> See, they used to log these woods with a logging tram. All right, you work both sides of the tram. You've got a team foreman on one side and you've got a team foreman on the other side. And these fellows had to be pretty tough because sooner or later somebody was going to call their hand, you know? And either you had to be able to pack your stick or they'd send you to the house. When that guy loses his temper, he's gonna whip you. He might come at you with a knife or he might come at you with something else.

The most popularly visible members of the logging crew were the tree fellers, or "flatheads."[2] Working two men to a saw, they tended to see themselves in a somewhat special light, echoing in this their more colorful Northern counterparts. All trees were cut with a two-handled crosscut saw; the flatheads preferred to work at about waist level for their own comfort, while the crew bosses

The nimble but snail-paced Shay locomotive

insisted they get more value out of the tree by cutting it closer to the ground.

Supporting the flatheads were the saw filers—a small group of well-paid experts who kept the saws sharp and clean. Considering the dozens of saws and the hand filing each one required, this was no easy task. It was not uncommon for these tough old trees to take the bite out of a saw's teeth within a couple of hours.

Catering to the flatheads, although they would probably have said the flatheads catered to them, were the equally proud teamsters. These came in two varieties: mule skinners and bull whackers, both of whom were so named for their prowess with a whip. The debate over whether mules or oxen were best suited to lugging trees across the forest floor was colored by the peculiarities of both beasts. Oxen were strong but more stubbornly resistant to command, while mules were more malleable but not as powerfully built. The Buchanan mills favored mules, which were also cheaper to buy and maintain. The mules' job was to pull either large wagons equipped with enormously fat wheels—to resist sinking into the all-too-prevalent mud—or two-wheeled, brace-type devices under which the leading end of a felled tree was hoisted, allowing the rest to be dragged on the ground. The whipping prowess of the mule skinner had to do not with actually striking the hide of the animal, but rather coming close enough to flick a fly off its back from twenty feet.

Southern lumberjacks, nicknamed flatheads

Scurrying around the teamsters were swampers, men who cleared away debris from in front of the wagons, or freed the logs of any snags on the ground.

A crucial part of this whole operation, the felling and transporting, was the scaler. Equipped with calipers or other measuring devices, he calculated the board feet contained in each tree. This was for more than just record keeping. Many of the woods workers were either part-timers or free-lancers and as such were not on payroll. Their income depended on how many board feet they could cut or haul each day. The relationship between these men and the scalers covered the gamut, since the accuracy of such a measurement was quite naturally subject to opinion.

Otis Richardson, writing about a non-Buchanan logging operation of the same time and area, remembered learning to be a scaler under the watchful eye of an old-timer named Tom: "After I spent a few hours under his tutelage, Tom felt confident enough to take off on other duties, leaving me with the job. However, in reviewing my record book later, Tom made certain alterations. 'We always take off some,' said he, 'and give it back when they have a bad day.' "[3]

Of course, not all scalers had Tom's paternal instincts, and those who did not were often not the most popular men in the woods.

At rail-side, in the early days, one of the more dangerous as-

Two mule skinners with their teams. Notice the logs hung from a pair of tongs below the carriage on the right

pects of the job came into play—getting the logs onto the railroad cars. Two skid poles were leaned against the car to act as a ramp for the log. The mule team was taken off its wagon and led to the opposite side of the car. Then a chain, attached to the far side of the car, was snaked under the log, run back over across the car, and attached to the mule team. As the mules walked away, the chain tightened and gradually rolled the log up the skid poles and onto the car. That, of course, was the theory. As with all things involving men, mules, and twenty-foot-long, one-ton cylindrical behemoths, opportunities for mishaps were great. Nonetheless, the system worked for years before a flatcar-mounted crane was introduced to speed things up and reduce the risks.

Those, with two important exceptions, were the basic components of a logging crew. The exceptions were the rail gang, responsible for laying and maintaining track, and a small army of boys who dashed around the forest delivering water kegs and supplies or gathering highly flammable pine knots for the locomotive's furnace.

There was one final hierarchical detail: with few exceptions, those who worked the trees were white, while the rail gangs and those who loaded the cars were black.

The hazards of this work were tremendous—worse, in fact, than in any other phase of the entire lumber-producing business. Hands and feet were crushed, people were mangled by axes and falling or shifting trees, hernias and back injuries abounded. The

The hazardous cross-loading operation. The mule team, attached to a looped chain running over the flat-bed car, is about to roll a log up the ramp

environment itself added to the mayhem with copperheads, cottonmouths, rattlers, mosquitoes, malaria, yellow fever, centipedes, scorpions, tarantulas, and even alligators in the swampier areas. All that was in addition to hot, humid, and occasionally stifling summers and frequently bitter winters, cold enough to freeze water, but not cold enough to bring work to a stop. "It was killing. I can remember the woodsmen coming by, and I know they were young men—they were as bent as badly as I am now. And it was just from work. As a little child, I'd think they were old men."

The hardships were not restricted to humans. Unlike many of his contemporaries, Buchanan never used a steam skidder to mechanically drag logs along the forest floor to rail-side. But in exchange for his sparing both his crews and his land from this highly dangerous and destructive monster, he had to fall back on large numbers of work animals, many of which died on the job.

> I wonder sometimes if it wasn't harder on the mule than it was on the man; I don't know. A lot of them died. I've had those things bog down in the mud—just pile up on one another. I couldn't do much with them. There wasn't much

A Bodcaw steam crane in the 1920s, a welcome improvement of the cross-loading strategy of old

anybody could do. I'd just back off and let them kick and break and tear up and bawl.

As difficult as it was, at least the Buchanan employees were covered by some slim company benefits. This wasn't true for the free-lancers. Farmers frequently showed up at the mills or in the woods, often with teams in harness, to fill the financial chasm that stretched between growing seasons. The real threat to these people was that if something went wrong and either they or their animals became injured, they had no security to fall back on.

It was an awesome scene to visit. The once serene and towering trees fell, one by one, in slow, rushing crunches to the slicing of the saw. The air was filled with locomotive smoke, the tang of pine resin, the shouts of men, and the jangle of harnesses. The saw filers' rasping, the cracks of the whip, the long whistle from the train about to depart—all crowded around as in a factory without walls or roof.

All that effort had a dramatic impact on the forest, like a huge, slow-motion scythe ripping through tall grass. As the trees fell, the filtered light disappeared, replaced by the harsh glare of an

A parklike forest no longer, the crop is ready for the teamsters

unforgiving sun. The once lawn-smooth ground became buried under flammable debris: abandoned tree tops, limbs, and powdery sawdust.

When the loggers left a site for the last time, it resembled a battlefield, torn up and blasted. People who had cut down trees all their lives acknowledged the desolation, even convinced as they were that there were too many trees in the first place. Despite the fact that it could all grow back eventually, those who cared knew that what was gone could never return. What had been taken was nature's best—the survivors of hundreds of years of quiet evolution; what would grow back would be crop—fast-growing saplings adapted to wastelands and valued as pulp.

The log trains came to the mills several times a day, depending on the weather, the number of logs held in reserve, and the demands of the market. They stopped on an inclined embankment that tilted them precariously sideways, on the edge of a large pond. Parallel to the tracks and emerging from the water was a ramp made of heavy, evenly spaced beams—the reverse, in effect, of the skid poles that were used to ease the logs up onto the cars. With a clang of hammers on steel pins, the chains holding those logs in place were sprung loose, and in a thunderous rumbling, the logs rolled crashing into the water.

Inevitably, the odd tangle would occur, and one of the black laborers would have to climb gingerly between the beams of the ramp, somehow loosen whatever was holding the logs in check, and then quickly duck down between the beams, allowing the logs to roll by above his head. As several witnesses recalled, he didn't always make it in time.

Log ponds, for the most part, were artificially created. Usually, that was a simple matter of damming a nearby stream or spring. In a few cases, the water was piped in. The Bodcaw pond, a part of which survives today as Lake June, measured in its prime some eighty acres and was capable of holding many days' worth of work for the mill.

That, naturally, was the primary reason for its existence—as a holding tank for timber for those inclement times when the logging crews couldn't operate. But there were fringe benefits to preferring log ponds over storage yards. The most obvious of these was maneuverability: it was far easier to shove around a twenty-foot-long tree that was floating in the water. Cleanliness was another. The logs were encrusted with dirt after their treatment in the woods, and the water washed them off somewhat, giving the mill's sawblades a slightly easier and cooler time of it. Lastly, keeping the logs almost totally submerged prohibited their invasion by highly destructive beetles, bugs, and worms.

The floating timbers were managed by men in small boats. Equipped with pikes, they separated the logs by date of arrival and sometimes by length and corralled them behind lines of logs chained together. Seen from the air, the effect was of lily pads in a pond, each pad representing a huge gathering of logs.

The destination of all this was the mill, which loomed on the water's edge. The mills were generally three stories tall, with the third floor appearing as a smaller penthouse perched on top. A jackladder—or in Bodcaw's case, two jackladders—extended from the second floor of the mill and sloped down into the pond.

The jackladder was a long trough containing a continuously running, hooked chain at its bottom. The logs were nosed into the trough, snagged by the hooks on the chain and run quickly up to the second floor of the mill, as if they were riding an escalator.

The trough ended up on the log deck, where the mill scaler assessed the number of board feet contained within the log and where a cutoff circular saw was used to bring the log down to a specific length. At that point, a mechanical log-kicker booted the log out of its trough and sent it rolling down the slight incline of the log deck to a holding point just parallel to a machine called the "carriage."

At the Bodcaw mill and other larger outfits, the log deck fed two carriages and thus was sloped to either side of the trough, one reserved for longer logs, up to forty feet, and the other for shorter ones. The kicker then could boot logs one way or the other, depending on their length. Most of the Buchanan mills, however, were "one-saw" mills, and all the logs followed a single line of production to the end.

The carriage was the most critical piece of equipment in the mill. It, and the band saw it worked against (called the "head rig"), produced the raw slabs to be converted into finished boards down the line. The carriage was a large, sliding log holder; it grabbed each log as it rolled off the deck and held it firmly in position as it was pushed by the band saw, producing a board or beam. On each successive pass at the saw, the log was realigned.

In later years, all this was done mechanically with a mass of hydraulically powered hooks and levers and grips, manipulated from a booth by one man at a control board. In Buchanan's day, it was a man-power operation.

The carriage rode on two railroad tracks, parallel to the band saw. On it rode the sawyer, the man responsible for deciding how each log would end up, and his blocksetters, who after each pass repositioned the log and clamped it into place with two lever-activated claws. Once the log was ready, the piston operating the carriage let fly and the carriage sailed by the saw at high speed, coming to an abrupt halt on the other side. It then shot back for a repeat performance.

Aside from the precision of the job—which made the head-rig sawyer, along with the saw filer, among the highest-paid workers in the mill—the most demanding part of the carriage job was

The log carriage. Beyond it, sheathed in a wooden shaft, the large band saw awaits the logs piled to the left

merely holding on. There were no seat belts or guardrails or tethers to insure security, and many times one or more of the men would take a spill. With a one-foot-wide band saw screaming inches away from the carriage, a fall in the wrong direction could be fatal.

The sound of that saw was a significant factor. It was an enormous piece of machinery. Driven by a power source on the ground floor and going all the way up to a third-floor pulley before circling back down again, it could be forty feet in length, and moved at a rate of thousands of feet a minute. The noise was so overpowering, in fact, that survivors of the experience say it vibrated the skull. Verbal communication was out of the question, so the men at the head rig resorted to hand signals and lip-reading to coordinate how they wanted each log cut. After a long time at this type of work, one former blocksetter admitted he could read the lips of actors in silent movies. The question should have been whether he would have been able to hear the dialogue if there *had* been sound.

Located on the third floor, just above the head rig, was the saw-filing room. Here, somewhat protected from the noisy chaos below, worked the filers, men valued for their expertise and paid accordingly. Day in and day out, they sharpened all the blades of the mill, one tooth at a time, checking for chips, cracks, or metal fatigue. At least twice a day, more often if the mill was operating overtime, the saws would be pulled for sharpening and cleaning. The reasons for this attention range from the obvious to the frightening. The obvious was that sharp saws cut better. They also cut cooler, and if this detail was not attended to, the friction of a dull saw against highly resinous material could cause a fire in short order. Also, the saws were terribly expensive, being of high-grade steel, usually imported from the North, and they operated under great stress. One former mill worker remembered when a large band saw gave way at full speed; once the explosive noise had subsided and all raised their heads, they found the remnants of the blade sticking clear through a ten-inch-thick chunk of wood.

The unformed slabs left the head rig in two basic shapes—as boards and as beams. Some of the beams were left as such for future use as railroad ties, ships' keels, and trestle posts. Others were routed to the gang saw. The gang saw was made up of several parallel saws, all working in unison and located just an inch or two apart from one another. The squared beam went in one end whole and emerged as six or eight side-by-side boards. This treatment was usually reserved for the smaller logs and to produce low-quality boards for making boxes and the like.

Larger boards left the head rig and were directed, mostly on gravity-feed rollers and chain conveyors, toward edgers and trimmers and cutoff saws that further defined their shape and length. This was not a haphazard process. Each board's appearance, at each step along the way, was analyzed for its best possible grade. Instant determinations were made deciding whether a certain board would be more valuable as a twenty-footer, three six-footers, an eight- and a ten-footer, or whatever. Widths also were a factor in future value, as were thicknesses. Tied in with all this, the men making these decisions also had to be aware of the inventory, and of which areas needed resupply. All down the line, the watchword was profitability—how to get the most money for the board foot.

And yet, for all of this scrutiny and attention to value, the waste was overwhelming. Boards that today would find a home in a lumberyard were relegated without hesitation to the scrap heap. Estimates vary, but anywhere from 40 to 60 percent of the original tree didn't make it to the lumberyard at the back of the mill.

Not that all this waste wasn't put to use. The sawdust, which was sucked away by cyclone fans and carried throughout the mill in a network of large overhead air pipes, ended up as fuel for the burners powering the mill's generators. The same fate awaited the bark and scraps which were initially ground up in the "hog" and reduced to more easily burnable chips.

The process by which this rejected wood was separated from the merchantable lumber was a curious throwback amid all this mechanization. In a fact-based novel about the Good Pine Lumber Company and town, Stuart Purser introduced his primary character, a teenage white boy, to the rigors of mill work by placing him at the roller table that received both good and bad wood. His job was to separate the two.

> Some of the slabs and rotten strips of lumber and bark . . . were so heavy and clumsy to handle that they almost carried me over the roller onto the table below. For the first few days, . . . my arms felt as if they were being torn from their sockets. We worked six days a week, ten hours a day, starting at seven and quitting at six, with an hour off for lunch. After the first two days, all my muscles and joints were like boils. At night I fell into bed without even eating. I was so numb in the mornings that I would walk out of the house stiff and staggering.[4]

The boy adjusts with the help of a fellow worker who teaches him to move with the weight of the wood. Shortly thereafter, that same worker gets his glove entangled in the dangerously exposed gears of the power rollers and has his hand ground off to the wrist. The most popular nickname for this particular part of the mill was "the bear pit." Compared with actual testimony of conditions in the mill, this entire fictional episode is indistinguishable from fact.[5]

Rejected boards and beams piled up outside, for sale to

whoever wanted to cart them off. Some of the lumber went for eight dollars per thousand feet, some for one dollar per wagon load. In many instances, entire houses were built by enterprising farmers using nothing but this rejected wood, and some of those houses stand to this day.

Indeed, one of the key bywords of the Buchanan companies was their standard of high quality. People remember clearly seeing boxcar after boxcar heading out to market, filled with nothing but knot-free lumber. Today, such an excess of perfection would be economically suicidal.

The boards surviving this scrutiny emerged from the back of the mill headed for drying, either in the open air or in a kiln. In both cases, they were picked up by the largely black yard crew who used two-wheeled, mule-drawn carts to move them to the appropriate spot. Estimates are that the larger of these mill yards reached one hundred acres in size. Survivors of the era recall looking out across the mill site and seeing stacked lumber as far as they could see.

The yard crews moved fast. In many cases, they were contract workers, paid by the thousand board feet, so time quite literally meant money. This, as it turned out, could be a two-edged sword. While for the most part it insured that lumber stackers would show up early and leave late if they could, it also gave rise to a few who would happily quit once their own private quota had been reached. In these cases, the men at the back of the mill could only watch and shake their heads as, come midafternoon, those particular stackers dropped whatever they were doing and headed out to do some fishing.

Stacking was an art in itself. The idea was to place layer upon layer of flat side-by-side boards, each layer separated from the one above with a row of thin wooden "stickers" which allowed the air to circulate between the boards. The stacks reached up sixteen or twenty feet, and even with the occasional use of elevated walkways, or "tramways," creating such a pile could be daunting. But the two-man stacker teams usually did it with no visible strain, one man using leverage and momentum to tilt and swing twenty-foot boards out of the mule carts and sailing them up to his teammate on top of the stack.

All this was the fate of the more common grades of lumber. The best wood was routed to the dry kilns. These were long, narrow, hangar-sized brick or wooden buildings with double doors at each end which could accommodate several stacks at a time. The stacks were usually piled on top of low, wide railway cars and then rolled into the kilns. There, surrounded by miles of switchbacking steam pipes, they would bake for days in some instances, and be rolled out, as one man remembered, "almost scorched."

From the kilns, the lumber was moved to the planing sheds and given its finished appearance. In most cases, that meant looking much like lumber does today. But there was also a large commercial demand for fancy molding that has since gone out of popular usage. The planing mills therefore always had a number of machines that produced such molding day in and day out.

One of the most memorable aspects of the planing mill was, once again, the noise. Unlike at the head rig, however, here there were many machines all working at once, and at a much higher speed. Former residents of the mill towns rarely said much about the sound from the lumber mills, but few of them could forget the distant screaming of wood being carved into shape in the planing sheds.

The last stage of production was shipping, and that, as William Buchanan had realized, along with all his competitors, was the key to success or failure.

Buchanan was perfectly content to let the day-to-day management of his mills be handled by his staff, although they were required to file with him biweekly reports of their activities. But all the shipping from those mills was handled from Texarkana, where William was more directly involved.

To go into the details of how lumber was routed and sold, and to make the process clearly and simply understandable, would be like asking someone to successfully complete a crash course in Sanskrit—it might be possible, but hardly useful. The system was complicated, not only in and of itself, but by a regular and shady use of rebates, kickbacks, and arcane double-dealing.

Most of this activity had been ruled illegal with the passage of the Interstate Commerce Act in 1887, which established the first permanent administrative board of the federal government, the Interstate Commerce Commission. Typically, as with most seemingly pro-consumer bills of the period, there was less here than met the eye. Enforcement of the law was left to the courts, with the burden of proof and prosecution being the commission's responsibility. But the courts, somewhat startled at the appearance of this regulatory animal, began to challenge some of the orders emanating from the commission. As a result, before the commission could even begin to hunt down the lawbreakers, it found itself being hauled in before the judge. One by one, its powers were whittled down to size. When it was able to perform its function, more times than not it lost its case. By 1905, fifteen of the sixteen cases appealed to the Supreme Court had been decided against the commission. In its own annual report in 1898, it admitted its mission had been a failure.

Considering the confusion all this created and the surefootedness required to tiptoe among the rules and the loopholes, experts in the area (like Buchanan's own traffic manager, B. S. Atkinson) were truly worth their weight in gold.

Buchanan also had an old and trusted friend to help him out with his sales. W. T. Ferguson, his much-valued brother-in-law, had set up a wholesale lumber business in St. Louis and served as William's agent at that end of the line. St. Louis was a key city for commerce, still being at that time very much the "gateway to the West" as well as the marketing funnel for the South. Few people realize that there were no bridges crossing the Mississippi south of St. Louis for the first third of this century.[6]

Not that crossing the river was ever a major factor in William's overall sales strategy. Buchanan lumber for the most part didn't compete in the long-standing and highly competitive eastern market. When it wasn't absorbed by the cities on the Mississippi and Missouri rivers, it headed west. One lumber dealer in Lincoln, Nebraska, ruefully admitted that in his opinion, every house in town had been built with Buchanan lumber.

Nevertheless, competition remained cutthroat, so much so, in fact, that trade associations began to sprout like mushrooms in an effort to control prices and production. It proved, however, to be an uphill battle. Lumbermen by nature were an independent lot, being for the most part self-made and proud of it. The business they were in was also a sensitive barometer, quick to respond to any economic ill wind. Added to this was the fashion in which many of them, Buchanan included, set up their individual empires.

Buchanan was a rather good example of how potentially weak a one-product empire could be. He established himself during the Southern lumberman's version of the gold rush, where foolishness could cause instant ruin, but boldness often met with amazing gain. Unfortunately, when some of the shine tarnished with an ebbing market, a depleting resource, and the dawning of a truly gigantic competition in the Pacific Northwest, many of the bold became highly nervous.

The major problem was overhead. While times were good, the man with the biggest operation grabbed the most and made a fortune; when the market began to fluctuate, the same man found himself standing atop a very shaky scaffold. He had no diversification, and all his money was tied up in equipment, plants, real estate, salaries, taxes, and interest payments. As he watched the market drop and the price of lumber drop with it, his profit margin grew slimmer and slimmer, and there was little he could do about it except hold on and try to ride it out.

Riding it out could entail a variety of options, some of them drastic. He could freeze or reduce wages, lay off his workers, close or sell some of his plants, unload his less productive properties, find a market outside his usual network, or even, as a last resort, burn some of his property for the insurance. William Buchanan, at various times, did most of these things, and his son, allegedly, did the last.

Of course, for short periods of time, producing lumber at a loss was better than sitting idle and letting the bills pile up. So, often, Buchanan and others like him kept turning lumber out in the absence of a market, betting that when it returned, it would be fast-moving and hungry. This process had one obvious drawback: if it was kept up for too long, the lumberyard became glutted. In that case, spare railroad cars were used for storage, and once they were filled, they were sent out on the road along the most circuitous route possible. While in transit, the lumber was sold to whoever was interested, and at increasingly lower prices the closer they got to the end of the line. One ex-employee of the L&A who worked in Texarkana recalls entering William's office to tell him no buyers had yet been found for such a shipment. William, stretched out on the couch, one arm across his eyes, merely waved his hand and said, "Go lower, go lower."

Another story reflecting how close to the bone William's operation could cut is told by a man who worked as a general clerk. While visiting some friends in the claims department, he noticed floor-to-ceiling racks of unpaid claims sent in by businesses in receipt of damaged goods; the businesses were demanding adjustments on their already paid bills. The clerk asked one of the men why the company didn't just pay off the claims. "Are you kidding?" the man responded. "The only way we can operate is on the interest we owe on all these claims."[7]

This helps explain an odd dichotomy with which William had to deal. The huge dividends mentioned earlier were not necessarily signposts of good health. They were the only way he could get money back into the hands of the people who had invested in him, some of whom had done so quite generously. So when the market dropped, as it routinely did, the dividends were apt to keep coming, despite the fact that their suspension would have helped in weathering the slump. There is no telling how many times this Russian roulette strategy came close to being fatal, but it does help to explain why, when the Depression of the 1930s finally hit, these companies had so little protection against the storm.

William was not alone in his constant financial predicament, although he is credited with being cleverer than most. The economic buffeting the industry constantly underwent became more than even the hardiest individualist could withstand indefinitely. Salvation, it was hoped, could be found in unity, and a rapid growth of trade associations was the result. By responding in this fashion, the lumber industry joined what was becoming a nationwide trend. From the syndicates of the super-rich to the unions of the beleaguered working class, the country at the turn of the century was organizing.

The trend setters were mostly the rich. Early on, prospering capitalists saw that if supply of a given commodity were successfully controlled, the price tag given that commodity soared. As the export/import business rose in importance, these men saw their monopolies threatened from overseas competition. In defense, they enlisted politicians who could control this flow through the creation of tariffs. The resulting collusion between business and government led to a closed-off community of high prices, low wages, and gross social inequality.

The next step in this inevitable progression of push and counterpush was the gradual organization of the working classes. As relentlessly as their privileged counterparts, they began to find strength in numbers and to exert their new power. For them, too, there were politicians ready to carry their banner.

The lumber business, as did many others, found itself squeezed in the middle. On the one side unable to present as unified a front as could steel or oil, it feared on the other being dismembered by the unions.

For lumber's one critical weak spot as a potential industrial monopoly was the very nature of its product. Boards and beams made from trees, unlike rails from steel ingots, could technically be produced by anyone with a saw and some time. So for every magnate like Buchanan, capable of some clout, there were dozens of small-timers with portable mills who eroded any potential unified market strategy with their heedless independence. It was a case, quite literally, of the Davids outnumbering the Goliaths.

Nonetheless, the Goliaths sought comfort in each other's company. In 1890, the same year the Sherman Antitrust Act became law, the Southern Lumber Manufacturers' Association (SLMA) was formed, one of the earliest and most aggressive of the regional lumber-trade groups. Its major goals were to categorize all lumber into a finite number of grades and to fix its various prices industrywide.

It is an interesting insight into this period that while the latter goal was flagrantly illegal, it was nevertheless attempted—the struggles of the Interstate Commerce Commission were not to be unique. Indeed, whatever John Sherman's intentions were when he sponsored his famous bill, its wording was so vague as to border on allusion. Its effect was that Congress handed the prob-

lem of policing the monopolies over to the Supreme Court. And in an age when all conspired to honor capitalism, the Court was just one of the crowd. From 1890 to the end of the Taft administration, it proved the point by using the act most often against the unions, claiming that picketing, boycotts, and strikes were restraints of free trade.

Despite this advantage, the SLMA made little headway with its plans. Even millionaire lumbermen proved a cantankerous crowd, brought up in a dog-eat-dog tradition. To ask them to lay down their capitalist ambitions and cooperate with their competitors was too much. The lumbermen's association never did successfully fix prices, and it took a full nine years to only partially establish a grading standard.

But while a failure as a monopoly builder, the SLMA was to fill a crucial role as a union buster. The nation's economy, despite Big Business's manipulations—or because of them—continued to fluctuate badly. Labor unity grew stronger: in 1894 the famous Pullman strike occurred; in 1898 Eugene Debs formed the Social Democratic party; in 1900 he ran for president, and the United States Industrial Commission concluded that strikes and lockouts were more prevalent in this country than in any other industrial nation in the world.

In 1906, the Southern Lumber Manufacturers' Association changed its name to the Yellow Pine Manufacturers' Association (YPMA) and created an offshoot, the Southern Lumber Operators' Association (SLOA), with the sole purpose of combating

Smoke-shrouded panoramas of the Trout Creek Lumber Company

organized labor. While the lumbermen were slow to band together against a volatile market, they now enthusiastically ganged up against their workers. At around this time, even William Buchanan let go of his cherished independence and joined the YPMA.

In June 1910, the first battle line was formed in Fullerton, Louisiana, when the newly formed Brotherhood of Timber Workers attempted to unionize one of Buchanan's competitors, the Gulf Lumber Company. One year later, less than 5 percent of all the mills in East Texas and Louisiana were operating full-time. Eleven thousand people were out of work, and the industry was rife with strikes, shutouts, blacklists, and violence. By 1912, the killing had started.

In 1911, Buchanan had his one and only taste of that general turmoil. The L&A Railroad shopmen working out of Stamps went on strike. Details are vague, but witnesses remember William standing on top of a boxcar telling the strikers they had one month to change their minds or they'd lose their jobs. One month later, he had them replaced.

But while "creeping unionism" generally passed them by, the Buchanan mills were not spared the hysterical paranoia that gripped both sides. A resident of Jena recalled one particular night.

> Those companies were against labor unions, and most of those men in authority were too. I know my father was. One particular night, I remember, they were fearful there would

be outsiders who would come in and try to organize. There was a warning that the individual homes might be raided or something and those who didn't have guns were furnished guns.

That night, everything was locked and barred, and later we heard a "thump, thump, thump" on the front porch, just as though somebody was trying to do something. It later developed that it was our old dog Towser, thumping his tail on the front porch.

The Brotherhood of Timber Workers failed. By 1913–14, it ceased to exist. It was a bitter irony to the unionists that it was more the weather that beat them than the Southern workers' inbred reluctance to organize. Just when the brotherhood tried to shut down the mills with strikes, the mills found it to their own advantage to shut down anyway. Extremely rainy weather and a soft market made production a costly waste of time. When the weather finally let up, the market was so starved for new lumber that prices shot through the roof. Mills, once idle, went into overtime and double shifts, and workers climbed all over each other showing up for work.

Not that unions stood much of a chance in any case. The South, with its rooted, rural, largely uneducated populace, was no hotbed of radicalism. People had been bred for generations to believe in the rightness of a ruling class, and had even fought a war to protect it. Unionism would come eventually, but like most things in the South, its advent would be gradual and cautious.

Unfortunately, lumber mill workers could have greatly benefited from the unions, even those loyalists who worked for Buchanan. For while the Buchanan mills were head and shoulders above most, they were still pretty casual with the welfare of their employees.

Take wages, for instance. In 1890, the first year of William's success, lumber industry "common laborers" earned an average in Louisiana of just over 16 cents an hour (equal to $1.84 in 1984). Fourteen years later, in 1904, that average was 13.7 cents an hour ($1.57 in 1984). By 1930, wages had climbed to an average of 23 cents an hour, but inflation had gone up too. In 1984 terms, those workers were making $1.44 an hour—40 cents less than they'd earned forty years earlier. And the real crunch of the Great Depression had yet to come.

> I started out at $3.55 a day—that was for ten hours. Then they cut it down to $2.25 [in the mid-1920s.] Then they cut it down to ten cents an hour. That was in the Depression.
>
> The white man, he had a better thing all the time. He'd go in there and get a job and they'd pay him a little more money, working right along there with me. I was working for $2.25 and he was getting about $3.00 and something. They didn't know how I could live on that, . . . how a black could feed a family of seven children and a wife.[8]

The answer was that many people either lived out in the country and raised their own vegetables and livestock, or they did so in the backyards of their company houses. As the same black man put it at the time, "If I can't make it here, I can make it somewhere." That was the saving grace of the entire nation before and during the Depression: for the most part, people like these had never had anything. This was just more of the same.

An additional aspect of this wage picture is that all the above figures reflect what was in the company books, not what the workers actually received. In fact, the men in the Buchanan mills rarely received their full wages in cash, and sometimes never received cash at all.

In the early days, at the turn of the century and before, payment was commonly made in script, redeemable only at company stores. The exceptions to this rule were contract workers and the higher-echelon men. It was possible, in some instances, to turn in the script for cash, but only at a loss.

This practice eventually came under fire and was technically eliminated. What replaced it was a coupon system. Each worker was paid in cash on Saturday; if, however, he needed funds in the middle of the week, he could only get coupons, again only usable at the company stores. The value of the coupons would be deducted from his Saturday paycheck.

There were three advantages to this system: (1) the company avoided putting as much hard cash aside for paychecks as it might otherwise, and therefore used that money elsewhere; (2) the worker was tied to the company more securely than through simple loyalty; and (3) the company stores were guaranteed business and rapidly became significant income producers.

As bad as it sounds, this sytem was considered the cream of the crop by Buchanan employees, and to this day he is highly praised by many of them, black and white. In other mill towns, the coupon alternative was often a flat-out sham—company paydays were six months apart, as against every Saturday, virtually guaranteeing an entire work force of debtors. Additionally, Louisiana, which produced the most lumber coming out of the South, paid out the highest industry paychecks on the average. Buchanan's wages for blacks, traditionally lower than those for whites, met that average, meaning the whites all did slightly better.

That, to some of Buchanan's executives, was not something to be proud about. "Mr. Gallaher [one of the headmen and a shareholder of the Trout, Good Pine, Tall Timber trio of mills] was heard to say, even as late as the thirties—he stood up and said it at the barbershop—that no laborer was worth more than one dollar a day. And he was a big churchman."

Benefits, to use a distinctly modern word, were on as slim a footing as wages. They basically consisted of access to the company doctor, which privilege was paid for with an automatic monthly deduction from wages of about a dollar per person. The care received was not of the best.

> They'd get out there and work their butts off. They'd have a guy, like a timber cutter or some guy rolling a log, and he'd rupture himself. They'd have the company doctor there and he'd say, "Aw, you just strained yourself, that's all. Take off a couple or three days." And he'd go back out and start to work again.
>
> Those doctors—they sure wasn't no De Bakeys. Hell, I've seen people die in these sawmill towns just for lack of a hospital. If you'd been someplace where you could have hospitalized them for four or five days, they wouldn't have died.

A case in point was one woman's seven-year-old sister, sick with typhoid fever: "The old doctor at Trout—I guess he knew what he was doing; he was the best they had. But they say he gave her what they called calomel, which I think is quinine. And it salivated her. This doctor, he had been to school a little, I think. He did the best he could, I'm sure."

Calomel is not quinine; it is a mercurous chloride compound—a highly poisonous cathartic. By administering it, the doctor had insured that the child would die from any one of three causes: by acute dehydration through use of a strong purgative, by mercury poisoning, or by the fever itself, which the calomel wouldn't have treated in the first place.

While ill, a worker could expect the company to cover his medical expenses, but his wages were suspended the moment he stopped working. And if he died as a result of injuries, his family knew better than to look to the company for help. "The way they'd do that is they'd go out and take up a collection of all the workingmen and pay for the funeral and any other expenses that incurred. That was the extent of it. Naw, the company never took care of anybody."

That was mostly true for the laborers and the lower-skilled workers, the "back of town people." The upper echelons fared much better. Not only were stockholders' widows allowed to retain their late husbands' shares, they were occasionally invited to loan money to the company to insure themselves of a tax advantage and a steady interest income as well.

Accidents were plentiful and mostly avoidable. Reminiscences abound of dangerous working conditions, unsafe equipment, and a slowness to respond by those in charge. But all this—the physical hazards, the high death rate, the official lack of interest, the abuse of human resources—was par for the times.

These were, after all, the years of sweatshops and child labor, of convict leasing and yellow-dog contracts.[9] Malaria, smallpox, yellow fever, and the flu washed through communities with monotonous and deadly regularity. So too did men, and occasionally women, armed with knives or guns or whatever fell under their hands; their frustrated response to the heat and the oppression and the racism was spontaneous violence.

With all that taken into account, and with some truly execrable examples to hold up in comparison, the Buchanan mills, for all their flaws, don't look too bad. The best witnesses of this—those men and women who had experiences outside of Buchanan territory—all attest that what William Buchanan had to offer, slim as it was, was about the best that could be expected.

4 / Mill-Town Life

William Buchanan, through his companies, created seven wholly independent communities. The town of Buchanan, Texas, was an unstructured, tiny affair that grew haphazardly out of circumstance. Others—Stamps, Springhill, and Selma—had their beginnings, however minute, before Buchanan's arrival, and the most impressive, the grouped trio of Trout, Good Pine, and Tall Timber, were carved right out of the forest.

With the exception of Buchanan, Texas, of which few details survive, all these towns, including that part of Minden, Louisiana, which the lumber mill dominated, shared a physical and sociological similarity.

In appearance, these towns might be most kindly described as "practical." Laid out generally in square grids of interchangeable "shotgun" houses,[1] the grids were further split into quarters, and then again according to the race of their inhabitants. Each house faced a street and backed on an alley and had a small yard and an outhouse at the edge of the alley.

> Sanitary conditions were very bad. The outhouses were on flat ground and there was a little ditch that run down the back. Usually it was slanted one way or the other, and ours—we lived on the end house—ran east for a block. Then it turned north along back down into the millpond [also a popular swimming spot]. There was a man come in with a two-wheeled cart once a week—every Thursday. He'd scoop all the stuff out and throw some lime in. But there were flies everywhere and we didn't have screens anyplace. We did have mosquito bars over our beds.

They cleaned it as much as possible, but how we lived, I don't know. That ditch got pretty ripe.

The yards were fenced, some better than others, and were populated by chickens, pigs, cows, horses, and other animals, the smaller of which were protected behind wire from marauding dogs; the others were let free to roam the streets or the fields beyond the town limits.

Also roaming free, and accounting for a good many health problems, were clouds of mosquitoes.

> They were worst in the fall of the year, when there was a lot of water standing—late evening, around sunset. There was a world of people around Trout who bought mosquito bars, and I could see all over the nigger town that they'd have some kind of big old buckets and put something in that wouldn't burn but would just smoke. That drove them away. But it was bad.

In the early days, most of the houses were painted a uniform gray, with the exception of the black quarters, which curiously were usually red. The black housing was also inferior in size and quality, and as improvements like running water and electricity were introduced, black households were always the last to benefit. Even then, distribution was scant. In Tall Timber, when water finally did reach the black quarters, it was in the form of one pipe for every three houses. If someone wanted an individual outlet, he had to rig the appropriate plumbing himself.[2]

The towns were set close to the mills, allowing the latter to share electricity and affording the inhabitants easy access to work. By the same token, the noise, fumes, and debris from the plants became an inescapable part of everyday life. The most prominent, and best remembered, of the sounds were the company whistles. Every day, blasts from the steam whistles dictated life, from getting up in the morning to breaking for meals to warning of accidents and death in the workplace. They became, for long-term residents, as reliable a dictator over time as the sun itself. They were also used, all too frequently, to warn of fire.

Plan of Trout, Good Pine, and Tall Timber Mill Towns

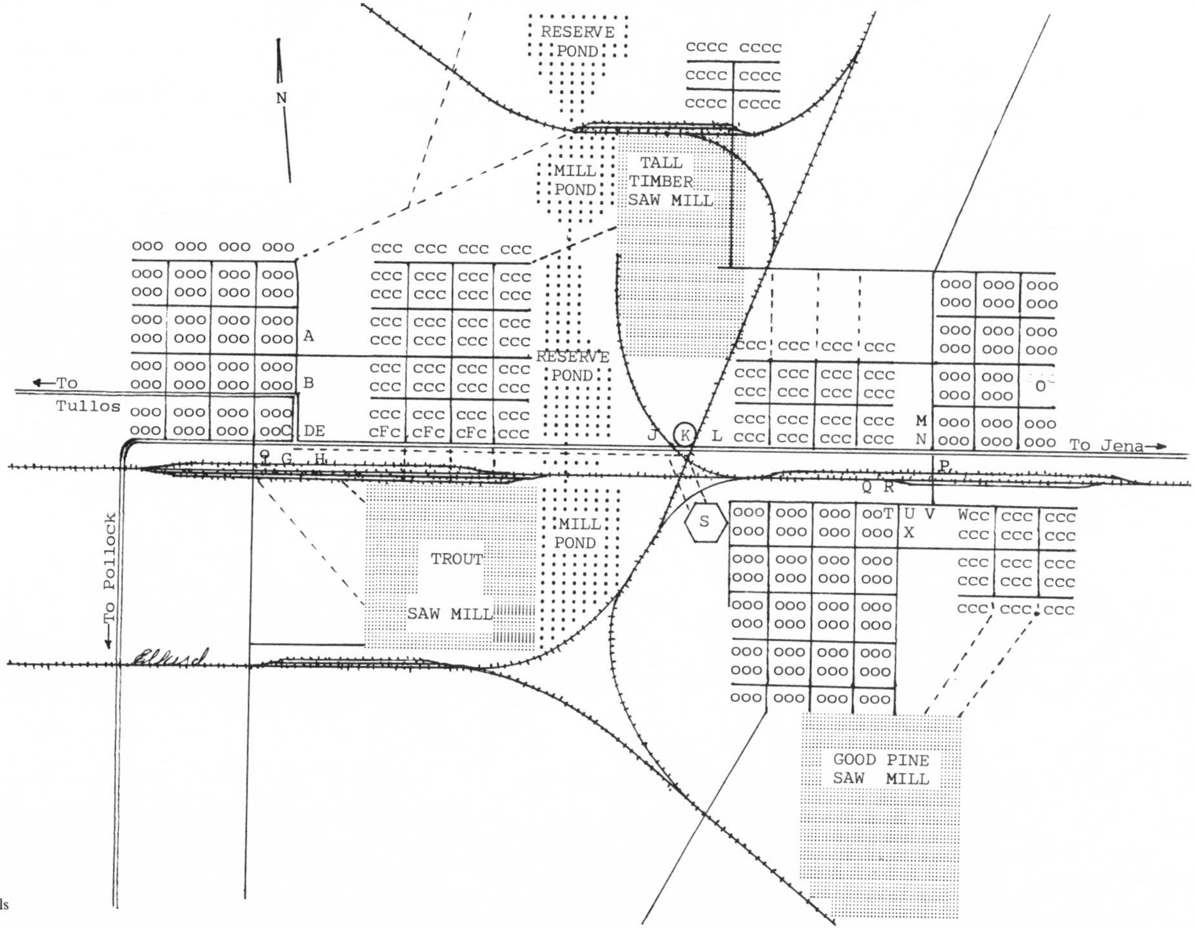

KEY

A Masonic lodge
B Methodist church, white
C Trout hotel, white
D Doctor's office, barber shop
E Trout post office
F Trout hotel, black
G Company office
H Trout commissary
I Trout depot
J Methodist church, black
K Good Pine high school, black
L Baptist church, black
M Methodist church, white
N McIntire house (Supt.)
O Good Pine commissary
P Good Pine depot
Q Baptist church, white
R Company office
S Trout–Good Pine high school, white
T Good Pine hotel, white
U Doctor's office, barber shop, post office
V Theater
W Pressing shop
X Ranch (bachelor quarters)

LEGEND

═══ Major highway
——— Street
——— Railroad
ooo ooo Company houses, white
ccc ccc Company houses, black
--------- Trail

Map by James Ellard, courtesy of Leland Nichols

> The night watchman sat up there in that tower, and if he would see a blaze of fire anywhere in the town, he'd go to ringing this bell just as hard as he could. And then all those whistles that were over there would take off with the most frightening sound you've ever heard. I used to stick my head under the cover so I couldn't hear.
>
> I can remember at night when it was storming, and lightning would strike something and the fire would start somewhere, and that little bell would start clinging and all of us children would start yelling. Because we knew what was coming. Well, you can imagine. There was a whistle for every one of them plants over there, and they were all toned different. But they were loud, earth-shattering loud.

Two other memorable aspects of town life were the smoke and the dust. "When the wind was out of the south, and it was out of the south most of the time, those cinders from the smokestacks would get everywhere—that and the smoke. Everything had a dullness about it. There wasn't any keeping it off of you. It was just there. If it wasn't moisture in the air, it was smoke."

The smoke, others have acknowledged, was often carried away by the breezes. This was not the case with the dust, ground into a fine talcum powder by an endless passage of carriage wheels. Housewives reported a perpetual warfare with the stuff, which piled up in miniature dunes in every nook and cranny of their houses.

Cleanliness, however, was not an issue for most of the populace, especially among the lowest-paid mill workers, who could ill afford it, and the children, who naturally avoided it.

> We didn't have baths. Actually, we didn't take baths. My bath came as soon as the weather started changing—I'd head for the pond and the creek, mostly Trout Creek. That's where us kids spent our time.
>
> They had a shower at the barbershop. A lot of adults would go down there. They charged a quarter, I think. That's where Dad went. He'd go a week without shaving, and then he'd go get a shower and a shave and they'd maybe

The first Bodcaw Lumber Company commissary in Stamps, Arkansas

> have a little something to put on to smell good. I loved Saturdays because Dad always got his shoes shined too.

Beating the dust and searching for a place to shower was less of a problem for those living toward "the front of town." Generally, the main street separating town and mill was gravel and somewhat less dusty. The company officials, living in larger, front-row houses, were usually supplied with indoor plumbing and electricity from the start. The social pecking order, and the physical amenities, descended the farther one got from that front row. Often, real problems arose from simply moving to the next block:

> My husband won an electric refrigerator in a contest, but we didn't have electricity. So after we got this refrigerator, he went to Mr. Brown [the superintendent] and asked him if we could make this move another block away—they had a transformer there so we could hook the refrigerator up. And he let us move.
>
> The reason I'm telling you this is that we had another friend that was trying to make a move. She wanted to move there too and, I think, then buy a refrigerator. And Mr. Brown wouldn't let her have the house. He let us have it. I just about lost a friend on that deal.

Inside the Trout Creek Lumber Company commissary

An irony in this scenario, and one which would be unacceptable to today's upper crust, was that this privileged location automatically put one closest to both the sounds and pollution of the mill and the railroad tracks which often straddled the main street.

The use of domestic help was less exclusively a luxury enjoyed by the highest echelons, due to the startlingly low wages charged. A black woman did a week's worth of laundry for fifty cents or ironed all day for ninety cents—and considered herself well paid. "They would get there and have to do everything—wash clothes, bleach their clothes, boil them in the pot outside, get the wood for that. Two dollars a week. You had to do that to hold a job, and plenty of them did it."

This highly stratified societal pressure cooker was typical of company towns in the South run by operators like Buchanan, and it wasn't restricted to the living quarters. The company owned virtually every commercial enterprise in town. This high degree of control over everyday life forced people to conform to the company's way of thinking.

The recently discovered key to industrial success, later parodied in Charlie Chaplin's *Modern Times*, was to reduce all movement, both human and mechanical, to a form of productive purity. Thus a man trained in a single gesture, standing in a line of similar men trained in related gestures, would be more efficient, and a lot cheaper, than a machine.[3] What worked most famously for Henry Ford's assembly lines applied equally well for almost every form of manufacture, including lumber. It was an easy step carrying this attitude over into the private lives of the workers, controlling their environment to insure tranquility, harmony, and company support.

And, by and large, it worked, especially in a rural South well-trained by years of modern feudalism. P. A. Speek, an investigator employed by the United States Commission on Industrial Relations, toured many of the lumber towns in East Texas and western Louisiana in 1915 and reported: "The land and all buildings—houses, hotels, churches, schools—are owned and controlled by the company. . . . [The people] are depressed, shy, and on the surface appear to be satisfied with their lot. There is no organization, no open criticism of the company."[4]

In Buchanan's case, the best example of a company's efforts to control a town appeared in Springhill, starting with its rather abrupt renaming. One non-company-related resident of the town recalls:

> They wouldn't let anybody come in close and put in a business of any kind. My daddy built his house and little store on the other side of town. And several others did that. He moved that store two or three different places over a thirty-year period until he finally settled on what we call The Hill. Some others joined him. They needed a bank, and my daddy and some other business people got together and organized a bank and put it up there.
>
> Well, [the company] saw that the town was going that way, so they made them a proposition that if they'd put the bank down close [to the mill] in the main part of town, they'd sell them the lots.

It was also in Springhill that the company faced its first defeat paying script to workers. One of the local merchants began accepting script from company employees who were sick of the commissary's high prices. When he submitted that script to the company in exchange for its value in legal tender, there was little they could do but comply.

Perhaps as a result of the town's independent spirit, the Pine Woods commissary eventually established a reputation for fairness, efficiency, and a certain amount of flair that brought it business from people from all around—a rare tribute to an institution that often was accurately accused of highway robbery.

Springhill, however, was an exception. Most of these company-dominated towns were content to sit back and ignore that they might have an existence outside of the company. Even Minden, the one fully legitimate town that Buchanan invaded, had doubts about survival following the mill's burning in 1918.

In some respects, it's hard to fault this surrender of independence. Our modern abhorrence of dictatorships damns that political philosophy across the board—no exceptions. But in the turn-of-the-century South, generic dictatorship was about the only system going; one either lived with it or starved. Northern mill towns under similar control seethed with resentment and were usually ripe for unionization. Southern equivalents were not.

Much of this was a reflection of simple inheritance. In the North, the population was largely in constant transit—families came and went in perpetual pursuit of a better way of life, and society as a whole was more regularly injected with immigrants bearing new ideas. In the South, this was less true. Ambitions for self-improvement were blunted by an isolated, insulated, routine way of life. Sons and daughters followed their parents down a path worn deep with repetition. Gradually, a mill owner who in the North was seen as a ruthless exploiter, took on in the South the aura of a father figure.

The entire state of Louisiana, in fact, owes the basis of whatever status it has in this world to such an undemocratic system of government. Huey Long will probably forever remain the preeminent example of an American dictator.

And just as there were, and still are, thousands of people with love in their hearts for Huey, so there are many survivors of the Buchanan mill towns with nothing but fond memories of their regimented society.

One might assume that an obvious and predictable exception to this rule is the blacks, many of whom still live in the now-sagging houses built for them in the early 1900s. For many, however, that is not so.

> In my way of thinking, them sawmills was the first ease that black people got. Because they was dying down on the farms, you know, slaving for what they could get.
>
> But as long as you worked for the company, as long as you stayed there and *worked*, you was all right. Wasn't nobody goin' to bother you. The company *did* pay what they promised, and that's the way the black man got away from the farm.

Not that mill-town life for blacks was a sudden bed of roses. As mentioned earlier, the whites of Springhill protested Buchanan's importation of black workers; in the Jena area, things were considerably rougher.

One of the distinguishing features about that locale, especially at the turn of the century, was the ethnic mixture of the populace. Primarily white Anglo-Saxon, it was infiltrated from farther south by both the Cajuns and a less definable group from the Catahoula Lake–Nebo region, a people notorious for their clannishness and short tempers. Competition among these three had existed for years, and violent conclusions to disputes were commonplace. Buchanan's introduction of a large black population on the one hand and his hiring of former black farmhands on the other did not go over well.

The very first night blacks arrived in their new quarters in Trout in 1904, threats of violence were made against both them and the company. The result was a company curfew, the construction of fences around the compounds, and the hiring of armed guards for protection. Out of economic necessity, the protests didn't last long, and soon blacks and whites were working side by side. But the friction remained, and as blacks ruefully point out today, Jena is still, for all intents and purposes, a white town.

It used to be a very rough town. Tales abound of shooting incidents in broad daylight, of Klan meetings, of knife fights. Blacks were careful to step off of the sidewalks and into the street at the approach of anyone white, and even the white mill-town girls were often afraid to venture into Jena. The confrontations didn't stop with the workers; the local sheriff intervened enough times in the mill towns (once shooting a man in cold blood) that the company quarterboss ordered him out permanently.

That, along with the building of fences to protect and control their own workers, was a demonstration of just how autonomous the mill towns became. They had their own rulers, their own law, and their own justice, all of which, according to both white and black witnesses, were far better than anything they got outside. Nevertheless, if a crime involved murder or reached outside the company premises, local officials were made a part of the judicial process.

All Buchanan mill towns, from Stamps to the three near Jena, had quarterbosses to police them. With few exceptions, these men are remembered for their restraint and lack of vindictiveness; several are also credited with turning a blind eye, whether paid to do so or not, to the gambling that cropped up on Saturday nights. There was a realization by all concerned that men who worked hard should be allowed to blow off steam.

Still, when times got lean, as they often did in the lumber business, blowing off steam could get downright bloody. Older residents of these towns, especially those in the Jena area, admit that what they lived through was reminiscent of the Wild West, including the frequent carrying of guns.

C. Vann Woodward, in his *Origins of the New South,* points out that statistically, "the South seems to have been [by 1900] one of the most violent communities of comparable size in all Christendom."[5] He also adds that the casually racist assumption that all or most of the violence came from the blacks is not borne out by the facts.

That may have been true statistically, but it is easy to understand how the misconception held water, especially regarding company-owned, all-black quarters. For one thing, if all the residents contained within a restricted compound are black, it stands to reason that blacks will figure prominently in the crime figures. For another, if this concentration of blacks is located in

Young Buchanan mill workers at Good Pine Lumber Company's planing shed—good examples of why a large family was a financial plus

an area populated by hostile whites, it will be scrutinized under a twenty-four-hour social microscope and subject to much abuse. Cases abound where whites and blacks were arrested on similar charges, but where only the blacks ended up facing a judge. Also, many legal altercations stemmed from whites invading the privacy of the black compounds and behaving in a fashion unacceptable in the white sections of town. Not surprisingly, the blacks occasionally fought back.

Lastly, and this was especially true during hard financial times, non-company-affiliated blacks, some with rough-and-tumble pasts, often used the company's black quarters as temporary refuges from life on the road. Considering the roads they were traveling, these men were rarely squeamish.

> One time, a fellow got off a train—you know, people used to be awful bad about riding freight trains—and somebody snitched on this man and said, "That's a bad nigger there." So the quarterboss said, "I'll follow him down the road and get him."

> He went down the road and found him and took a forty-five [revolver] off him and said, "You hit the road." The black man just turned around and went walking on.
>
> But before the quarterboss got back to town, that black man snuck around and met him and he said, "Well, we're even now—I let you look good. But you'd rather live than keep that gun, wouldn't you?" And the quarterboss gave up that gun.
>
> Then the black man said, "Now you go back to the quarters and tend to them, and I'll tend to the road."

As unappealing as all this is, it was merely a facet of life back then, as in context with the times as rampant disease, open sewage, political corruption, and any number of other "inconveniences" that today are labeled intolerable.

The poet and author Maya Angelou, a former resident of Stamps, remembers the town of her youth all too well in this light:

> Stamps, Arkansas, was Chitlin' Switch, Georgia; Hang 'Em High, Alabama; Don't Let the Sun Set on You Here, Nigger, Mississippi; or any other name just as descriptive. People in Stamps used to say that the whites were so prejudiced that a Negro couldn't buy vanilla ice cream. Except on July Fourth. Other days he had to be satisfied with chocolate.[6]

This view of the South is an enigma to most older Southern whites living today. To them, their early years were populated by hardworking, God-fearing whites served by contented, childlike, and occasionally contentious blacks. If, for some reason, those blacks were entirely excluded from some portions of society, that was merely as it was meant to be.

No history of Southern forestry or its lumber trade is considered complete without some mention of Henry Hardtner, who will be dealt with later in chapter 6. His company, Urania Lumber, which was located just a few miles northwest of Jena and the three Buchanan mills, is heralded as a model of early commercial forest management. Hardtner himself, long portrayed as a saintly figure even during his lifetime, has long been called the "father of Southern forestry."

Urania is remembered as a model mill town, peopled with loyal, dedicated workers, willing to bite the bullet when money was scarce, and rewarded by the fatherly beneficence of their boss. Ironically, few chronicles of this haven even mention the fact that Urania was exclusively white—and actively so. One black former resident of Tall Timber recalled the town's lack of hospitality:

> In Urania, we were passing through there once in a car and one of my brothers says, "I want a pack of cigarettes." I said, "Oh, William, you can wait 'till you get somewhere else." "No, I want one now," he says.
>
> So we stopped the car in Urania and he got out and went into a store. Two-dollar bills were in circulation then. He bought a pack of cigarettes, threw the two-dollar bill down, and waited there for his change.
>
> They said, "What the hell you waiting on? You'd better get the hell out of here."
>
> That pack cost him two dollars—wasn't but fifteen cents normally.

Urania wasn't unique. Several black witnesses recall that a standard routine while riding the train through Georgetown, a town next to Selma, was to get down on the floor of the passenger car to avoid being shot through the window.

In this light, William Buchanan is glimpsed as a liberal social equalizer, dedicated to giving the black man a fair break. That, of course, is untrue. Evidence suggests that William was, from his cultivated manners to his elegant goatee, the perfect image of a Southern aristocrat—a God-fearing and paternal gentleman, solicitous of and loyal to his employees. He was also a member of, and the main contributor to, a Texarkana church that had a strict segregationist policy.[7] In this and other areas of his private life, there are no indications that his views of white racial superiority were in any way different from those of his peers. His only distinction in this regard was his general benevolence to all.[8]

His extensive employment of black workers had roots both in Southern culture and in hard-nosed economic thinking. The use of blacks as slaves, after all, had not come about from mere whimsy. Initially, according to one school of thought, it was the Irish who were supposed to populate the cotton fields of the South. But African blacks proved better suited for the role, not only because they were supposedly used to the climate, but because, in Anglo eyes, their appearance, customs, and languages placed them comfortably in a social stratum between animals and humans. The white Southern slave owner never had to rack his conscience over enslaving a people who spoke his tongue and shared his skin tone. Blacks as slaves were a part of God's strategy, and all was well with the world.

When slavery was abolished, this attitude merely needed a few minor alterations. From quasi-animals of labor, blacks were upgraded to workers, and as such received pay. But their social stratum remained the same. They were still regarded as plentiful, controllable, and cheap—in fact, cheaper than they'd been as slaves. They were, in other words, the perfect work force.

That view did not go unnoticed by white laborers—whenever layoffs occurred, whites, routinely higher paid than blacks, were always the first to go. William Buchanan may have had the paternal instincts of a plantation owner of old, but he was nobody's fool in getting the cheapest labor money could buy—or in his case, import. Nor was he inclined to change that advantage by improving the status of the blacks in his employ.

That was of scant comfort to white laborers, forced to compete with, and often lose to, erstwhile black slaves. The resulting resentment, which flashed angrily with sorrowful monotony, blew up one night in 1921 in the Jena area.

The details leading to the incident are garbled, but the flash point was reached with the shooting of a white man in a boardinghouse in one of the black quarters.

> I don't know how that happened. You had a place down there, Miss Eunice's Boardinghouse, that played a lot of music and going on, you know? Just had an old gramophone . . . music playing. I think he got too much to drink. . . . Anyway, he got killed, and that's when the powder keg exploded.

Instantly, people began pouring all over town, arming themselves, inciting others to join. Allen Brown, then superintendent over all three mills, slapped a 4:00 P.M. curfew on all black housing and closed down all lumber operations.

> One fellow got in a crowd and said he'd furnish enough rope to hang a hundred fifty [blacks]. When that got back to Mr. Brown, he give him to stay away from Good Pine. He didn't even allow him to come to the post office—he had to get him another box. He told him, "Don't never put your foot on this soil no more as long as I'm here."

Brown put guards around the quarters, emptied the boardinghouses, and parceled out the boarders to any black families who would take them. He lodged the remainder under protection in the mills.

> And then he [Mr. Brown] said to the black race, "I've done everything in my power . . . can't do no more. . . . If you've got guns, you'd better keep your hands on them."
>
> And he told the whites, "When the sun goes down, don't be caught in them quarters, because I've done give the order to shoot any face that pops up down there. I've got to do something to protect my people." He said, "Now I've done talking to y'all. They ain't coming up here—don't y'all go down there."

They didn't. The curfew was maintained while the mills reopened. Blacks nervously went to and from work and slept uneasily at night until, eventually, the crisis passed. Life returned to its lopsided normalcy, dances and music were heard again in the boardinghouses, and the usual back-of-town knifings and fisticuffs reappeared for their Saturday night appointments.

Without Allen Brown, things would have turned out quite differently, and for that, most credit William Buchanan. As one person put it, "I've always thought that [Buchanan's] best asset was the eye he had for competent people. He had a knack for picking out very good people and then letting them run these companies."

This was especially true of people with a technical prowess.

E. E. Fitzgerald, the man Buchanan lured away from Minnesota and the Alis company and whom he installed as one of the head men at the Minden Lumber Company, was an engineer of no small merit. In 1893, he was issued a patent for an improved band saw that significantly affected the entire industry. This saw was installed in the Minden plant and in subsequent Buchanan plants thereafter. Names of other uniquely qualified men abound throughout the company rolls.

A smaller group, of which Allen Brown was a part, fit in among the best of these men. They were the ones whose technical abilities, in the eyes of the workers and their families, played second fiddle to their qualities as compassionate human beings.

J. F. Giles, the man in Springhill who for years filled out the company minutes all alone in an empty room, cheerfully admitted that his reason for not joining the "big brass" in Texarkana was that "I'd rather be a big fish in a small pond than a little fish in a big one." As such, until his death in the late 1920s, he proved a kind and public-spirited leader.

Another was Tommy Gillespie, the last of the superintendents of the Bodcaw Lumber Company.

> He was one of the best public relations men they had. He had a kind, helpful feeling for everybody, and anybody that needed any help went to him to get it. They didn't go to the Buchanans or Brown to get it; they went to Mr. Gillespie. And he managed to get some, one way or the other. He was quite endeared to all the employees. They thought if Mr. Gillespie couldn't get it done for them, forget it.

But the highest marks remain with Allen Brown, the son of Stamps lumberman W. C. Brown. Having come to the Jena area as a young man with the opening of the Trout Creek Lumber Company in 1906, he quickly won the hearts of those with whom he dealt. His was a mixture of dedication, friendliness, hard work, and, most important to the blacks, a sense that he truly cared for their welfare.

From his handling of the near riot mentioned earlier, to his sharing with anyone the headphones of the first radio in the area, he left behind the impression of a man whose goal it was to leave things better off than the way he had found them.

> Once, he was watching some kids playing baseball in a field, using old brickbats and God-knows-what for equipment. And the next thing they knew, a few days later, he called them all together into the post office and he had purchased a whole bunch of bats and mitts and balls and bases and the whole bit. That was typical of the man.

Everyday life in the mill towns was no endless string of gunfights and mayhem. The principal purpose for living there was to turn out lumber, and that, for the most part, is what everyone did. Six days a week, from 7:00 A.M. to 6:00 P.M., with a one-hour lunch break at noon, men and boys, black and white, transformed millions of feet of timber into boards, ties, beams, molding, and whatnot.

When the weather was prohibitive, the market flat, or the log pond had run dry (which happened during early droughts before pumps were brought in to keep the ponds full with well water), the mills fell quiet and everyone waited. Pay was suspended, so the hours were not spent watching the clouds float by. Those who could returned to their farms or went hunting in the woods for food; those whose only ties were to the town tended their gardens and their limited livestock and tried to find paying odd jobs. It was during these lulls that the commissary system of purchase on credit proved an immediate blessing and a long-term bane.

Families tended to be large. Unlike in the 1980s, the cost of having lots of children was less of a burden, while the benefits could be significant. In an era with no child labor laws, children under ten were frequently seen on the job site involved in menial tasks. The added income they provided, especially when the main wage earner was injured or sick, often made the difference between having a meal on the table or not.

Also, less fortunately, having lots of kids insured that some would survive to maturity. Infant mortality was tremendously high, among rich and poor alike. One Tall Timber resident, whose father worked in the woods, was a boy of ten when they came to Tall Timber in 1923. His mother had recently died giving birth to her seventeenth child, eleven of whom survived to maturity.

> The sawmill was very classified—the big boys in the front row, then the assistant bosses next, and on down the line. We lived on the next to the last row. It was a three-room house—two bedrooms. The five girls had the front room with two beds. The six boys and my dad had the back room, with five or so of the smaller boys in one bed. And we had a kitchen. We also had an outhouse—a two-hole job. For water, we had a shelf on the back porch and a pipe coming up with a faucet. Our house cost us five dollars a month. That included the electric, water, no taxes.

The same man recalled the regular beat of daily life.

> My sister would get up, I think at four-thirty. And my brother. The alarm would go off and he'd get up and build a fire in the cookstove. My sister didn't have to get up until the fire got going—too cold. They'd have the oven open to warm the kitchen up. Then she'd get up and start making biscuits. And she had some great big pans that could hold two dozen to a pan. She'd make two panfuls. By the time Dad got dressed to go to work, she had the biscuits made, some bacon fried, and some eggs fried. And coffee made. And she had some molasses. Dad would get up and eat, and she would put him some biscuits and syrup in a bucket—a regular lard bucket for a lunch bucket. And he'd get on that train—they rode the train out, back and forth, in a regular boxcar with benches in it. Then they'd start getting us kids up to eat our breakfast.

Cornbread and pork were the two most widely used staples in the South and managed to find their way into most meals. Balancing this nutritionally, rice, beans, and flour were standards; vegetables, fruit, fish, and game were available seasonally. While a reasonably rounded diet, it was not free for the taking, and many of the poorer workers went without much of it. For them, scrounging became a standard activity, one many of the kids took entirely for granted.

> When Mr. Sullivan would go to town, we boys would raid those apple trees. From when they were green till they were gone—we started hitting them early. Mr. Sullivan knew it, but he didn't fuss at us too much. That's where our fruit came from.
>
> Off season, when they'd open the store early to clean up, sweep up, etc., I'd go down to the back and hit the trash holder. There might be a half-rotten apple or a spotted orange or grapefruit. So we had a pretty good diet.

For the adults, these needs were less easily satisfied. The commissaries carried an enormously varied stock list, from groceries to clothing to caskets, but the prices were often high and some people were leery of the alternatives to paying cash. A well-known but unwritten rule was frequently violated by the purchasing of goods from independently owned stores in the area.

Schools, on the other hand, were free. Rudimentary, they were usually small single buildings with, for example, the elementary grades on the ground floor and the high school on the second. In Stamps, the Presbyterian preacher opened a private school, but that was unusual and reflected the comparative wealth of several of Stamps' residents.

In most mill towns, the schools were controlled by the company, usually to bad effect. In the Buchanan towns the control was there, but apparently with little or no damage. Former students of the system report that all teachers were carefully screened and were highly regarded. In Selma, the local high school was creditable enough to be the designated high school for neighboring Georgetown as well.

In the Jena area, aside from Jena's own schools, Trout offered the only available education for years.

> I remember we didn't start school until nine o'clock then because people did have to walk a distance. The Good Pine and Tall Timber children had to walk farther—the school was behind Trout over on the hill. On a rainy morning,

A touch of gentility amid utter destruction—a Sunday outing to one of Buchanan's logging spurs

sometimes they couldn't make it until it stopped raining and the water ran off a little. They had to go across the millpond and around it most of the time. And some of the kids were small. So the people complained that they didn't want their children coming that way. So for about a year they had

> school in what they called the Yellow Hotel at Good Pine. Then they decided they'd build a new school and put it somewhere between the two towns.

That was in 1917, but it still wasn't a high school. From the beginning it had only gone up to the eighth grade. Choices beyond that were limited to the Jena High School and the prep departments at area colleges. In 1919, a souvenir booklet was issued listing seventy-two students and three teachers. The local board, made up entirely of company leaders, naturally included Allen Brown. By 1921, it had become a high school with a first graduating class of six. Eight years after that, a sturdy fence was built to keep livestock out of the playground.

Typically, the blacks were not so fortunate. Where the white schools were financed early on by the companies, the blacks had to canvass their own people for the funds to pay a teacher. This was cumbersome and led to arguments, one of which concluded with the burning of a schoolhouse outside Jena. In any case, what schooling there was ran only three or four months out of the year, versus the full nine for the whites. Things for the blacks improved over the years, but it wasn't until 1971 that the Trout–Good Pine High School integrated.

Reminiscences abound of white and black children sharing the same swimming holes and playing games together, but the mutual antipathy didn't take long to surface, especially when segregated schools were located near one another.

> The niggers went to school in what they called the middle school—now, of course, it's integrated. And us whites went on the other side of the track over there. Them niggers got out of school in the evening right there and we got out right there and we had a boardwalk that would come back up to the old commissary. We met right there on that boardwalk. If you don't believe there was some fighting going on, brother, then you don't know what was going on. They didn't back up. I'll tell you, boy, them nigger boys could fight. And the white ones could fight. It got so bad there when school was out that that old quarterboss had to come down there every evening at three o'clock to that boardwalk.

During nonschool hours, children occupied themselves according to what was available. From town to town this varied greatly, but two constants were millponds and lumberyards, both of which received a great amount of juvenile attention. The ponds, with their sweeping acres of barely floating logs, proved as irresistible to young boys as a flame is to moths; playing tag across the logs or rolling them like the fabled lumbermen of the North were favorite activities. Unfortunately, as with the moth, the outcome was occasionally very sad. After a few fatal accidents, such excursions across the water were forbidden.

Fishing was not, and was plentifully practiced, as were boating and swimming in the summer and ice-skating in the winter. On many a cold Sunday, groups of people built bonfires on the shore, roasted hot dogs, and watched the skaters sail by. "At Good Pine—Mr. Brown had this done—they put in two bathhouses down there [at the pond], one for men and one for women. It was a beautiful place, and that's where I learned to swim when I was a kid. That was one of the biggest forms of recreation we had. We just went all the time."

Visits to the lumberyards only occurred on Sundays, when the mill was quiet. Hide-and-seek was a favorite activity there, as was climbing the towering piles of drying lumber, but mostly what is remembered is a sense of ritual awe. Usually accompanied by an adult, kids entered this huge and usually bellowing domain as they might have approached the dreaded dragon's den—both excited and a little scared.

> Walking across the mill yard took all afternoon, if you walked clear back to the sawmills. Of course everything up there looked huge to me. We'd go down in these boiler rooms where they were shoveling these shavings to keep up the steam. They had this colored man that worked on Sundays. They'd open those doors and throw that sawdust in there and I thought, when I was a kid growing up, "Well, that looks like what Hell must look like—all that fire and everything."

Religion was a mainstay of mill-town life, often preceding the building of the town itself. In Springhill, a Methodist preacher was holding weekly services in the planing shed before the lumber mill was even officially organized. Generally, each town's early years were marked by an unavoidable religious fraternity—one church building serving the needs of Baptists, Methodists, and Presbyterians alike. "They didn't have a church, so Mr. Giles built one. He was a Methodist, and it was really a Methodist church, but it was a community church. All the denominations used it. We had the first and third Sundays, and the fifth Sundays, and the Baptists had the second and fourth Sundays, and we all had Sunday school together for years."

It was a system few of the participants enjoyed, however, and as soon as it was financially possible, each congregation built its own place of worship. This sometimes led to interfaith bickering and a high-minded moral tone, especially in the flagship town of Stamps.

> I remember somebody wanted to go swimming on Sunday and my father said, "No, that's Sunday. That's a rest day. That's just against church rules. Nobody goes swimming on Sunday." It was that way all around town. Of course some of them would go swimming on Sunday and they'd talk about them: "They're not good Christians."
>
> Everybody went to church. The colored people had their churches over there too. Everybody went on Sundays and on Wednesday night [attended] prayer meeting. And [later] everybody had their own church—the Methodists didn't go to the Baptist church and the Baptists thought all the Methodists were sinners.
>
> Mr. Boney was a Methodist and he was about the strictest man—he was always saying anybody'd go to Hell who went to a dance.

Stamps was an exceptional case. As with most of Buchanan's far-flung operations, the individual town leaders tended to set the moral tone, and most were not as rigid as Mr. Boney. One former resident of Trout Creek recalled, "People wasn't very much church-related because when a fellow works sixty hours a week, he wanted to rest on Sunday."

Recreational opportunities were often supplied by the company, which hoped the alternatives might prove more attractive than the bottle. Again reflecting the autonomy of Buchanan's mill managers, the variety and quality of these outlets was truly a grab bag, from men's clubs to tennis courts. "When we first moved to Good Pine, no one ever went to play tennis without a shovel; it was standard equipment, along with the racket and tennis balls. . . . As the town developed more civic pride, pressure was put on the people in the community to keep their cows in lots or staked out in the meadows west of town."[9]

Stamps, being the queen bee of all the operations and the hometown to several of the founding fathers, had the most to offer, including a truly impressive YMCA.

> Everybody went down there on Mondays, Wednesdays, and Saturdays because those were bathing days for the public. You'd see men with those little handbags and you'd know they were going to the "Y" to get a bath. Everybody came down there. Some would get a shave and haircut and a bath. They had about twenty shower stalls—didn't have any tubs. There was a roller-skating rink . . . they played basketball—had a team. It was two stories tall. There was a clubroom and reading room upstairs. Downstairs was the pool tables and bathhouse—a swimming pool too, indoors.
>
> But the main attraction in Stamps—which at its peak when the railroad was going good and the mill had about three thousand people—the big event would be when the circus would come. It came every year—Ringling Brothers' Circus. The mill would shut down and everybody'd go to the circus.

Another popular pastime, at which Stamps again outstripped the others, and in which it took a highly competitive pride, was baseball.

> The company let some of the local college stars come in there and gave them jobs and then would let them play ball. Being a hometown boy, I didn't get any pay—I was the only one on the team not paid. I played second base. The manag-

er was the drugstore manager. He gave me free chocolate ice cream sodas. So I played semipro baseball for chocolate sodas the whole summer.

But generally, the off-hours were spent at picnics, strolling among the towering pines, meeting the trains at the station, or just whittling pieces of wood in the shade.

For the more romantic, content to sit quietly outdoors of a summer's evening, there was also a routine sight unique to sawmill towns. The mill's refuse stacks were kept burning all through the night, in order to keep up pressure in the boilers and to process the daily avalanche of scraps and sawdust. Each stack was immense, measuring from fifteen to twenty feet across and stretching one hundred feet into the sky. And each was covered with a domed wire mesh to prevent the burning ash from escaping. These domes were what caught the eye at night, semispheres of glowing cherry-red held up on ebony columns beneath a star-packed sky. It must indeed have been a pretty sight.

For the more energetic, evenings were also taken up by movies, which were first shown outdoors against sheets and later in auditoriums like those at the Stamps Opera House or the Mason's Hall. People danced, too, but often surreptitiously due to Mr. Boney and his austere kind.

The black community participated in some of these activities. Blacks were allowed, for instance, to watch movies, but only from the balcony accessible by an outside staircase. With typical Southern ambivalence, whites still have fond memories of dancing late into the night to the lively music of an imported Natchez black band, while black mill employees were not even allowed in the hall. When it came to supplying the blacks with their own recreation hall, however, the company stopped shy of actually constructing it, as they had many similar buildings for the whites, and merely delivered the lumber free of cost.

It was also deemed entertaining and acceptable to visit the black quarters at night and watch its residents play music and dance; the reverse, of course, was unacceptable.

The blacks did rule one day of every year. On June 19, Emancipation Day ("Juneteenth"), all the Buchanan mills shut down, free railroad passes were handed out, and the day was filled with festivity. The trains shuttled the 150 miles between Stamps and the Jena-area mills, stopping at towns along the way, bringing families and friends back in touch for a moment. Stage platforms were erected, bands played for hours, company-supplied ice cream and barbecue and soda pop were consumed by all. For those who became too rowdy, several boxcars were set aside as temporary cooling-off spots. Whites generally didn't participate, but took advantage of the day's leisure.

Over virtually all these activities, with the possible exception of strolls in the woods, the company exercised some form of control.

> On top of that picture-show building, the whole top was a big dance hall. And we got a band out of Natchez and we'd have that thing full sometimes. You know, all sawmill people knew each other, and they would come from all those places—not a whole lot, but a few from all of them.
>
> It wasn't company-sponsored—it was the boys that got it up and paid for it. But you couldn't come without an invitation, and you couldn't get on the list unless Mr. Brown okayed you.

The extent of control was psychologically debilitating to town residents. As the companies foresaw the end of their mill operations—something they envisioned far in advance of the workers—their enthusiasm to spend money maintaining these recreational facilities began to wane. Old-timers recall an inexplicable sense of desolation that started afflicting the towns as the ponds went unstocked, the grass took over the tennis courts, and aging movie halls were left unrepaired. Only long after the companies had closed up and left them to their own devices did residents begin to understand how drained they'd become of any self-determination.

And yet, there is little bitterness. Some of this is due to the passage of time—the witnesses to those days are nearing the ends of their lives, and have little time for acrimony. But the primary reason they don't view the mill towns with the same skepticism of their grandchildren is because those towns—for black and white alike—represented salvation: "Everybody worked at the sawmill and the sawmill was everything. And it was good. The way I look at it personally, they were a lifesaver."

5 / The Good Life

William Buchanan once told a friend that the first fifty thousand dollars were the hardest he ever made. Considering that he probably didn't reach that mark until he was well into his forties, that was an understatement. And yet, he no doubt realized that the impulsiveness that finally marked him as a great entrepreneur was the same characteristic that had made him spin his wheels for over twenty years before the Bodcaw Lumber Company came along.

Judging from the historical footprints he left for others to study, William emerges as a man of clear vision. He was not, like the stereotypical self-made millionaire, a compulsive workaholic; nor was he consumed with an insatiable need to acquire more and more. It seems, on the contrary, that once he hit his stride with the establishment of the Bodcaw mill, his goal was to become impressively wealthy, and then to enjoy life as fully as possible. That, in any case, is what he did do. In his later years, he frequently headed out for days on end of hunting or fishing, telling his secretary not to disturb him with anything shy of a total catastrophe.

Of course, if that was his goal from the start, those early years must have been studies in frustration. Certainly his restlessness betrays that: one or two years in Forrest City; one or two in Texarkana; a few in Buchanan, Texas; one in Fort Worth; several months in Leadville; then back to Buchanan. He appears all through those years as a man on the prowl, looking for his break.

When it came, he hit it in full stride, building plants, buying land, creating a railroad, hiring thousands of people, establishing a marketing network, striking deals with monied men. At times, this eagerness to move quickly caught even his trusted lieutenants by surprise. One of the Brown brothers, returning to Stamps from Washington, D.C., received a short handwritten letter from William on the eve of his departure: "Go by Detroit and buy a locomotive. Give my regards to Sally when you get home."

He created a tightly knit organization that was both light and fluid, and yet rigidly one-dimensional—except for a failed attempt in the 1920s to profit by the oil craze, the sole Buchanan business was lumber or lumber-related. And this specialization was fully supported by his backers; through decades of stockholder lists and management rosters, the same names appear again and again, a testament to rare and mutual loyalty.

That last characteristic—loyalty—is what truly distinguished William as a human being. It imbued him with a uniqueness in the eyes of his employees, his colleagues, and even his family. As tough a businessman as he obviously was, he would go to extremes to take care of those close to him who needed help or whose vices had to be overlooked.

J. F. Giles, the oft-mentioned manager of the Pine Woods Lumber Company in Springhill, is a case in point. The self-proclaimed "big fish in a small pond" who spent all those years writing up, and not writing up, company minutes, also overlooked paying taxes to the state of Arkansas for the years 1907, 1908, 1911, 1912, and 1914.[1] In addition, in 1917, after William had appointed two men to appraise each company under his control, he had to enlist Giles to help examine Pine Woods because only he could decipher the books.

Tommy Gillespie was another man William valued deeply, flaws and all.

> Tommy Gillespie was running the Bodcaw mill, the big mill, at Stamps. And Tommy had a drinking problem. Now Mr. Buchanan had a flat rule that anybody who drank was to be terminated. The people who worked with Tommy at the mill were very fond of him, so whenever Mr. Buchanan came over there, they'd hide Tommy if he'd been drinking. They always made some excuse—he was out in the woods or he was here or there. Of course, one day Mr. Buchanan came in unexpectedly and found him and he had been drinking, and he told him, "Well, Tommy, you know the policy and I'll

William Buchanan with granddaughter Mary Seeger, in 1919

just have to terminate you. As much as I regret it, there are no exceptions." And Tommy was terminated.

Almost the day Tommy left, performance at the mill started downhill. They tried to find a suitable replacement but nobody could get it back to the operating level it had been at when Tommy left. So finally, Mr. B. admitted he was going to have to swallow his pride and get Tommy back. Unfortunately, they couldn't find him and finally resorted to running ads in the *Southern Lumberman*, a magazine that everyone read at the time. The ads asked anybody knowing the whereabouts of Tommy Gillespie to please advise the William Buchanan organization in Texarkana, and gave a brief description of his age, height, slightness—he was a very slight man.

They heard nothing for some long time—I don't know, months—until they got a call from a sawmill operator in South Louisiana, who said, "I think the man you're looking for is working for me. He's not here under the name of Tommy Gillespie, but from the description, I'm almost sure he's your man."

Mr. Buchanan told Mr. Boyce to go down and get him, so Mr. Boyce went down and went into the mill owner's office, who said, "He came by and told me he was an expert sawyer and wanted to know if I had an opening." It so happened there was an opening and the owner took Tommy on. One week later, Tommy marched into the office and said, "You're not grading your lumber correctly and you're losing a lot of money because of it." So the owner answered, "If you're so smart, you grade it."

Well, Tommy did that and a number of other things, and soon enough the owner found he'd never made so much money as he was making now. But, as he admitted, "The Buchanan organization is so big I knew that ultimately they'd find him, so if you'd like to talk to him, you can."

Mr. Boyce went out and found Tommy, who saw him coming and merely said, "Hello, Jim."

"Hello, Tommy."

"What are you doing down here?"

"Mr. Buchanan sent me to ask you to come back."

"Well, I don't know if I want to come back or not."

"He's willing to let bygones be bygones."

"I'm not going back if he's going to criticize my drinking. I just won't do it."

"Mr. Buchanan said he'd be willing to waive the policy in your case."

So Tommy then went back to the Bodcaw mill and was there until the mill shut down several years after that.

This leniency, of course, was somewhat selfishly motivated, but that too was typical of both the man and his times. The lumber business, being the unregulated mess it was, had a hysterical rhythm of economic peaks and slumps, some separated by mere months. Profit margins, per thousand board feet, could vary from $1.51 to $5.45 from month to month and from timber stand to timber stand. Of course, it could also dry up entirely—one person claims that when the Bodcaw mill cut out in 1930, it was getting ten dollars per thousand feet for lumber that was costing it fifty dollars per thousand in the pond, prior to milling.

For a mill with a 350,000-board-feet daily capacity, that was a definite problem.

So, when it came to the Gillespies of the world, flawed men with money-making talents, exceptions were found. Such was not the case with the common mill hand.

This is not a condemnation. Buchanan was a paternal industrialist. Within the moral structure of his era, he stands as one of the brighter lights in both the South and the nation. While it is true that recreational facilities were primarily introduced to mill towns on the principle that happy workers are more productive, it is overly cynical to limit Buchanan's compassion to that extent. He was not, as were many of his peers, the old "massa" on the hill, whimsically seeing his workers as slaves and ruling them with a heavy, omnipotent hand.

He was instead, as countless people recall him, "a gentleman"—gentle, solicitous, almost grandfatherly, with a predilection for calling everyone "son." An example of his style is remembered by a then-new member of the L&A Railroad payroll.

> He was the nicest old man you ever saw almost. Just an example—I was a telegraph operator in the Shreveport freight office, a new building. And he came up there one day to use the telephone. I was in there at noontime, and everybody had gone to lunch except me. The operator had to stay on duty. Old man William came in and he said, in a real warm friendly way, "Hello, son, I'd like to use your telephone a minute, if you don't mind." That's the kind of man he was.

There is, to us now, an absurd element here—after all, all the man did was ask to use the phone. But the distinctions of employer/employee, of upper-class/working-class, and of rich/poor are so tangible as to make this anecdote almost painful. As far as can be determined, Buchanan never did anything to dispel this aura—he did not, for example, make a practice of laughing it up with the boys in the pool at the Stamps "Y"—but, to his credit, he also did not abuse the position that Southern social mores had granted him. While his business decisions may have cost people their jobs, and his complacency about worker safety their limbs and their lives, he was never, unlike his son, personally offensive or cruel. And that fine point—which, unfortunately for those times and the people in them, was an exception—marked a major step toward progress.

He was no pushover. The majority stock position that he almost unanimously held was used frequently as a bludgeon. He made it clear several times that if a shareholder objected to his plan of action, he would happily write a check on the spot and buy the nay-sayer out. The only noted exception to this pattern was his involvement with the Grant Timber and Manufacturing Company in Selma, Louisiana. "Anybody that wanted to know something, after they went to him—his word was law. It didn't make any difference what he said, it was right."

The knack to this brand of autocracy is in showing some degree of temperance and in setting a perfect example. The following tale, apocryphal or not, fits the hallmark of William Buchanan to a T:

> Now Mr. Lillyhand had something on his mind, so he goes up to Texarkana and demands to see Mr. Buchanan. "Mr. Buchanan," he says, "about this railroad of yours." And he laid down the law to Old Man Buchanan.
>
> Mr. Buchanan looks at him and asks, "Are you telling me how to run my railroad?"
>
> "Yes, and faith and bejesus, you're going to listen."
>
> And they say Old Man Buchanan listened, and from then on, that was Old Man Buchanan's favorite engineer. Just because old Lillyhand went up and laid it on the line. That shows what kind of man Mr. Buchanan was. He was always open to listening to people and courteous and considerate and kind and thankful. That's my impression of the old gentleman.

People who knew him better were not quite so adulatory. They also saw him as aloof, domineering, somewhat dictatorial, and occasionally hot-tempered. He was a stickler about being on time, a disciplinarian with his children, and wouldn't allow his wife any charge accounts. The difference, and it was one he managed to preserve to the end, was that his employees saw him the first way, while only family and peers were privy to the latter perspective.

This, however, is a credit to his self-control, rather than to any coldhearted manipulation, for another dominant trait of the man's personality was his sentimentality. A hapless teenage victim of the Civil War, born of a romantic age violently put to an end, he seems to have been particularly attuned to the sensitivities and misfortunes of his peers. He visited new babies born to the management people, used his private railway car for occasional missions of mercy, and commiserated with the deaths of his friends' children. He was, in fact, personally familiar with that particular pain, having lost his first two children, Lillie and Cora, aged ten and eleven, both to "appendicitis" in the early 1890s, just as he was hitting his stride.[2] It is the sad and baffling dichotomy of both his era and his class that William's humanitarian streak extended only tentatively toward his common laborers.

He was also highly religious, a devout Presbyterian whose observance of the Sabbath reached every corner of his organization. Even when he was out in the countryside enjoying himself, Sundays were a time for religious observance.

As a Presbyterian he was part of a definite minority. The South was dominated by Methodists and Baptists; in fact, even his two brothers were Methodists. But there again, the difference is appropriate—William was a natural for the patrician and loftily democratic Presbyterian church. His brothers, notably less perfect in the eyes of all around them, preferred a more grass-roots approach to their God.

Ironically, William's humble interaction with his church was to be as domineering as his conduct in business. For while he always refused the honor of being elected an elder, his routine contribution of about half the church's annual income had an anesthetizing effect.

> There were numbers of people who joined that church and belonged to it because they had a feeling that Buchanan was paying most of the costs of operation and therefore it wasn't obligatory for them to contribute much of anything.

[After he died], when they found they were on their own, then the church really began to grow.

It's hard to know how many other people were put in the shade of William's oversized shadow—certainly his two brothers and his son Will. Remembrances of the "Old Man" in public often bring forth vague saintlike images that some people probably found highly irritating. A favorite among these stories was his habit of riding the L&A rails, sometimes in a handcart ahead of the train, surprising the black track gangs at work. He'd get out among them and "talk to them like they were some of the family," before gliding away and leaving them in awe.

It seems that toward the end of his life, this kind of detached, almost celestial paternalism rose more and more often to the surface. He allowed certain company children and their parents to tour his lavish private railway car, carried the families of management employees on trips to Ringling Brothers' winter camp in Florida, and invited others to join him on extravagant hunting and fishing trips to places as exotic and distant as Yellowstone Park.

Business, quite obviously, had begun to take a backseat in his priorities.

> One of the big sawmills, I've forgotten which [Minden, in 1918, five years before William's death], caught fire and burned to the ground. They called up Mr. Boyce and told him. It was Mr. Boyce's job to go ahead and tell Mr. Buchanan. As Mr. Boyce told it, "I went in and told him, and Mr. Buchanan said to me, 'Son, that sometimes happens.' "

What did hold his attention those last years, almost exclusively, was his cherished railroad and a long-standing love affair with the outdoors.

The railroad has been touched on before. He had two private cars in succession, some say three, the last of which was called the Catahoula, after the lake of that name near Jena. They were equipped with beds, a dining room, a sitting room, a kitchen, and a bath, and the Catahoula had a deck off its rear complete with a searchlight that played on the tracks and an oversized speedometer for the amusement of the passengers.

Meals aboard were sumptuous affairs, prepared by a staff cook who lived in a small cubicle at the front of the car, and served on china by waiters in uniform. The generous extravagance was catching.

> [B. S. Atkinson] would go up there and stay on that private car while [Mr. Buchanan] was being treated at the Mayo Clinic in Rochester. I remember [Atkinson] saying he had a colored chef that was real good. Dick—I forget his last name. [Atkinson] said he told Dick one day, "Our grocery bill sure is high each week." He found out Dick was feeding all the colored folks in Rochester. They'd come down there and he'd give them food—it was some of the best eating you ever had."

Riding this miniature mansion over some of the best-manicured rails in the nation, Buchanan was truly in his element. In 1922, he made the decision to move the L&A shops from Stamps, which was by now at the tail end of his operations, to Minden. There he had built some of the best facilities money could buy.

> Buchanan was great to work for. I never saw anybody on the railroad that didn't like him. That old man—if they were told something, that's the way it was. They didn't have bosses that didn't know what they were doing. And they had the finest mechanics that ever were—ever—working on any kind of railroad.
>
> We could make furniture or anything. We built several private cars from the ground up. The only thing they didn't do was pour the wheels. But we could build a flatcar, boxcar, gondola, didn't make any difference. The machine shop could overhaul a complete engine or anything you wanted done. It was one of the finest shops in the U.S.

His other love, the outdoors, was the object of equally lavish attention. He had always enjoyed hunting and fishing, but his increased distance from company affairs allowed him to indulge himself as never before.

> He had gone up to Jackson Hole country one year and fell in love with it and decided next year he was going to go back. But he was really going to go in style. So he went to Abercrombie and Fitch and bought an enormous inventory of flies and all the most expensive kind of fishing rods, reels, and then he had a truck fixed up with a body—what we'd now call a camper body. Inside, he had rows and rows of little drawers, each drawer containing a different fly. He had a notebook with all the flies marked down—this kind of fly in drawer number two, number twelve, etcetera.
>
> He put that truck on a flatbed railroad car—of course, he could do this, owning a railroad (you could drag those things around for free)—and he took it up to Jackson Hole along with a couple of blacks, sort of manservants. And they would go out, and he would take one of the blacks with him, and if he saw a fish feeding on a certain kind of fly, he would look at his little book and say, "Go and get me the fly in drawer number thirty-two." This guy would then jump in the car which he had up there and go back to the truck, get the fly, and bring it back to Mr. Buchanan.
>
> Well, he wasn't having any luck. So he was in the grocery store there which was then sort of an all-type store, visiting with a man who was having a lot of luck, and admitted he didn't know what the problem was.
>
> The man said to him, "I'll tell you what the problem is. Throw all that goddamned junk you've got away and go and buy some of the equipment they've got here. They've got what they've got because it works in this area."
>
> So that's what he did, and he had a marvelous month of fishing.

His pursuit of fish and fowl led him from the marshes of the Louisiana Gulf Coast to the wilds of the American Northwest. Even visiting his mills near Jena, he couldn't resist a few days off to go fishing on the banks of Hemp's Creek. But wherever he went, he was accompanied by the trappings of his success—guides, servants, cooks, traveling companions, and an inordinate amount of hardware. He returned to his early haunts on the Sulphur River, near the spot where he'd sat watching the rising water threaten both the log boom he'd erected and the future he'd staked out for himself as a lumberman, and he set up a floating camp with a houseboat and a small fleet of motorboats.

His finest hour came when he heard of a property a few miles northeast of Texarkana that was covered by thousands of acres of cypress trees and swampy water. The man who owned the area was all set to harvest the cypress when Buchanan intervened, marveling at the place's potential as a hunting and fishing preserve. Apparently, the owner agreed to sell out for the value of the land, plus the profits he would have gained had he cut the timber.

> At the time that they got it, Robert and William and Jim fell out over that lake. William had all the money he wanted and liked to shoot ducks. So did Robert—he liked to shoot ducks, but he didn't have all the money he wanted. So William wanted to make a shooting lodge out of it and Jim did too. Jim, I think, always sided with William—I think he was afraid of him. Robert said, "We can't afford to leave all that fine timber up there so you guys can go up there from Texarkana and shoot dumb ducks. I like to hunt ducks too, but I get out on somebody else's rice farm and shoot ducks." Robert never did join.

The preserve, nicknamed Grassy Lake, was and is amazing to behold. Formed by a geological upheaval in the early 1800s that caused some six thousand acres to drop several feet—and supposedly allowed the Mississippi River to flow backward for a day—it is the vestige of some undisturbed primeval world. Miles of water, alternately clear and covered with a thick verdant growth, form the floor of a forest of ancient towering bald cypress trees. Birds of all colors crowd the branches and hammocks, and alligators lie motionless, basking in the sun.

William immediately formed a club, with fifty membership shares (of which he instinctively held the majority), and had a large lodge built on the shore of the lake. There, for season after

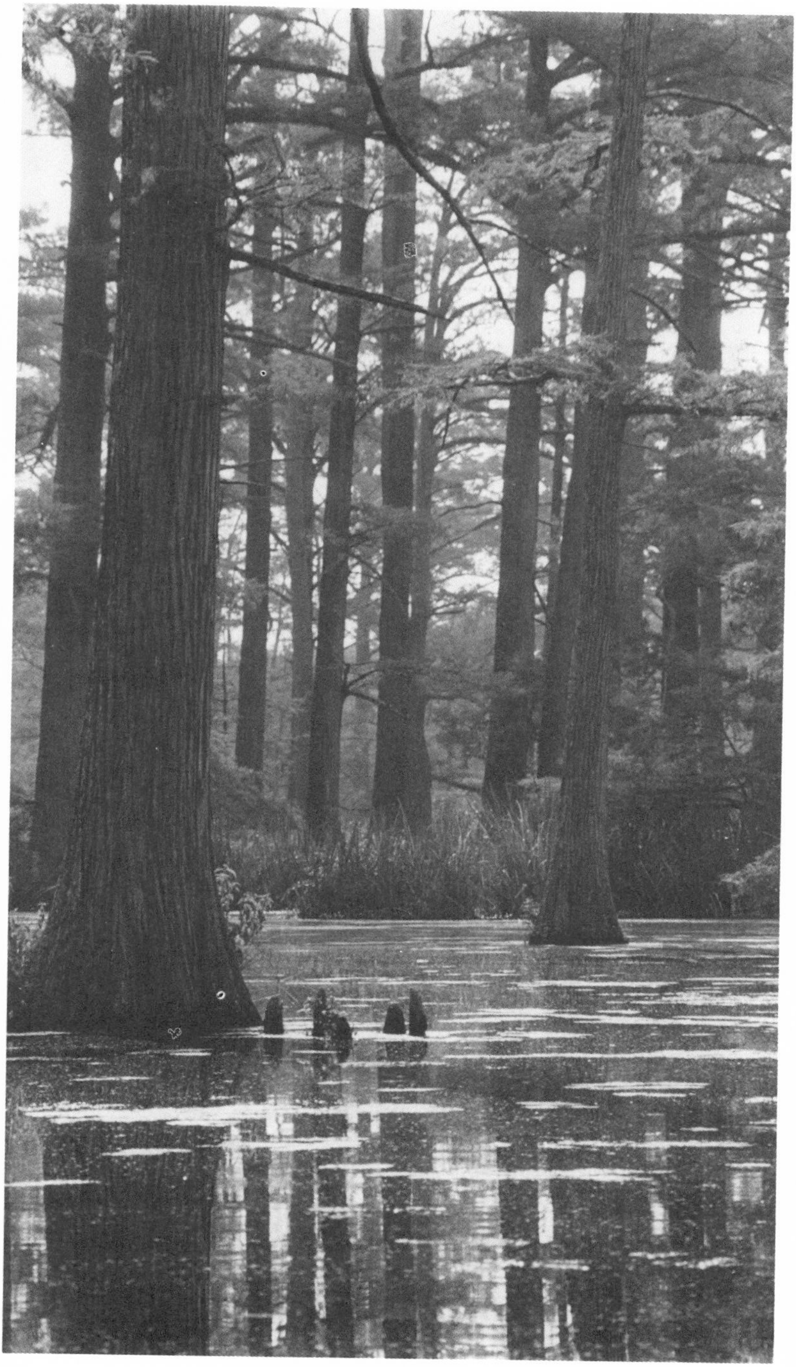

Grassy Lake today, near Texarkana

season, he and his family and friends convened to enjoy the same natural serenity that his logging crews were so busily destroying further south.[3]

Duck hunting was the major attraction, and it was handled with the industrious zeal William used on all his activities. Dozens of duck blinds were constructed, teams of blacks were hired as guides and helpers, kayak-style boats were brought to the lake, sick and injured ducks were nursed back to health for future use as live decoys. Hunting parties started at 2:00 A.M. with the arrival of black cooks in the kitchen to prepare huge breakfasts and picnic lunches. At four o'clock, guests were woken with bedside offers of hot coffee, and by five-thirty most were being paddled out onto the still-dark lake by their guides. There, in teams of two, they huddled in their blinds, keeping their hands warm over smoky smudge-pots, waiting for dawn.

When it finally came, and the ducks with it, the results were usually pure carnage. In those days before limits, morning bags of from fifteen to fifty birds were not unusual. J. K. Wadley claimed he once shot 48 one afternoon and 125 more by eleven o'clock the following morning.[4]

The one guaranteed interruption to all these leisurely pursuits came, as always, on Sundays. It wasn't until years after William's death that this one tradition was finally breached. But even he didn't let it slow him up for long. During duck season, he'd return to Texarkana on Saturday night, spend the next day in town, and be out by the lake twenty-four hours later.

During the last eight years of his life, the Buchanan home in Texarkana was the single most unusual house in town. Legend has it that on an earlier trip to a summer camp in Saginaw, Michigan, William took a fancy to a building he saw in Oak Park, Illinois, designed by Frank Lloyd Wright. In fact, the house was most likely in Decatur, Illinois.

Built in 1909 and called the Irving residence,[5] it was actually designed by one of Wright's associates, Marion Mahony. It unmistakably reflects Wright's style, however, and it is almost a dead ringer for the house Buchanan eventually had built for himself. Decatur is on the way to Chicago and Saginaw, although via a slight detour, and it is possible he saw the Irving house during a stopover or a change of trains.

In any case, in 1914, he sent a Texarkana architect named Bayard Witt to carefully photograph the house and set him to work duplicating its exterior.

The property the house was to crown first attracted Buchanan's eye in 1887, when he purchased a portion of what was then a suburban block on the Texas side of town bordered by Maple Street (now Texas Boulevard) on the east and by Seventh and Eighth streets on the south and north. Over the years, he continued to nibble at the entire block, and in 1914, the actual year of construction, he bought out a small bakery on the corner and assumed ownership over all.

For the next full year, builders were at work, tearing down the old two-story family house and replacing it with the red-roofed Wright facsimile. The choice of this particular architect's style is intriguing,[6] especially considering that the interior Buchanan chose was not what one associates with Frank Lloyd Wright. Decorated and furnished by Tiffany Studios, it did not reflect Wright's penchant for oriental-influenced furniture of his own design.

It was, however, fancy. Costing one hundred thousand dollars ($1.03 million in 1984 terms), it featured dining, living, and music rooms, a library and a kitchen downstairs, and four complete bedroom suites, complete with separate baths, upstairs. The place was covered with vast oriental rugs, the floor of the dining room was laid in ebony, and a single huge cedar closet took up a large chunk of the second floor. Outside, there was a separate garage and servant house and a large screened porch festooned with the ducks and quail of William's outings. As final attractions, the whole thing was perched atop a low man-made hill and fronted the only paved street in all of Texarkana. The opening of the house in 1915 was apparently the talk of the town, being "the most colorful and largest house party ever given in the city."[7]

This last was unusual for Buchanan, for despite his sometimes extravagant expenditures, he was generally headline-shy.

The same could be said of his wife, Hannah Ferguson

E. P. Irving home in Decatur, Illinois, built in 1909—the most likely inspiration for Buchanan's home in Texarkana

Buchanan. Remembered in her later years as one of the town's *grandes dames,* she had a distinct sense of propriety which sometimes clashed with her less than regal upbringing.

> You couldn't say "damn" or "darn" or anything. She'd say "Oh shit" when she got really mad, but "darn" was out. She'd sit in her chair upstairs and sort of receive all the time, and when Gloria Swanson or Mary Pickford were on at the movies, she didn't want anyone to know she'd go to see something like that, so she'd quietly take us kids in her electric car.

Her struggle to maintain a high-society image was revealed fairly often. It was not, after all, until she reached her thirties that her husband's fortunes pushed them both to society's forefront. Life up to then had revolved around Buchanan, Texas, hardly the social apogee for people far and near. It was, in fact, enough removed that she arranged with the railroad engineer's wife to do her shopping for her in Texarkana in the morning and to dump it off on William's sawdust pile as the train made its return trip in the afternoon.

William Buchanan's home in Texarkana, reminiscent of Frank Lloyd Wright's style

Those lean days bred independence, tough-mindedness, and a reputedly hot temper, as well as a few somewhat less refined personal habits that dogged her in later years. "My father ran a grocery store on East Broad Street and for years Mrs. Buchanan would come in and buy a bottle of snuff. Then one day, he made the mistake of saying, 'How are you this morning, Mrs. Buchanan?' When she found out he knew who she was, she never came back."

Apparently as devoted to the church as her husband, she regularly taught Sunday school and, after his death, maintained his generous contributions. Money, however, was a less expendable commodity with her. "When they'd have a flat tire, which was pretty routine on those gravel streets, and Louie [the chauffeur] told Mrs. Buchanan they'd have to buy a new inner tube, she didn't like that. That was throwing money away."

She also kept a key ring by her side, with which she controlled the servants' access to some of the house's more costly items as well as the grocery money needed to keep the larder stocked. This attitude, while not uncommon, had an additional explanation, involving a one-million-dollar foundation that William created shortly before his death.

> There were a lot of people that tried to get their hands on that money. I know a fellow came into my office one time and wanted to know where Mrs. Buchanan was—he was trying to get hold of some money. Everybody was after her from all sides. Well, I said a very foolish thing—I meant well—but I said, "Mrs. Buchanan is in Mineral Wells." Well, in those days, you didn't just get on your mule and light out for Mineral Wells, or your automobile—the roads were terrible. I thought that would stop him. So help me, the guy got on a train and went to Mineral Wells and tried to get hold of Mrs. Buchanan. I never forgave him.

Despite this type of harassment, she was highly conscious of her "position" in local society, and while she didn't get out much, especially after her husband's death, she did go to pains to keep herself in the proper light when entertaining guests. Several visitors remember her grand entrances down the main staircase and the studied graciousness of her demeanor.

One wonders, for those reasons, what she thought of her brother-in-law James, who lived across town on the Arkansas side. Also ensconced in a magnificent mansion, albeit more traditional in appearance, he built a reputation as a playboy gambler with little interest in the day-to-day activities of his eldest brother's empire. James was variously characterized by family members as "a wild man," "a gay blade," and "an idiot—a dressed-up dandy"; the contrast between William and himself must have made Hannah, among others, shake her head in wonder.

From the very start, James never demonstrated much interest in carving out his own slice of the pie, and for that, William is perhaps partially to blame. Seventeen years William's junior James was just coming into his majority when his older brother purchased Bodcaw. At the same time, their father's budding banking career collapsed, and William pulled James into the lumber business behind him, loading him up with stock and responsibilities.

That well-meant effort apparently didn't pay off. Despite hav ing taken a business course in preparation for his duties, James wandered from job to job within the organization, never staying long at one thing and never leaving much of an impression, except one—which might have foretold of his eventual preferences.

He, like both his brothers, spent a good deal of the early years out of doors, personally handling those details that would eventually be passed to lesser management. The one memory of him that stands out from these days is a fine high-pitched singing voice. On the road, scouting for new land purchases or helping plot the future course of the railroad, he entertained those country people who took him in for the night with a bevy of songs—a welcome sound during hard times.

His one fond reminiscence of Stamps was the railroad. Writing a friend in 1945, he recalled with pride laying the first ten miles of the L&A "with a good bunch of colored boys" and running the locomotive himself. Throughout his life, the L&A remained as close to his heart as it did to William's.

But slowly, those pioneering days gave way to routine and to the hiring of people who presumably did a better job. James wound up managing the commissary during the first years of the new century until even that was handed over to C. L. Cabe, who had been running it for the most part anyway.

Former residents of Stamps assess James variously from those years, from a rather condemning "He didn't know much about working" to a more charitable, and most likely more accurate, "He didn't have much to do."

> Jim—he wore a little white mustache, clipped very short, trimmed and taken care of—freshly shaved every morning. He was more talkative than any of the rest of them. We didn't stand off in awe of him; he was a little more friendly. The others—they didn't have much truck with the local people.

Aside from his dapper appearance, children from that time recall a strict Sunday routine he held to.

> Every Sunday, Mr. Jim would take Earl, my brother and me and maybe one other walking through the mills. Now he

wasn't necessarily outgoing and fatherly or anything; he just went walking by himself and didn't mind us trailing along. Anyway, afterwards, he would come back and go to the commissary and open up the candy counter and we'd all get some candy free.

Around 1907, he finally threw in the glove, moved to the Arkansas side of Texarkana and had constructed a truly monumental mansion, complete with ballroom. He was now about the same age William had been when he'd purchased the Bodcaw mill.

Curiously, this move may have improved his standing with William, who began to use him—taking advantage of his brother's easygoing talent with people—as a frequent go-between in various company dealings. He became, unofficially, a public relations man who could speak in William's name and allow William to maintain his aloof fatherly image.

After William's death, he played largely the same role for William's son, Will, who took over management of the business. It was James who ran interference with people like Huey Long and H. L. Hunt, keeping the first on friendly terms with the company and introducing the second to Will, who later signed an oil deal with Hunt.

The trade-off, unfortunately for James, was a widely perceived image of himself as a glorified step-'n-fetch-it man. Most reminiscences dismiss him in this fashion, even those covering the years following William's death. Despite both his continued presence in the minute books among the prominent shareholders and the leadership titles he held in many of the companies, he was never seen as the man in charge. In the short run, this attitude no doubt encouraged him in his self-indulgence; in the long run, it led him to a violent break with the family.

But until that time, he and his wife Ludie and their children led the life of "socialites—entertaining country club people," frequently on the move, traveling to Chicago, Florida, and Long Beach, California, where reputedly an offshore gambling boat added to the attraction.

This combination of an eagerness to please (especially to

please his brother) and a propensity to gamble is found in an anecdote appearing in a syrupy biography of millionaire J. K. Wadley, who as a young man had been an employee of the Buchanans and even briefly an in-law.

> In 1913, Wadley accompanied William and J. A. Buchanan on a duck hunting expedition on the Sulphur River. Breakfast was late and J. A. Buchanan became very impatient because he did not want his brother William to be waiting on him. After breakfast, J. A. Buchanan started off in his car at a rapid speed, and after going two or three blocks on Hickory Street, he made a right turn which was down hill and almost turned the car over. When they came in sight, William Buchanan had his chauffeur start driving at a rather fast speed, and in trying to keep up with the front car, J. A. Buchanan occasionally would run off the road, prompting Wadley to suggest that he should drive the car. Wadley pressed this suggestion several times because of the difficulty J. A. Buchanan was having in controlling the car. About six or seven miles out of town the accident happened. Buchanan ran off the road and tried to cut back too quickly and the car flipped over, coming to rest across the chest of Wadley. . . . Buchanan and a colored man named Tom were thrown out of the car.[8]

Everyone survived the accident, and Wadley spent a day in the hospital recovering from his ordeal. It is not revealed whether he ever rode with James again, but it has been pointed out that the younger Buchanan's behavior at the time was not out of character.

This pre-jet-set life-style was clearly addictive and led in the early 1920s to a significant clash between brothers. William, his eye fixed on a developing trend in the industry, began to push for a move to the Northwest. James, a major stockholder and thus a necessary ally in such a decision, opted for a life of pleasure that by now had become second nature. William reportedly was livid at the impasse, and what might have developed had death not intervened is anyone's guess. But William did die, and with his passing James was allowed to pursue an empty and meaningless life, concluding, as will be treated in a later chapter, on a sad and bitter note.

Robert was radically different from James. Gruff, uncouth,[9] bullheaded, opinionated, and—that peculiar social sobriquet—"uneducated,"[10] he came to Stamps to oversee the woods operation and never strayed from his assignment. As the years passed, his responsibilities grew to include the logging divisions of both the Pine Woods mill and the one in Minden, but he never left Stamps and never took on additional duties.

His course in life, though less successful than William's, paralleled it rather closely. Starting out by selling peanuts to soldiers during the Civil War, Robert went on to secure a contract for cutting railroad-trestle ties, and finally ended up for a few years running a modest lumberyard in Paris, Texas. It was there that the Leadville bug bit him in the late 1870s, and he headed north.

Obviously he kept in touch with the rest of the family, since William knew to join him in Colorado. But his independence was such that one wonders: if his mill had not burned in Thornton, Arkansas, in the mid-1890s, would he have joined William's enterprise at all?

Certainly, he didn't have much to do with his two brothers once he arrived, and it seems clear from family testimony that the feeling was mutual. A Methodist like James, he wrote off Baptists and Presbyterians as "low-down people" and was constantly after William for "playing cow pasture pool when he should have been tending to business." He was also irked at William's familiarity with the black workers, and his coming across like "Mr. King."

Less prominent than William or James as an officer and a stockholder, he was also less interested in the workings of the company outside of his own area.

> They had these stockholders meetings, and in the later years, they'd hold them down in Good Pine. And they couldn't get Mr. Robert to go down there. Finally they succeeded, and he said at the meeting, "Take a good look at me. This is the last time I'm going to attend a stockholders meeting down here."

This cantankerousness wasn't limited to his brothers and colleagues, as evidenced by the following two reminiscences:

> He was a peculiar fellow. He wasn't a mixer with people, that's all. He wasn't very friendly with anybody.

> He was a very austere looking old man, tough looking, and he wanted everybody to know it. No foolishness about it. He was tough on his family too. The children really had to walk a chalk line.

And yet, there are positive memories, although they frequently needed some time to evolve.

> The YMCA had a small swimming pool. That's where I got to know old man Bob Buchanan. He used to come down there. He was an old bald-headed grouchy fellow. Had two boys, William and Robert. One of them was younger than me and the other was about my age. He used to come down and swim with us. There'd be thirty or forty of us going in that pool every afternoon during the summertime. The old man would come there and sit around with his feet dangling off in the water and he'd walk around the pool.
>
> I hadn't learned to swim yet, and he says, "You ever going to learn to swim?" He stopped by there by the side of me one day. I said, "I guess so, Mr. Buchanan, but I don't know when." He said, "Well, you never will learn how sitting up here on this bench."
>
> He picked me up and threw me into the pool. Scared me to death and made me mad too. But of course right then I swam out of that thing. Of course, he got in there with me—he wasn't going to let me drown. I learned in one afternoon how to swim. I almost hated that old man. Later, I said, "Well, you sure did me a favor."

In a similar vein, an old black woman still living a few miles below Stamps, whose father used to sell timber to Robert, remembers one time when Robert displayed more sensitivity than was normal with him. One sunlit, warm-weather Sunday, he broke from his austere, hardworking schedule and brought his family down for a picnic in a field across from the black woman's home. She watched them enjoying themselves for most of the afternoon, the children frolicking in a sea of cotton blooms.

Nonetheless, he was a hard man to approach and seemed to cherish the image. Despite that, he was given the best of life's opportunities by his older brother—a truly fabulous income, a nice home in a thriving but unpretentious rural town, and a job with men who enjoyed reputations like his own.

Whether Robert ever did so or not, others have acknowledged William's faithfulness to his family. While never sacrificing any of his ambitions, he looked out for them. It seems, from their viewpoints, that he succeeded.

But fundamental questions do lurk beneath the surface, the most prevalent being: why, since William is reported to have been such a prince among fellows, was he surrounded by a family so overloaded with insensitive, boorish, and self-centered people?

The answer, if it ever existed, has been long lost to time; even the question, to some living family members, appears combatively one-sided. But the fact remains that both of William's brothers and both of his children who survived to adulthood developed into pretty unpleasant individuals. With James ranking as the least unpleasant and William's son, Will, as the most, the overwhelming testimony reveals a family churlishness of impressive proportions. William's role in this would be intriguing to know.

6 / The Bell Tolls

William Buchanan died in his home in Texarkana at 7:30 A.M. on October 26, 1923. He was seventy-four years old and was killed by cancer of the lower esophagus and stomach, probably due to his use of chewing tobacco.

He had been in pain for a long while. In September of 1922, he returned home from visiting a trouble spot on one of the logging roads where some thirty miles of track had disappeared under swamp water. He had a temperature of 103 degrees. Three weeks before, an outbreak of dengue fever had been reported in the area, and he was convinced that was the cause of his discomfort.

He was wrong. For a long time before this attack, he had acknowledged a fragile stomach. In fact, it had turned him into an absolute teetotaler—his infrequent nips of old had begun to burn on the way down. But with the onset of the "fever," he began to experience real problems. He became exhausted, constipated, and regurgitated his food on occasion, eventually losing thirty-three pounds. He also felt a drawing pain down under his ribs.

At the end of that year, he was back at Grassy Lake duck hunting, feeling better and regaining some weight, but still aware that something was wrong. His son-in-law, Dr. Stanley Seeger, whom his daughter had married in 1918 and who practiced in Milwaukee, looked him over and suspected a neoplasm. He urged William to get medical attention, but William, now claiming simple old age, put it off.

By the time he checked into the Mayo Clinic in Rochester, Minnesota, in April, 1923, it was too late. He was gaunt and exhausted, sleeping only four and a half hours each night. He could barely swallow, he was in pain, and his stomach was massively enlarged by a large solid tumor.

Leading a small team of doctors, Dr. William Mayo, whose specialty was abdominal surgery, opened Buchanan up. What he found was beyond hope; the mere examination caused complications and the incision had to be rapidly closed. A tube was inserted through his abdomen to allow nourishment to bypass the closed-off throat. In early June, William was discharged so he could die at home.

The last months of his life were spent mostly in bed, although he made one final tour of his favorite haunts.

> The last time he came down, he parked his [railroad] car over there at Good Pine. Papa went over there—Papa told me about this—and old man Buchanan said to him, "Well, Jimmy, I won't be down here anymore because I've been to Mayo and they say I won't be here much longer."
>
> And Papa said he and old man Buchanan got to crying. Two big old men, and he said they just bawled like babies.

He also visited the new L&A railroad shops, just nearing completion in Minden, and had himself driven to Grassy Lake one last time. There, reclining on a mattress, he was placed in a boat and was paddled out for a private farewell among the tall cypress trees he so loved.

One of the saddest aspects of all this is that it was quite possibly avoidable. Had he appeared at the clinic a full year before he did, as his eminently qualified son-in-law, a former Mayo Clinic resident, had urged, his chances of survival might have been quite good.

But this was typical behavior. Buchanan's interaction with the Mayo brothers began in 1909, when he limped through their doors with kidney and bladder stone problems. That time, he had waited two and a half years before conceding he had a problem, suffering several excruciating attacks which he treated with morphine and chloroform. The result of his visit was an operation removing a stone the size of a pecan from his right kidney.

In 1916, he was there again, this time with an abscessed jaw. Some sixteen months earlier, he had developed a toothache which had swollen his gum tissue and forced a local dentist to evacuate a large amount of pus. True to form, despite continuing drainage for months—indicating an ever-worsening infection—William did nothing about it. Only a second, severely painful attack convinced him to travel back to Rochester for care. The result of this trip was the removal of a piece of dead bone from the ridge of his jaw.[1]

This pattern of self-neglect was an invitation to trouble, and in 1923 it finally arrived. The impressive thing was he survived that long. Reflected in his medical files at the clinic are several observations concerning his lack of personal care. Despite an outwardly robust physical appearance, his teeth were riddled with cavities, he smoked cigars and chewed tobacco excessively, and by 1920 was suffering from Parkinson's disease, none of which seemed to concern him.

From a historical viewpoint, his death was an appropriate piece of timing. He represented with his life span, by simple chance of birth, the growth and evolution of an era. In the 1870s, as he entered the lumber business, the South was about to steal from the Great Lakes region the title of largest lumber producer. As the railroads and Northern capital discovered the South, Buchanan was there, building his own road and benefiting from the sudden flow of cash. In 1909, Southern lumber production reached a peak of almost 20 billion board feet; in 1913 Louisiana produced the record high for any one state with 4 billion board feet; and William Buchanan's mills turned out their top number of just under 335 million board feet in 1915. That last figure, by the time of his death, was off 25 percent and declining fast.

Also by 1923, the South had lost its preeminence to the Pacific Northwest, which had been growing rapidly since the turn of the century. With the 1914 opening of the Panama Canal, this process accelerated, since western shippers now had a cheaper, shorter route to East Coast markets. Additionally, conservationists, fearful of the consequences of an unchecked "cut-and-run" policy, were raising the specter of a "timber famine" in the South that made the clear-cut acres of Maine and the Great Lakes region look good in comparison. One of the results of this hue and cry was to further convince lumbermen that the South was on the brink of logging out.

As time has told, this was not the case. It might have been, however, had the Depression not caused everyone to stop their headlong rush toward materialism. Already by 1920, 13 million acres of Louisiana's virgin forests had been reduced to sunbaked fields.

Concerns about cutover land were not restricted to conservationists. The lumbermen themselves knew something had to be done, and by 1917 the Southern Cut-Over Land Association was formed with the heavy backing of the Southern Pine Association. This attention to denuded land was disingenuous, however, since few of the lumbermen involved had any intention of reforesting their properties. The idea of the association was to promote the acreage as good farming land, which, of course, it was not. While Buchanan was not a member of the group, he independently participated in the same scheme, something his neighbor Henry Hardtner referred to as a "skin game."

The irony of all this was that the lumbermen were cutting themselves right out of business, just as historically they always had done. The tree-harvesting attitudes during World War I were little different than forty and fifty years before, when trees were considered an inexhaustible resource.

Hardtner was a glaring exception. Starting in 1904, he began experimenting with reforestation on some thirty thousand acres of his own cutover land. The times were propitious for such a move—Teddy Roosevelt's conservationist attitudes were beginning to catch on, schools of forestry were beginning to appear, and, also in 1904, Louisiana created a department of forestry designed to preserve the forests, fight fires, educate the public, and provide penalties for arson. In true bureaucratic style, no funding was granted this department, but at least it was on paper.

In 1908, the state improved on its performance. In the wake of a couple of White House conservationist conferences hosted by Roosevelt, Louisiana created a temporary Commission for the Conservation of Natural Resources, with Hardtner at its head. Over the next two years, he and his team formulated a forestry plan which was to become one of the nation's best, although it took the legislature thirty years to enact all its recommendations.

Keeping his crusade going, Hardtner in late 1909 got himself elected to the state legislature as a representative of the newly formed La Salle Parish, which he had also helped create. Located within La Salle Parish were Hardtner's own Urania Lumber Company and the three Jena-area mills of William Buchanan. His term of office was only sixty days, but in that short time he managed to sponsor both the Commission for the Conservation of Natural Resources and Act 261, which provided for reforestation contracts between the state and any landowner whose denuded land was worth five dollars an acre or less.

This special contract provision stated that in exchange for a low tax assessment agreed upon between landowner and police jury—no more than one dollar per acre annually—the owner would plant or maintain seed trees or seedlings in a manner prescribed by the state forester. The contract could last forty years at most and entailed cooperative fire control and timber maintenance agreements with the state as well. No cutting of trees was allowed except when it benefited the crop; at the end of the contract, regular taxation would be resumed.

Hardtner's other great landmark was the 1910 severance tax, which called for a diminishing of land taxes in exchange for a tax on any timber cut for profit. The tax was to go into a conservation fund for the preservation of forests, although part of it could be used to compensate those local governments who felt they had lost revenues on the deal.

As with the 1904 legislation, problems arose. The severance tax was initially deemed unconstitutional. Once it cleared that hurdle, revenues ended up not in a conservation fund, but in the state's general fund, which proved of no benefit to the lumbermen paying the tax. This situation wasn't rectified until 1918.

As for the reforestation contracts, not a single one was signed until Hardtner himself took out a couple in 1913[2]—the first and last until 1922. One reason for the general lack of interest was that denuded lands were taxed about the same as contract lands, so there was no evident advantage in taking out a contract; additionally, it allowed the state to meddle in one's private business affairs—a time-honored anathema. There was also the age-old argument on the part of most lumbermen that trees took a minimum of one hundred years to mature. In that light, the contracts wouldn't be of much use to anyone living anyhow.

Hardtner's activities, combined with the state's lethargy in following up on them, made him a folk hero in the parish. The *Jena Times,* published in a town that should have spoken of little beyond the three huge Buchanan mills on its outskirts, focused instead on Hardtner with impressive consistency—he was the "father" of La Salle Parish, of forestry in the South, and of the severance tax. In comparison, the Buchanans rarely even appeared in the paper.

Of course, Hardtner had a gospel to preach, and he did so with great inventiveness. Road signs erected near his mill read, "The Pines are Coming Back," and, "Grow a Crop of Timber in 40 Years"; he gave lectures and tours of his land and named certain lots after famous forestry-oriented people; and he invited the Yale Forestry School to establish a yearly summer program for its students.

If all this struck fellow lumbermen as meddlesome, hyperbolic nonsense, it did not so affect their workers. "Everybody thought Hardtner was just *it* because he seemed to have a mind for the future, where ours didn't seem to be doing that too much. There was a lot of discussion about that—an awful lot. It just seemed like it was mismanaged."

To a certain extent, this comment reflects the classic adversity of labor and management, with each party convinced the other is feathering its own bed. It is true that management was trying to make as much for itself as possible; nevertheless, many a flathead shared the cut-and-run attitude of the lumbermen and viewed their greed and destructiveness with a philosophical shrug.

Not that general apathy lets the lumbermen off the hook—Hardtner's activities saw to that. Before his experiments at Urania, timber barons could claim ignorance; by World War I, that excuse was gone. By then, the Southern pine tree, and in particular the loblolly, had proved how fast it could mature—in fact, the forty-year limit of the reforestation contracts was twice the time necessary to grow pulp trees for the newly developing paper industry. Buchanan and others like him were forced to fall back on old arguments like high taxes and interest rates and fierce competition to justify their lack of interest in reforestation.

And often they were good arguments. Certainly without some

radical rethinking by people across the entire banking, lumbering, and legislative spectrum, most of these mill owners were indeed stuck in their old pattern. Hardtner was a special case—his overhead was restricted to one mill and about 120,000 acres. And, in 1924, a large gas well was discovered three hundred feet from his land, leading to 110 wells inside his boundaries within two years—a nice little subsidy for his philosophical position.

For Buchanan to take Hardtner's lead, he would have been forced to pare down his operations, massively refinance, swallow several years of red ink (not to mention his pride), and rethink the philosophy of a lifetime. That he didn't do so should come as no surprise.

> They were just stripping it all out and not replanting a thing. We would sit on the porch and watch them cut those pretty pines. It would hurt my father's feelings a lot. It troubled him—about the reforestation. He at that time had some pretty pines growing around in the yard and around back—he'd done it to see how fast they would grow. And he talked about it many times with Mr. Gallaher [one of Buchanan's head men], but Mr. Gallaher wouldn't hear of it. They all kind of stuck together on those things—except Mr. Hardtner. He just went straight to it.

Ideally, in the story of a man of the times, like William Buchanan, the torch should pass to a younger and more progressive heir who takes the old business and adapts it to new practices. In this case, that evolution took place only after skipping a generation. The intervening eighteen years, represented by J. A. and Will Buchanan, almost marked the death of the entire Buchanan empire.

It is not unusual for the passing of a commanding paternal figure to leave a void in its wake. As we saw with J. A. Buchanan, the effects of living in William's shadow for years could be psychologically debilitating—the sudden removal of that shadow had no less an impact on Will.

William's death doesn't seem to have affected J.A. much. He was, after all, fifty-seven years old and pretty set in his ways. Will, on the other hand, was twenty years younger. No callow

Will Buchanan, William's only son

youth, he had nonetheless been brought up knowing but one style of life—that of a very rich man in a very class-conscious society. He had also been brought up with preordained responsibilities. His role, it was clear from the start, was to take over the business and, by his early to mid-twenties, he was well on his way.

But it was evident to all who knew him that he was not sitting comfortably. Early memories of him are of a troubled, angry young man who gradually developed into an overweight, mean-spirited, alcoholic bully.

One major problem, many remarked, was that he didn't have any interest in the lumber business. Sent down to Good Pine by his father to learn the ropes, his enthusiasm was underwhelming.

> I remember when Mr. Will—"Little Will" is what we called him—came down there to learn the lumber business. He'd come over to Trout and Papa would take him out on the lumberyard and try to teach him grades of lumber and so on, but Little Will couldn't be bothered about all that. He didn't last long. He went back to Texarkana.

Yet, he was never openly rebellious. He did what his father told him, kept his drinking at a socially acceptable level, and ended up as president of the Tall Timber Lumber Company in 1912.

In 1923, that all changed. The transfer of power created a curious dual management—J.A. appeared as head of several of the companies and as an officer in most of them, while Will was regarded by one and all as the inheritor of his father's mantle. Robert, as before, tended to business in Stamps—and continued to do so until his death in 1930.

The problem with this arrangement was that no one person was left in charge of all the mills. J.A. remained content with his wandering, self-indulgent life-style, and Will, when he bothered, was more interested in securing quick cash. The mills were left to carry on as before. For the short haul, this was fine—William had staffed his companies well—but overall a sense of direction was lost, and with it any chance of salvation in the face of what lay ahead.

And the future did not look good. In 1925, the post–World

James Buchanan

War I lumber-producing spree hit an end. Not only was construction off, but excessive competition among lumbermen had glutted the market and filled yards to overflowing. Furthermore, it looked like time wouldn't help as it had in the past: building materials other than lumber were being introduced rapidly, and were gaining wide acceptance. The lumber business, and the South that depended so heavily upon it, were in trouble.

Other timber barons began to move defensively. Reforestation gained acceptance as a hedge against depression, the federal government was invited to help out after years of being told to mind its own business, and alternate sources of revenue raising were researched. With the exception of the last, the Buchanan empire did none of these.

The obvious place to look for more money was in the ground. Since the first discovery of the turn-of-the-century oil gushers, lumbermen had toyed with the idea of drilling a few holes. But until the 1920s the incentives were slight. The failing lumber market changed that.

William Buchanan had just begun following this trend at his death. In 1920, he created the L&A Oil Company to take over all the mineral rights of his lumber companies in order to make them more attractive to oil drillers. But no Spindletop-type well had yet been discovered in the area, and it was hardly swarming with hungry oilmen. The few who did take leases on Buchanan land came up dry. The L&A Oil Company dragged on for nine years and finally died of its own inertia.

The same fate was awaiting the Buchanan mills. For years, they had been nibbling away at around six hundred thousand acres of timberland owned outright, gradually transforming the countryside into bare rolling hills extending as far as the eye could see. Towns which had pushed aside trees to fit in were slowly gaining views of up to ten miles all around.

The mills kept cutting, and processing, and shipping at ever less profitable prices. The books were juggled with depreciation allowances, tax avoidance schemes, and increasingly massive dividend payments. Salaries were frozen or cut, men were laid off, the lights in the towns, once available all night, were cut off at eleven.

J. A. Buchanan's mansion in Texarkana, 1925

The people in the mill towns watched and waited, at once resigned and mournful, as things began to slowly fall apart. Maintenance on the houses fell off, recreation halls were closed and allowed to decay, the baseball diamonds became choked with weeds. Gone was the shade the trees had offered in summer, and so too the protection they'd been against the winter's wind. Now people fried in dusty, unfiltered heat or huddled together under blankets in houses so cold the water froze in the washbasins.

> They just cut Trout out of the forest—the town of Trout. There were trees right up to where we lived. They were the biggest, prettiest pine trees you ever saw. Same way around the school. All in front, around the sawmill and on up the hill. They finally cut around the school. I can remember that feeling how everything opened up and it was suddenly so bright. It hurt my eyes.
>
> Long before that, we had this Arbor Day celebration. Mr. Baer, a bookkeeper at the commissary, stood on a platform. He gave a little talk about the beauty of the pines, and that impressed me as a child. I looked all around. I never had thought anything about them being pretty. But he said they

Behind this trio, as far as the eye could see, was once a verdant, virgin pine forest

were, and then I saw it, I think, for the first time. After they were cut, I was so sorry.

By the mid-1920s, Arbor Day celebrations were quietly retired.

In 1928, Will sold his father's cherished L&A Railroad to Arkansas magnate Harvey Couch. The terms of the sale are vague, as is the final amount paid. The railroad's assets were listed at $16.5 million, and Will's personal shareholdings at a par value of over $1 million (that's $99 million and $6 million respectively in 1984 terms). It's a sure bet that Will received something beyond his mere value as a stockholder, considering he was retained as a vice-president for several years after the sale, along with J.A., who had held about half as many shares as Will.

Whatever amount Will received, it was sufficient to finance a bash to end all bashes that he hosted in Cuba the same year. According to a family member, "They didn't spend it all, I don't think, but they probably made a dent."

Ironically, these were probably the worst times for Will personally. He has left nothing behind that allows any insight into his character, and there is no survivor of that era who was both a good friend to Will and a keen observer of human nature. But there are more than enough reports of his activities to reveal a deeply troubled nature.

As is usually the case, his problems didn't just suddenly appear. As a young man, he developed a reputation as a gambler, which football coaches found to their liking and headmasters did not. He was finally sent to the Bingham Military Academy in Asheville, North Carolina, presumably with the hopes that "a little discipline" would do him good. It did not.

His excesses didn't flourish until after his father's death. Before then, he is recalled as a fat, redheaded man with a fondness for gigantic plugs of chewing tobacco which, according to several sources, he couldn't seem to keep off his shirt front. After 1923, his lack of personal tidiness was the least of his offenses.

On a trip to the Mayo Clinic with his father in 1916, Will was treated for severe hemorrhoids, a problem which plagued him his entire adult life. At that time, during the examination, it was revealed that his smoking and chewing of tobacco were excessive, but that his alcohol intake was marginal. A few years later, he was diagnosed as an alcoholic.

> He had a friend whose father ran the drugstore next to the hotel [in Texarkana]. There was an alley between the two, and during Prohibition there was a fellow down at Garland City who put out a whiskey that he named Garland Pride. And every Saturday his truck would come there behind that drugstore and they would unload whatever Will and his friend wanted, generally in ten-gallon kegs. They were pretty good drinkers.

> He drank a whole bunch. The awful part was, he would keep the whiskey upstairs in the attic in Mountain Valley water bottles and the gardener was constantly drunk. His mother never knew all this. Nobody was allowed to go into his rooms except his flunky. There were Christmas presents in there he hadn't opened in ten years.

The drinking didn't help an already testy personality. Living in the Texarkana home with his mother, he came to dominate her in his father's absence, holding sway in matters concerning them both and so overpowering her with invective that she grew fearful of the slightest misstep. "One time in Milwaukee, which she used to come visit every summer, she lost her purse. And the only thing she was terrified of was, 'Don't tell Will.' "

His conduct in business was equally insensitive.

> He was pretty coldhearted. When this mill closed, some of the people who'd been working for them for forty years were in destitute circumstances. Wages were small and they were just barely living. We fellows that were on salary worked a little longer than the day laborers, [so] we paid in so much of our wages to help take care of the people who were in need, like for medicine.
>
> Mr. Smith, the manager at the time the mill closed, he went up to Texarkana and talked to young Will about helping the people out. He told Mr. Smith, "Hell, no. The company paid them everything they owed them, and we're not going to help them any." They couldn't help themselves. But we struggled along.

James Boyce, who was William's personal secretary and later became Will's, recalled one of the company land men coming by the office to have Will sign something. Will was out at the time, and the man decided to wait. Several hours later, Will walked in, went straight to his office and slammed the door. Boyce followed and informed him of the small piece of business at hand, and then went back outside. An hour later, Will left the office as abruptly as he'd entered, leaving the hapless land man still sitting in the reception room. Boyce's opinion was that Will didn't feel like seeing the man, pure and simple.

In Will's defense, he was not an ogre. Given the right timing and/or environment, he could be both caring and considerate.

> I [knew of] this boy who was in school in the College of the Ozarks up at Clarksville, Arkansas, who was fighting for his life—he needed eighty-five dollars with which to stay in school for the rest of the term. My salary was so small. I had three kids in college at that time too. I thought I'd go see Bill about it.

The State National Bank building in Texarkana. The Buchanan offices were on the fifth floor

So I went up to his office there and told him what my problem was and how much I wanted to help this boy get through school. "Well," he said, "how do you know that boy is going to make good?"

I knew that he had just come back from the Bahamas or somewhere down there at the racetrack vacationing, and all the rest that goes with it, so I said, "I can't guarantee it. But I do think that this boy has as good a chance as a racehorse in the Bahamas." He just sort of grinned and called his secretary and said: "Give this man a check for eighty-five dollars. And charge it to my mother's account."

He spent the majority of his leisure time at the Texarkana Country Club, which he and J.A. helped organize and which had developed into "the" gathering spot for the town's upper crust. Another member of the club remembered seeing him there.

I used to watch him playing poker. There were a couple of fellows who played regularly, and if he had a very fine hand and one of these fellows also had a fine one and got to betting to beat the band, I've seen Bill throw his hand in, because he knew the fellow couldn't afford to lose and he didn't want to take his money. He was very popular and very generous.

He was also, it seemed to others, on a lifelong slide downhill. As the market dried up and the mills began to close, the speed of his descent increased proportionally with his scramble for more money. In 1929, Trout Creek was sold to the Frost interests. In 1931, the Buchanan flagship, the Bodcaw Lumber Company, closed its doors and was dismantled. In 1932 Tall Timber's mills were boarded up and mothballed. In 1933, Pine Woods was shut down and the Grant Timber and Manufacturing Company began winding down operations, closing three years later.

Still, the cash was disappearing. Taking advantage of a recently passed federal law allowing the government to purchase private forestlands for the National Forests network, Will began selling off thousands of acres at a swipe, never at more than $2.81 per acre. The total acreage sold came to just under two hundred thousand.

In June of 1935, the most controversial of the mill closings took place. Starting early in the morning, the Good Pine mill burned to the ground. Fires were a commonplace occurrence and few of the seven Buchanan mills had not suffered from it, usually several times each.[3] The Good Pine fire was something more.

Immediately following the blaze, rumors began circulating as to its exact cause. The flames had first broken out in or near the pump room, which controlled the mill's internal fire-fighting system. One black man, years later, acknowledged that when he pulled out one of the nearby fire hoses, he found it had been cut in several places. An examination of the company's minutes reveals an unusual amount of financial shuffling six months prior to the fire, accompanied by the largest dividend payment in fifteen years, the second largest in company history.

Within weeks, Tall Timber, the newest and most modern of all the mills, reopened with the aid of Good Pine's insurance money, further raising eyebrows at the convenient coincidence. Nothing was ever proved—in fact, the question of arson was never officially raised. But in an era where mill fires were virtually a part of life, this one stuck out as suspicious in the minds of most who witnessed it.

With Good Pine burned, Tall Timber was all that was left of William Buchanan's former empire. From the sale of the L&A Railroad in 1928, it took his son seven years to dismantle virtually the entire operation, including a good chunk of the land. On paper, things didn't look so grim—with the exception of the Minden Lumber Company, all the companies were still happily alive, and turning out dividends. But they were also turning themselves inside out, something they could do for only so long.

There was one exception to the trend. After the dissolution of the L&A Oil Company, all mineral rights had reverted back to the separate lumber companies. But while oil royalties hadn't been able to keep a single joint oil company afloat in the 1920s, they began to show some muscle in the 1930s. As a result, some of Buchanan's companies were beginning to profit, albeit modestly, from oil revenues. This concerned major stockholders like the Packs, who felt that all the companies ought to benefit from the good fortune of a few. After all, the companies weren't in competition with one another, and they were each owned by essentially the same people. In response to this pressure, Will created the Good Pine Oil Company in 1932, along the exact same lines as the old L&A Oil firm.

The seemingly inconsequential birth of this new business was to prove one of history's small ironies. While Good Pine Oil displayed little more activity than its predecessor for its first eight years, in 1941, just before his death, Will reluctantly made a deal with oilman H. L. Hunt. The proceeds from that large sale of leases were to provide the one needed gush of oxygen that kept the ailing Buchanan enterprises alive through the Second World War.

During all this, the mill towns had been left to their own devices. Minden was the healthiest, having never been a hard-core mill town to begin with. It had other businesses to support it, not the least of which were the L&A Railroad shops, and it had been abandoned at a less dire time in history. The flip side of the coin was Selma, home of the Grant company. It disappeared so completely that several years after its death, former residents couldn't even identify where major structures had once dominated a thriving community. All that was left were the descendants of the original inhabitants—trees.

The others—Stamps, Springhill, Trout, Good Pine, and Tall Timber—suffered various degrees of trauma and reconstruction. The trio near Jena retained some identity but became suburbs to Jena's downtown, while Springhill and Stamps grew as independent and viable entities.

But all that lay in the future. In the mid-1930s, the end of each day was as far as anyone dared to look. A man who ran a grocery store in Jena recalled selling his empty flour and cement sacks to people so they could make shirts and dresses out of them. The infrequent trains began carrying hoboes who dropped off at the towns and went looking for something to eat, or steal.

> I remember one time some hobo was riding the train and fell off right there at that crossing and hit all that conglomeration of cross tracks and all, and it was like sausage. I remember there used to be a lot of hoboes on that train. And a lot of them would stop off there and rob or steal and go down to the houses. They broke into the little store one night and blew up a safe and took some stuff out. Had a lot of trouble with that in those days. During the Depression.

Violence and distrust increased. People began arming themselves against ambush and robbery. In small towns where unlocked doors had long been a way of life, locks and loaded shotguns became standard. The mills that did operate paid a dollar a day, but only opened their doors two days out of the week. Resentments between white man and black rose to the surface once more.

All this has become the cliché of the Depression: the Dust Bowl, the Okies, the hoboes' camp fires at night, the hunger, the anger, and the grinding need for relief. At the other extreme were the leftovers of the high-living 1920s. Like people nursing postparty hangovers, the rich and self-indulgent survivors of that era wondered what had hit them. Will Buchanan's behavior worsened as he progressed through the 1930s. Grassy Lake became as renowned for its drinking and gambling as it had once been for its hunting. When Will's private railroad car spent the night in Good Pine, local boys peeked through the windows, spying on Will and his friends entertaining their female companions. His drunken behavior became a standard item of Texarkana life, complete with car wrecks and nights spent in the police station drunk tank.

His desk grew high with unanswered mail, his philosophy being that if ignored long enough, the need of a response would vanish. Finally, mercifully, this apathetic neglect turned on him; in late 1940, his body gave in to the abuse.

The first sign appeared tame enough—he started to lose weight. One month later, he was having trouble swallowing, and noted that his throat would sometimes "fill up" and that he could vomit simply by tilting his head forward. Infrequent at first, these episodes increased, both in number and severity, and yet still he did nothing. His lack of response to all this is all the more shocking when one remembers, as Will must have, that his father had suffered the same symptoms for a full year before he was diagnosed.

In Will's case, the illness's progress, undoubtedly aided by his own unhealthy habits, was a lot faster. Six months after the first attack, he was at the Mayo Clinic—pale, short of breath, forty-eight pounds lighter, and extremely weak. For three weeks prior to his arrival, he'd only been able to swallow some milk and other liquids; alcohol had been out of the question for quite some time already.

On the last day of June 1941, he was informed he was dying of cancer of the lower esophagus and upper stomach, the same disease that had killed his father. He was released, to use the medical euphemism, to "continue treatment at home."

In a final bizarre twist to a sad and fruitless life, Will spent his remaining two months wrapping up a large oil deal with H. L. Hunt. Hunt, introduced to Will by James A. (who had met the oilman at a gambling table in Florida), had been pestering the dying man for months, trying to secure a lease for most of the Good Pine Oil Company land. Will, as he did with his mail, tried turning a blind eye. But Hunt was no inanimate pile of paper. He physically placed himself between Will and all comers, fearful of an approach by representatives of Standard Oil, and eventually

From left to right: H. L. Hunt, J. F. (Jick) Justiss, Hassie Hunt, and Attorney Phil Gaharan in Jena, Louisiana, in the early 1940s

won his way. His dedication was such that when Will was finally admitted to the Texarkana hospital, Hunt took the room next door. Before Will died, he leased almost 350,000 acres over to Hunt. That, however, was the extent of his paperwork. Lethargic to the last, he never got around to writing a will.

Will died on August 30 at 8:35 on a Saturday morning. His increasingly self-destructive behavior, especially toward the end of his life, bespeaks an extremely unhappy man. That, coupled with his very slow reaction in seeking medical attention, despite the obvious similarities between his symptoms and his father's, offers the strong possibility that he died not of cancer of the stomach, but of a disinterest in living.

7 / Rebirth

When Will Buchanan died, an interesting transfer of power took place within the family. Suddenly, the majority ownership of the companies, once equally divided among J.A., Hannah, Will, and Will's sister Helen, now tilted in Helen's favor. According to Texas law, Will dying intestate should have benefited both Helen and Hannah as his nearest living relatives. Apparently, Hannah passed this inheritance on to her daughter, because company records indicate Helen picked up almost all Will's shares upon his death.

Since 1923, when Helen had acquired her first stockholdings through her father's will, she had never demonstrated much interest in the business. She and Will stood on an equal footing with one another, and she was content to let him make decisions as he saw fit.

With his demise, she became concerned. He had been, for all his lethargy, the only obstacle in the way of J. A. Buchanan's growing desire to totally liquidate. By selling that huge parcel of land to the federal government and by closing the mills, Will had struggled to hold onto the company's remaining acres. Helen agreed with this goal, and realizing suddenly that speed was of the essence, she convinced her husband to quit his practice and move the entire family to Texarkana. Thus began a tug-of-war between uncle and niece that was to reach its conclusion a full four years down the road.

In 1941, Helen Buchanan Seeger was forty-six years old, Will's junior by six years. At the age of twenty-three, she married Dr. Stanley Seeger, whom she met at the Mayo Clinic in 1916. After the war was over and he was discharged from the army medical corps, they moved to Milwaukee, where he set up practice. As the years rolled by, he moved up in his profession, specializing in difficult surgical procedures and the treatment of burns, in particular of the young. In 1928 he was elected by his peers as chief of staff of Columbia Hospital and in 1934 as simultaneous chief of staff at Children's Hospital—a rare tribute to one man's capabilities.

In the meantime, Helen became a highly visible figure among Milwaukee's upper crust. She was an outgoing, free-spending, boisterous woman who enjoyed a good time on the town as much as her husband liked settling down in his library with a medical book. They had two daughters, Mary and Hannah, born in 1919 and 1921, and a son, Stanley, Jr.—nicknamed Joe—born in 1930.

The family's life-style reflected Helen's wealth. Although Stanley did well for himself, his double chief-of-staff jobs were nonpaying, and surgeon's fees in those days were a far cry from what they are today. The family lived extremely comfortably, the children were sent to expensive private schools, Stanley, an enthusiastic horseman, owned several polo ponies, and Helen indulged freely in a very costly fondness for clothes, furniture, and houses. In addition, both gave generously to causes that caught their interest.

In the late 1930s, Helen had plans drawn up for a $50,000 house to end all houses ($375,000 in 1984 terms). A Georgian-style mansion, it was built on the site of their previous house in River Hills, Milwaukee's most exclusive suburb, on their large estate at the Milwaukee River's edge. The talk of the town as it was going up, it also drew attention because of the several well-publicized arguments Helen had with the architect—she supposedly fired him twice.[1]

This aspect of Helen's character sticks most in people's memories. Various descriptions from "pronounced," "high-strung," and "colorful" to "demanding," "a hell-raiser," and "a bear-cat" followed her all through her life. A family nickname, although never uttered to her face, was Horrible Helen. In many respects, when she was at her worst, her similarity to her brother Will was striking. She was used to being obeyed and catered to and had, over the years, acquired an imperious disregard for other people's feelings. Many who were employed by her as servants remember an overbearing and often irrationally intolerant woman. Mercifully, she had a gentler side, which frequently surfaced in time to win over those who were tough enough to put up with her complex and abrasive outer shell. She was an extremely forthright person whose position in life sheltered her from what she meted out so freely to others.

She also dispalyed a curious and winning balance of pride and self-deprecating humor, as when she wrote to one of her favorite New York clothing stores in 1945: "Send me some sketches and try to trick me out a little bit in something besides my old uniforms! I need my face, spirits and tail lifted! Tell John to try to do something for the old girl."

Another family member recalls a complex, often mercurial woman:

> I remember one time she showed up at our house to take me out to the movies, and I was about nine years old or something. She pushed this picture of my great-grandfather William into my hands—this old man with a white beard—and she said, "Try to be like him."
>
> I almost laughed, you know, because I thought this was a pretty funny-looking old guy, and I didn't know what she was talking about. I was this little kid in a T-shirt. And my mother said later, "It's a good thing you didn't laugh."
>
> Then she took me to the movies, and it was a cowboy movie, and the cowboy stuck his pistol into his belt and she leaned over and said, "If he doesn't watch out, he's gonna shoot his you-know-what off." She was really kind of a salty character, and funny. But also, she could be really kind of mean and sarcastic.

The River Hills estate, which opened in 1939 with a monumental party, came complete with outbuildings, a guest cottage, and a polo field. The "Big House" was admired for its tastefully lavish appointments, including several complete bedroom suites, each with a separate bathroom—an unusual feature for the time—and a truly beautiful library, reputed to be Stanley's private corner of the house. Unfortunately, since it was completed

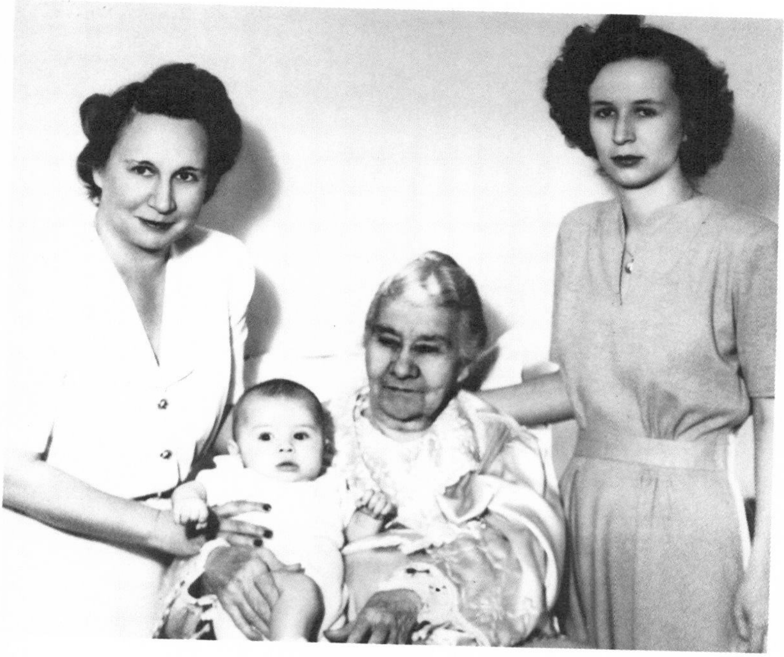

The matriarchal line, 1941: Hannah Buchanan (sitting, holding William O'Boyle), Helen Buchanan Seeger (left), and Mary Seeger O'Boyle

near the time of Will's death, the family had but a year or two to fully enjoy its comforts.

The decision to leave was a tough one for Stanley Seeger. Milwaukee was his home in the fullest sense. Born a Roman Catholic in the small city of Manitowoc, Wisconsin, his dentist father died when Stanley was three, and his mother when he was nineteen. Quiet, reserved, and studious, he pursued his medical career with devotion, becoming one of the most eminent physicians in Milwaukee. Respected not only for his medical abilities, he was known as an accomplished organizer, hence his simultaneous appointments as chief of staff at two hospitals. He was, in many respects, the exact opposite of his wife—diplomatic, calm, subtly persuasive and rather retiring. At fifty-two, he had reached the top of his profession in a town that counted him among the best of its citizenry.

But he was also a man of strong morals and dedication to his family. He owed much of his power and all of his philanthropy to his wife's inherited wealth, and now that her income was threatened, he was quick to come to terms with what had to be done.

Helen and Stanley Seeger in their new home in Milwaukee, around 1940

I don't think he felt he had any alternative. After all, it was a valuable estate, and it couldn't be ignored. So he pulled his roots not only away from his practice and medicine, which he really loved, but he pulled them away from al his friends.

It was not easy for him. It really was hard. He was a warm person and he had a lot of good friends in Milwaukee. And he thought a lot of his friends and enjoyed seeing them, being with them.

The impression I got was that Dr. Seeger was most reluctant to give up his medical practice. He decided to do it, not only because of his wife Helen's strong persuasion tactics,

Helen Seeger's showplace mansion in Milwaukee

> but also because he felt a responsibility to the younger members of the family. He also, I think, was kind of embarrassed by the way in which the Buchanan family had devastated the land, and he felt a social obligation to try to remedy that wrong.
>
> The sense of family responsibility was injected in large part by Helen, who was a very forceful personality and a woman accustomed to getting her own way. In this situation, her own way was along the lines of restoring these family businesses to a healthy state.

The first task, as Stanley and Helen Seeger saw it, was to stop the companies from vanishing altogether. After Will's death, the last of the mills, Tall Timber Lumber, had closed. All that remained, in fact, was the oil-leasing Good Pine Oil Company that Will had created in 1932. The other six firms, Bodcaw, Pine Woods, Trout, Grant, Good Pine, and now Tall Timber existed solely on paper; they all controlled their own acreages, were owned by the same people, and, being almost stripped of trees, produced very little revenue.

Once again, the major threat to survival was taxes. Since late 1939, the official start of World War II, Franklin Roosevelt had been preparing a reluctant United States to join the fight. As a result, the country's tax structure had undergone some changes by the time Pearl Harbor was attacked in December 1941—the same year the Seegers came to Texarkana to salvage the family enterprises.

One of these revenue-gathering changes was the institution of an excess-profits tax to be levied against companies making profits exceeding a set limit. Worried that an unpredictable wartime economy might expose some of their companies to this tax, J. A. Buchanan, the Seegers, and their fellow major stockholders sought the aid of an adviser. They found John Ohl, a tax lawyer from New York. He suggested they split their various companies into still smaller units. Each unit was designed to cover a specific activity or geographic portion of the overall operation. Thus, all the land belonging to the trio of Trout, Good Pine, and Tall Timber—minus its mineral rights— became the La Salle Land Company; Bodcaw's land, minus minerals, became the Stamps Land Company; the mineral interests that were tied up in the Little Creek oil field became the Little Creek Oil Company; and so on. The accompanying chart gives a better visualization of what went where. All these new companies were chartered as Delaware corporations, since Delaware had, and has, some of the most lenient laws governing business taxation in the country.

One anomaly had to be handled differently. Pine Woods had several shareholders unique to itself who were not eligible to share in the benefits of the other companies. So, rather than devising some complicated, and legally dubious, payment schedule, Pine Woods stayed apart until 1959.

The major thrust of the entire procedure was to break up the Good Pine Oil Company which, especially during a war, stood the biggest chance of increasing its profits excessively. As things turned out, this massive reshuffling of paper properties had both its advantages and its disadvantages, none of which were envisioned when the whole scheme came into effect.

In view of all this, the war years ironically turned out to be the leanest in company history. From over five thousand employees,

The Evolution and Interrelationship of the Various Buchanan Holdings

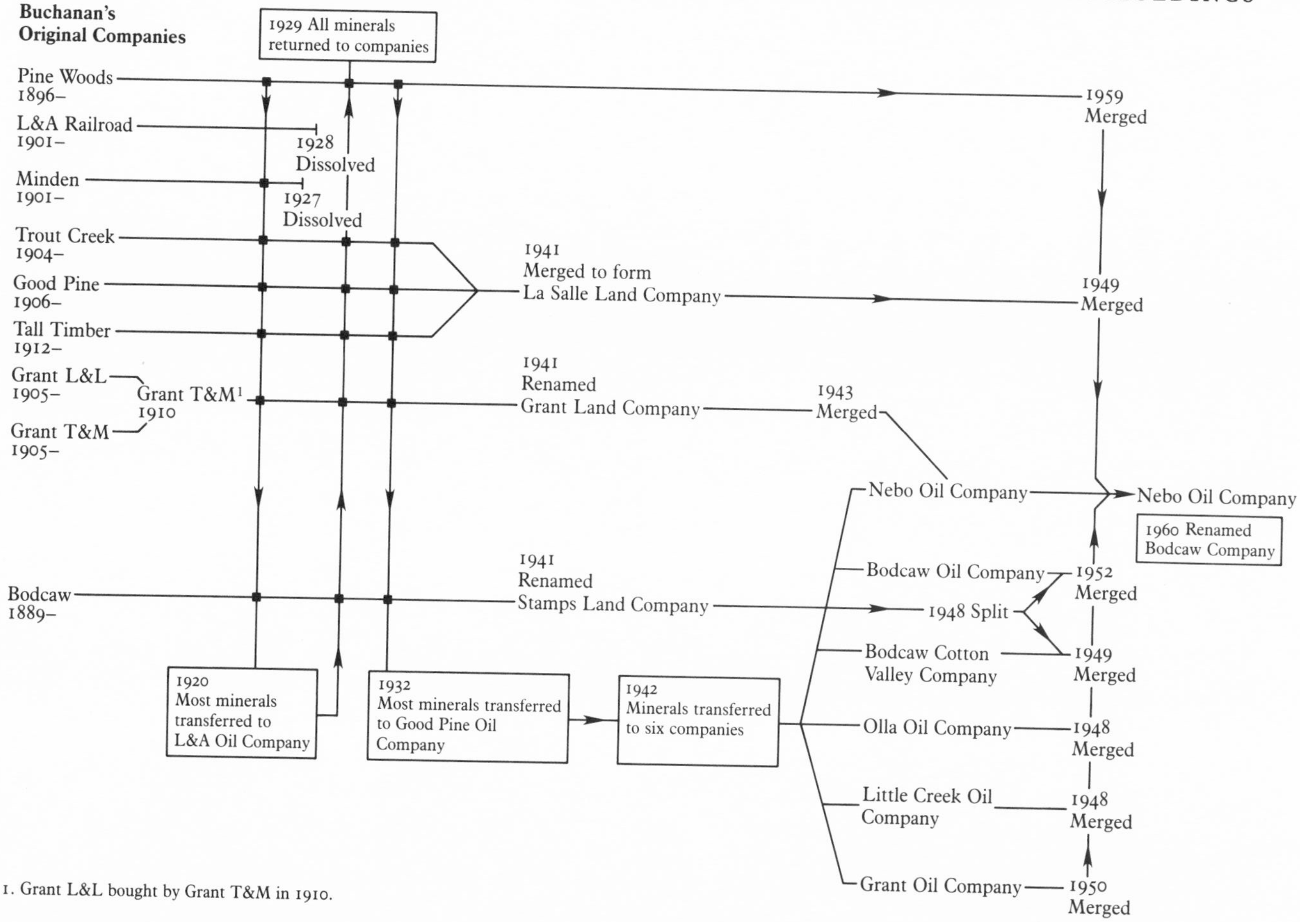

1. Grant L&L bought by Grant T&M in 1910.

the entire staff shrank to about five people. The lands were all but abandoned, stripped of 80 to 90 percent of their timber. The oil revenues amounted to a trickle of income. Until 1945, the only activity recorded was the selling of timber-cutting rights, town lots, and old mill housing. Here and there, a few acres were donated to a municipal cemetery or a local downtown development effort; Bodcaw's log pond was given to the town of Stamps and named Lake June, after one of the widows of the original three Brown brothers.

This slow deterioration began to grate on J. A. Buchanan, who was already unhappy at being usurped by his niece and her husband. His desire to liquidate increased with the lack of any movement on the part of the various companies.

In the fall of 1943, something happened which was to worsen James's outlook on life forever. In the late 1930s, he had taken under his wing a young protégé named Harry Ferguson—not related to William Buchanan's in-laws. Harry, by 1943, had become head of the land department, James's right-hand man and his constant companion. As such, he accompanied J.A. to Grassy Lake for the duck-hunting season that fall.

> They were both in boats on Grassy Lake and Harry was in the boat behind Jim and Jim had his gun loaded, cocked and everything else, sticking out of the back of his boat. Harry's boat rammed him a little bit and he got a twelve-gauge shotgun blast right in the face. It was too bad [Harry] didn't just plain die. He was a vegetable for years. It was awful.

According to all reports, J.A. went into an immediate decline. He was now seventy-seven years old. His eldest son, a narcoleptic, had died in an automobile crash eight years before, at the age of forty-one. With this latest loss, James apparently lost all interest, both in business and in life. The conflict between him and the Seegers rapidly escalated.

It reached a peak in April 1945. By this date, it was obvious the war would soon be over, government restrictions and excess-profits taxes would be lifted, and business would take a leap forward as it traditionally had following a war. The Seegers, whose influence was further swollen by Hannah's death in 1944 and the in-

John O'Boyle,
1944

heritance of her company shares, were ready to start gearing up for this event. J.A. was not.

Accounts vary. Some family members, eager to forget bad memories, contend that the inevitable showdown took place on the phone and was a matter of one short and quiet conversation. Most people, however, recall a far more rancorous parting. Certainly the fact that J.A. immediately sold all his stock to the Seegers and disassociated his branch of the family from any involvement in the company was not a happy sign. It was also the final straw for James in a recent string of personal calamities. On October 11, six months following what came to be known as "the fight," he died in Chicago at the age of seventy-nine—the last of the Buchanan brothers.

James's departure from the company gave the Seegers absolute power, an ironic position considering that neither Helen nor Stanley had any training or experience in running a business, especially one in deep financial trouble. For bad tidings were catching up with the company's long history of irresponsible tax dealings. From the early 1930s through the massive reorganization of the mid-1940s, Buchanan executives had been at best misserved by their legal advisers. The IRS was now demanding a reckoning.

Stanley's solution proved fortuitous. He contacted his son-in-law, John O'Boyle, and asked him to help save the company. In this one gesture, he not only got himself out of a very tight spot, he also revealed himself a judge of character in the mold of William Buchanan.

John O'Boyle in 1945 was a thirty-year-old army major working at the Pentagon for a secret unit called the Special Branch of the Military Intelligence Service. For two years, he and a hand-picked crew of other "bright young men"—mostly lawyers, professors, and newspaper people—had been analyzing and assessing intercepted and decoded Japanese messages. Special Branch was the American version of the now more renowned Bletchley Park unit in England which worked with the "Ultra" decoding machine against the Germans. Like their British counterpart, they were isolated from the military machinery and indeed from the rest of the world, becoming known to the public only a few years ago. The name given the American code-busting system was "Magic."

Born in Milwaukee in 1915, O'Boyle was the eldest son, in a family of four sons and two daughters, of a hard-driving, disciplinarian Irish Catholic father who coached his sons in elocution and debate and expected them to do their best at all times. A sometimes jovial man who played as hard as he worked, Oliver O'Boyle was, from 1931 until his death in 1956, Milwaukee's county corporation counsel and an outspoken pillar of society. Ever one to speak his mind, he never shied from confrontation and set an example his sons were hard put to overlook.

John toed the line his father drew, excelling in his studies and on the debate team at Marquette University High School. He was, however, blessed with some of his mother's gentleness, and presented a far more winning personality than did his more boisterous father. According to one glowing later appraisal, of which there were many, "John O'Boyle was as Irish as he looked. He was youthful in his attitudes, quick-witted, so charming as to make John Kennedy look dull."

From high school, John attended Holy Cross College and Harvard Law School, ending up as an editor on the prestigious *Harvard Law Review* and graduating in 1939. He spent a year as law secretary to Judge Robert Patterson of the U.S. Circuit Court of Appeals in New York (Patterson later became secretary of war) and finally returned to Milwaukee in 1940 and joined a small but highly regarded local law firm. That same year, he married twenty-two-year-old Mary Seeger, Stanley and Helen's eldest daughter.

Mary and John had fallen in love during John's law school days, when he would return to Milwaukee on vacation and join in the high-society party circuit. Enrolled in Vassar at the time, Mary transferred to Barnard after John's graduation so she could be nearer to him during his one-year stay in New York.

For those who knew him, John's presence on the party circuit was no surprise. A middle-class boy by birth, by college he had begun to show an interest in climbing the social ladder.

> I noticed that even in the way he would date girls. A bunch of us would date the local townies. That didn't grab John much. He'd line up dates in Boston. They'd always be girls from a finishing school—that was his level, his milieu. John was very careful to make friends that were going to benefit him. I don't think there was any fraud in him. He just liked those kind of people.
>
> He liked to know the people who were movers and doers, whether it was wealth or the Washington scene, like prominent lawyers. John was a little bit of a name-dropper—and liked to be associated with successful people.

Family members acknowledge that his increasing orientation toward the upper class was bound to end with his falling in love with a member of that group—the laws of probability all but made it inevitable. Equally acknowledged, however, was the deep and genuine bond that united the newlyweds. In Mary Seeger, John O'Boyle had a companion whose personality neatly dovetailed into his own. While not as outwardly charming as her husband, she was in many ways a much more open person, benefiting from both her mother's plainspoken sense of humor and her father's intelligence.

The marriage did not start out in the most conventional of manners, for by February of 1942, John had left the United States as one of the heads of the lend-lease mission to Australia, ending up his yearlong stay as acting chief. He then went to Algiers as special adviser to the U.S. minister on lend-lease affairs and became assistant chief and later acting chief of the reoccupation division in April 1943. It was then that he was tapped by Alfred McCormack to become a member of Special Branch. This impressive progression was marred by one stupid, sad, and—in the long run—fatal event. During his travels, John was given a contaminated yellow fever inoculation which resulted in a severe bout of viral hepatitis. His liver was extensively damaged, and for the rest of his life he was to wage an increasingly difficult battle to stay alive.

But this struggle was not to begin for several years, and in the meantime he remained as full of hope and ambition as before. It was clear to all, however, that he hadn't foreseen moving down to Texarkana to help salvage his wife's family business. Indeed, both he and Mary viewed Stanley's plea with reluctance, and only finally agreed on two conditions. The first was that the job be temporary—John would do what he could in a year or two, and then return to Milwaukee and his law practice. The second was that he would be allowed to bring a colleague down with him. Seeger agreed to both terms.

Stanley's eagerness to attract his son-in-law was based on more than the mere serendipity of having a lawyer in the family. As his budding but impressive career made clear, John O'Boyle was not one to avoid a difficult problem, and he usually came out on top. This had always been true, as one of his former college classmates recalled:

> He got things very quickly—he had the kind of mind that could get right to the meat of the matter. He was very good, especially on stuff like student council work, getting ready to present something to the faculty, fellow students or something. John would usually be the guy that would say, "They asked for too much; they're not going to get anything. Boil that down to this." He had that kind of mind. All business. When he got into something, he gave it everything. He was bound and determined he was going to succeed at anything he did. Maybe that's why he was voted "Most Likely to Succeed." He was ambitious.

When John made the condition about having a colleague come with him, he already had his choice in mind: his law school classmate, James Heldt.

The son of an agriculturalist, Heldt was a native of Scottsbluff, Nebraska, a Phi Beta Kappa graduate of the University of Nebraska, and a member of the Harvard Law Review with John. After graduating third in his class, he went to New York with John and joined one of the many law firms there. Uninterested in seeking a commission, he waited for the draft and, around 1942, entered the army as a private. He was working in the signal corps in Illinois when Special Branch, alerted by John, had him transferred to the Pentagon in 1944.

Jim Heldt at Grassy Lake, winter 1946

Heldt was not overjoyed by John's invitation to join forces in Texarkana. Now married himself, he saw a good future waiting for him in New York. The firm he'd left when he was drafted had since split in two, and both parties were eager to have him join them. But his fondness for O'Boyle was strong—they had been exceptionally good friends from the very start—and there were aspects to working in New York that were less than enthralling. "If I went back to New York, I was going to have to start commuting from the suburbs because you just can't raise a family in New York City. And that certainly was a horrible prospect."

Finally, he agreed, but with one familiar condition: he would try it for a year or so, and then would head back to New York, suburbs and all.

The coming of John O'Boyle and Jim Heldt to Texarkana was

Harvard Law Review, 1938–1939. John O'Boyle (third row, third from left), Jim Heldt (top row, middle), Bennett Boskey (third row, second from right)

like the ending of a long illness. Stanley and Helen Seeger, though remaining on all the boards and staying actively involved in the general goals of the business, gratefully handed over both the day-to-day operations and the tax problems to the two men.

This transfer did not happen all at once. John's discharge from the army preceded Jim's by half a year or more, so by late 1945, John was already a director of the company and had replaced the legal counsel of many years past, A. L. Burford. The other major decision taken prior to Jim Heldt's arrival in June 1946 was to do something constructive with the over three hundred thousand acres the company still owned.

Stanley Seeger felt rather badly about the state of that land. He more than anyone saw that the family had gotten rich from a terribly destructive practice. Yet, he still wasn't sure what to do about it. His solution, as it had been in dealing with the tax problems, was to hire someone.

First, he employed the firm of Pomeroy and McGowin to make a total survey of the land. This was not as straightforward as it should have been—the old Buchanan management had been as assiduous in keeping land records as it had been in paying taxes.

Once that task was finally completed, Seeger set out to hire a qualified forester to determine the fate of the land.

Johnny O'Boyle showed up one day in my backyard at Urania, and I'm not sure who he had with him, but I think maybe it was Seeger. They were interested in hiring a forester to look after their lands. A young man in Mississippi with the Forest Service by the name of W. M. Palmer, Jr., had been recommended to them as a man to consider, and they were told that I knew this man and knew him well because we had worked together on the East Coast.

My answer, very quick-like, was this: "Stop wasting your time in my backyard. Get in your car, drive straight to Mississippi, hire him if you can. You cannot hire a better forester in the South than W. M. Palmer."[2]

The advice was extremely accurate. From the time William Palmer, Jr., was hired in May 1946 to the day the company was sold in 1979, he put all his efforts into turning those hundreds of thousands of denuded acres into one of the best stands of timber in the South.

By the time of Heldt's arrival in mid-1946, enthusiasm was beginning to build. Most of the unproductive pre–World War II old guard had been removed, Palmer was hard at work "type-mapping" the land,[3] the tax problems had been identified, and a steady cash-flow procedure was being developed. The major project remaining was to come up with as many ways as possible to increase that flow.

Heldt's first job concerned the two hundred thousand acres of mineral rights that Will Buchanan had retained when he'd sold the land to the federal government in the mid-1930s.

Under Louisiana civil law, a reserved mineral right is not a property right. It's equivalent to an easement. If you do not exercise your rights on an easement in ten years, it expires. If you owned minerals and you did not drill for them once every ten years, you'd lose the right to them. We had these two hundred thousand acres of mineral rights under the

Kisatchie Forest. The sales had been made between 1932 and 1934.

About 1936 or 1937 the federal government wanted to build the Atchafalaya Spillway which drains excess water off the Mississippi and dumps it into the Gulf to stop the flooding conditions below. The people who owned the lands wouldn't sell them to the federal government because they were afraid they'd lose the minerals. So the government got a statute put through the Louisiana legislature which provided that if you sold land reserving the minerals and the sale was to the federal government or a branch of the federal government, then the minerals became what they call "imprescriptable." You owned them in perpetuity.

Well, here we had a legal problem. We had sold ours when that statute was *not* on the books. Before the ten years had run out it *was* on the books. Query: Did it apply to our sale?

John O'Boyle wrote to Jim Heldt while he was still in Washington and asked him to get in touch with the Department of Agriculture, which controlled the National Forests, and find out what the legal options were for clearing up this question.

The Department of Agriculture suggested that the only way to reach an answer would be for the company to sue the U.S. government and establish a legal guideline. Within two years, Heldt did just that, and won the case. The company suddenly gained an additional two hundred thousand acres of minerals to add to the three hundred thousand it already owned.

In the midst of all this, John O'Boyle came up with a third condition to his staying on the job: the company office had to be moved from Texarkana.

One could hardly fault him. Texarkana was an unusual city. Divided down its middle by the Arkansas-Texas state line, it amounted to two cities in one, a bifurcated municipality wrestling with itself.

Schools, police and fire departments, elections, and even zoning and planning are associated with a particular side. The airport, swimming pool, and the municipal auditorium are operated and financed by one side alone, while such services as garbage collection, hospitals, and the library are carried on privately or not at all. Only in the joint operations of food and dairy inspection, of the park system, and of the water and sewage system do the municipalities work together.[4]

This cumbersome, sluggish, and mutually destructive governing structure was further hampered by another disadvantage provided by the state line: criminals enjoyed the option of escaping the jurisdiction of one state by merely crossing the street into the other.

> According to the managing editor of the [*Texarkana*] *Gazette,* "Records of the Federal Bureau of Investigation will show that criminal activity in Texarkana is several notches above the average figures for cities of similar size." And he quoted a captain of the Texas Rangers as saying that Texarkana "has more human driftwood, more perverts, more ex-convicts, more petty thieves, more small-time gamblers than any other city in Texas with the exception of the larger cities, San Antonio and El Paso."[5]

This already sorry state of affairs was not helped by the fact that the city's population, due to a sudden increase in military personnel, had jumped 81 percent in five years to a total of a little over fifty-two thousand by 1945.

The choice of a different location for the company's headquarters was largely a matter of whimsy since at this point it basically didn't produce anything. Dallas, Texas, was chosen, however, because of its size and importance, factors John O'Boyle preferred, and also because it served as a base for H. L. Hunt, with whom both Heldt and O'Boyle wanted to keep in touch. The move from Texarkana took place in August of 1946, the same year William Buchanan's remarkable house was sold.[6]

Six months after the move, at the beginning of 1947, the company faced three major developments: (1) Bill Palmer and a small crew had typemapped the company lands, and he was prepared to undertake the next step, whatever that might be; (2) plans were being drawn up to unitize[7] the only oil-producing property of the Bodcaw Oil Company, the McKamie-Patten field; and (3) the Internal Revenue Service's demands for a settlement had to be dealt with.

The decision whether or not to reforest was ironically hinged on the potential value of the minerals lying under the earth's surface. As the Kisatchie Forest dilemma had made clear, if the company sold the land and retained the mineral rights, it would only have ten years to exploit them. Thus the advantages of profiting from a sale and not having to care for the acreage would be offset by the pressures of having to explore for oil in areas and at times not of the company's own choosing.

The question therefore became not whether to sell, but how to make the land an asset instead of a liability. Reforestation seemed the obvious solution, but it had its serious drawbacks.

> If you put [the land] back into production and did your reforestation, you wouldn't have much *ad valorem* tax problems for the first ten years because the striplings, the small trees, didn't have any commercial value. But when the trees got along to be about twelve years old, then you began to have added value because of the standing timber, and as time went on, the values became greater and greater. But until a tree is about twenty, it doesn't have any commercial value.
>
> We were all terribly worried that we'd get into a period there from say ten to twenty years when your *ad valorem* taxes would start escalating and you would have no way of getting any revenue to meet them.

All this assumed that the trees were successfully planted in the first place. Louisiana was an "open grazing" state which allowed a cattleman or a hog farmer or any other livestock owner to graze his animals on any unfenced land. Thus, fences were not erected to contain animals, but to keep them out, putting the cost of fencing on the person who didn't benefit from ownership of the livestock.

And that wasn't all.

> In the spring of the year when those little shoots of grass started coming up, there'd already be a growth of very tough old grass. And these cattle growers would just go through throwing matches and burn it so their cattle could get to the young shoots. When they did that, they also burned up all the young pine seedlings.

The good news was that if the company did embark on an intensive reforestry program, after twenty years it stood to gain—according to Palmer's figures—an 8 percent return on its investment for each one of those intervening years. But—and this was crucial—this optimistic scenario would only become real if the state of Louisiana could be convinced to pass both a forestry-favorable tax bill and a bill amending or revoking the open-range statute. The benefits of this legislation were so obvious to the company's new management that they envisioned little trouble convincing lawmakers of their wisdom. As it turned out, this was a tad overconfident. Nevertheless, full of good intentions, the directors gave Palmer the go-ahead to begin a reforestation program and alotted a special fund to support it.

The second major topic in early 1947 was the unitization of the McKamie-Patten field. Located in Arkansas and therefore on land of the new Bodcaw Oil Company, this oil field was the only productive acreage on that company's almost twenty-one thousand acres. Neither Bodcaw nor any of the other Buchanan companies was actually involved in the drilling or management of any oil fields, at least not at this stage. As mineral-rights owners, they sold leases to people to drill on their land, sometimes sharing part of the cost, and always benefiting in any discoveries.

With the McKamie-Patten field, the two largest leaseholders were Atlantic Refining, later known as Atlantic Richfield, and Carter Oil. The two of them had been considering unitization for quite a while, but negotiations had broken down, and by late 1946 they were at loggerheads. Heldt and O'Boyle, representing Bodcaw Oil, stepped in as arbitrators.

There were two major reasons for Bodcaw getting involved. The unitization process is a fairly straightforward one: several companies, all extracting oil from the same field, pool their resources, equipment, and personnel and act as one. The profits from the oil sales are divided proportionally. The savings in overhead benefit all concerned. The problem with McKamie-Patten was that the time had come to pressurize the reservoir, and in order to do that, teamwork was needed fast.

> In a field like that, if you don't maintain pressure somehow or another, you have what they call retrograde condensation set in and you lose an awful lot of the liquids in the reservoir because they settle. The liquids are originally under high pressure and exist in a gaseous phase. As the pressure drops below what they call the dew point, it'll drop out of the gaseous phase into a liquid phase, and then it's like sand at the seashore. It's damp, it's wet, but you can't squeeze anything out of it.

Unfortunately, since the concept of unitization was relatively new, the squabble between Atlantic and Carter had broken out over minor details. If Bodcaw Oil didn't step in, the reasoning went, the dew point would be reached and all of them would lose.

The second incentive for Bodcaw Oil's involvement was experience. For both Heldt and O'Boyle, the oil business was very attractive. Oil, as they saw it, was the way to get the overall company out of the red and to finance the reforestation program. McKamie-Patten didn't represent the biggest money producer of their handful of oil properties, but it was definitely one way to learn the ropes.

But unitization demanded that one spend money to make money. Expensive items like a gas-cleaning plant, a recycling plant, and other oil business esoterica were needed to make the unitization work. As with the reforestation program, a special fund was created to cover costs.

The last of the priority items facing the Buchanan companies was, as it was delicately phrased in the minutes, the "tax deficiency." It turned out that the New York tax lawyer who had designed the 1941–42 cluster of specialized companies in order to duck the wartime excess-profits tax had committed a blunder. A clause of that tax law exempted family-controlled companies, and because the Seegers held such an overwhelming majority of shares, all the Buchanan companies were considered family-owned. Adding insult to injury, the IRS's main complaint now was no longer the sins of old—those committed back in the 1930s—but rather the very reorganization that was supposed to have kept the IRS at bay.

Since they had already created special funds to cover the costs of the reforestation program and the McKamie-Patten unitization, Heldt, O'Boyle, and Seeger readily decreed a third fund to handle the tax deficiency. But while it all looked nice on paper, there wasn't enough money to go around—until the Nebo Oil Company came to the rescue.

Nebo Oil was the name given during the reorganization to one of H. L. Hunt's larger leases in La Salle Parish in Louisiana, and by the end of the war, its profits had started to grow. That in itself was fortunate, considering that several of the other oil properties, like Olla and Little Creek, were beginning to show signs of running dry. But the real beauty in Nebo's growth was tied in yet again with the 1941–42 reshuffling of companies.

There were two curious aspects to that arrangement. The first was that since some of the companies were solely oil properties and some were holders of unproductive land, that meant that the oil companies made money but paid no *ad valorem* taxes and the land companies made no money but paid the taxes. The second curiosity was that none of the major stockholders really wanted any dividends. Already well off, they were not keen on paying the maximum income-tax rate of 70 percent for money they didn't need.

The solution to these two problems lay in utilizing Nebo's success.

> [The reorganization] had indirectly a very beneficial effect which nobody even thought of at the time. I don't think it occurred to *anybody.* The company with the biggest income was Nebo. We had to figure out something to do with that income. So we decided the smart thing to do was to have Nebo buy up all the other companies piecemeal. We took all of Nebo's accumulated income and earnings and we'd buy, say, La Salle Land Company. That means the Nebo money

> that normally would go to dividends went over to buy La Salle Land stock. The stockholders [of La Salle, who were also stockholders of Nebo] then had a capital gains tax on it. The capital gains tax was a great deal less, maybe a quarter, of what the ordinary income tax was. So we got the money out of Nebo to the stockholders at a capital gains rate. We worked this over and over and finally bought out almost all the companies.

The end result of this elegant piece of paperwork was that the reforestation fund, the McKamie-Patten unitization fund, and the tax deficiency fund all ended up with enough money to serve their functions. Even the IRS, by 1950, declared itself satisfied.

As it turned out, it was a good thing the reforestation account was well padded, because it was going to need all the help it could get.

8 / Growing Trees

In 1947 William Palmer, one full-time assistant, and a small crew of hired hands planted just under three million seedlings on four thousand acres. In one year, the entire crop was dead, victim of a terrible drought. "He was just devastated. He could see Dr. Seeger just throwing him out and being completely torn up. But that wasn't the case at all. Dr. Seeger patted him on the back and encouraged him and told him, 'Let's do it again.' "

This combination of commitment and support was to be called upon again and again to rally the spirits of everyone involved in the reforestation program. In 1945, Pomeroy and McGowin, the original surveyors Seeger had hired, estimated that the cost of an intensive reforestation project would run about fifty-three cents per acre over a twenty-year span. By 1956, Palmer could report only eight thousand acres successfully planted, at a cost of $130,000, or $16.25 an acre.

The primary obstacles to Palmer's efforts were open-range livestock and arson.

> In the course of putting this land back into production, we were also trying to recover the basic ownership rights of the land. Because the company had not done anything for ten or fifteen years and had, for all practical purposes, abandoned the land, the local people had moved in and put cattle in and in some cases built houses and farms—whatever they felt like they needed. This was almost like eminent domain—they could just move in and use it.

The bad reaction to the company's reclaiming its own property was the result of deep and long-standing resentment. It hadn't been that long ago that the lumber mills had closed, that entire towns had been put out of work, and that entreaties for aid to

William Palmer

Hand-planting with a dibble

Will Buchanan had met with surly rejection. That recent legacy between locals and company was no spawning ground for future cooperation. The ironic historical fact that the mills had been responsible for whatever prosperity many of the communities had enjoyed in the first place was lost to time.

Palmer recognized this situation going into his job, although he probably underestimated the toll it would take.

The land he was to transform totaled some 320,000 acres. Of that, 70,000 acres were hardwood timber, of little interest to the old lumbermen and similarly ignored by Palmer until much later. Approximately 25,000 acres remained of the virgin timberlands of the Buchanan era, cutting rights to which Palmer immediately began selling to create some revenue. The remaining 225,000 acres were, as one man put it, "as bare as that floor," and represented Palmer's primary task.

The cutover land was fairly uniform in quality, lending itself to planting with most types of pine. Palmer's preference was for loblolly, a shortleaf variation valued for its adaptability, its rapid growth, and its supposed lack of appeal to hogs. This choice, however, was not available at the very start. For the first two growing seasons, the only seedlings he could buy in quantity were slash pine, a more resinous shortleaf best suited to deep sandy soil and areas with poor drainage.

He also experimented with a twelve-thousand-acre lot of longleaf pine—the largest, straightest, and strongest of the Southern pines. Why he did this is unclear. The tree, because of its special properties, was valuable for making poles, but in an age where as much timber was grown for pulp as for lumber, this feature wasn't overwhelmingly important. Perhaps more cogent was that the longleaf was king of them all—the perfect image of what a stand of regal timber should be.

Unfortunately, it's also difficult to grow. It can sit on the ground, barely distinguishable from the grass around it, for up to eight years, during which time it is susceptible to almost every hazard imaginable, including a fungus called brown spot.

The traditional method of planting seedlings in the early 1940s was by hand, using a tool called a dibble. The process was long and expensive, demanding many people and a lot of time. Typically giving in to a thirst for innovative solutions, Palmer traveled to Michigan where he had heard of new planting machines being used in the field. Too late to benefit the planting of the longleaf, but soon enough to be of major help elsewhere, six tree-planting machines were added to the company's equipment.

This was a significant investment. The entire heavy equipment of the company's forestry division in 1946 amounted to Palmer's 1936 Ford sedan and two other cars, four and six years old respectively. Palmer was to stretch his finances very thin very fast improving that paltry motor pool with jeeps, trucks, and crawler tractors. His being allowed to do this reflects again Seeger's commitment to the project and to the man he chose to head it.

Thirty-six years old at the time he was hired by the Stamps Land Company, later called Nebo, William Palmer, Jr., was a native Pennsylvanian with a forestry degree from Penn State and ten years' experience with the U.S. Forest Service. He was a tall, balding, rather severe individual, rarely given to emotional outbursts. His approach to the job was to make it as productive and as lean as possible, frequently to the discomfort of his employees. Accepting the fact that his turnover might be high, he paid his foresters comparatively little by industry standards and went to no pains to make them feel overly appreciated or secure. He was, however, a fair man, a hard worker, quick to use new methods, and utterly dedicated to creating the best timberlands he could. These attributes, coupled with the excitement of the project at hand, made his stern, tightfisted personality bearable to his young co-workers. Turnover was, in fact, very small over the years.

Nonetheless, his rigidly cool and moral stance kept his colleagues at arm's length.

> He was an ultraconservative individual. He just couldn't help it. It would almost break his you-know-what to say to somebody, "You did a nice job." He could be most concerned about somebody that he knew was ill and be as solicitous as a preacher. But then he could turn around and be as cold as a cucumber.
>
> I remember Jick Justiss—owns Justiss Oil—used to and

Stanley Seeger's dream: newly planted trees flourishing in spite of arson, hogs, disease, and drought

still does quite often at Christmas time send a ham or turkey to people he does business with. One Christmas, Bill called me into his office and said, "Mr. Justiss has sent me a turkey." Or ham—I forget which. And he said, "You know, company policy is we don't keep anything. I'm going to send it back to Mr. Justiss. Do you think that would be all right?"

I said, "Bill, if you want to insult the man, the thing to do is to send it back to him. Because he certainly will be insulted." He eventually gave it to someone around here who was taking stuff up for the children's home or something.

But that shows you. That's the way Bill was. He wasn't going to take a ham or a turkey because he didn't want anybody saying that somewhere down the line he had taken something from somebody he did business with. He was as honest and straight as a string could ever be.

That dogmatic quality may have caused some complaints within the company, but it was the perfect antidote in the years-long struggle against local animosity and mischief. Fighting arson, tree damage, vandalism, and threats of physical harm, Palmer's men were instructed to just keep working. As one former forester said with justifiable pride, "We never took a belligerent attitude. We took an attitude of understanding—trying to understand their problems and asking them to please try to understand ours."

It wasn't easy. The same forester recalled just how difficult conditions could become.

> The first job he gave me was to survey and supervise the building of an eighteen-mile fence that enclosed twelve thousand acres. I recall we would work until noon, and then from the afternoon on into the dark I would take fire crews and fight fires on into the night. But we never stopped that fence-building crew. They kept building fence regardless of what.

By the mid-1940s, arson was a long-lived Southern tradition, accounting for 73 percent of all the fires occurring in Louisiana.

> In those days [around World War I] fire was looked on as an aid to living. Turpentine men burned over the woods to open them so their turpentine hands wouldn't have to struggle in the woods, be bitten by rattlesnakes, and so on. The cattleman burned the woods because it was necessary for good grazing to fatten his cattle early in the spring. The farmer burned the woods because the turpentine men and the cattlemen were going to burn, and the fire would reach him if he didn't burn first. . . . It was also used by hunters in the woods and was used always as a fine way of venting spite against anything, anybody, or against the world in general. . . . None of these fires were the terribly disastrous fires that we hear of and see in the West. They were ground fires and they had been going on ever since the Indian days, actually. There was never wholesale destruction of standing timber unless the stands were very young—then it might wipe them out.[1]

That last point became the crucial one after the virgin forests had been replaced by plantations of seedlings.

> When you get forty thousand or fifty thousand acres . . . of planted forest as dense as it can be, young and tender, that could make a fire that would burn people up—burn homes, schools, cattle, and everything else. The reason we didn't have those fires in the old days was because we had annual burning and there wasn't any fuel on the ground to make heavy fires. The trees that were there had grown up through fire and were accustomed to it. The limbs were way high above the ground. It was rare to see a crown fire. But when second-growth forests came, all that changed; it can burn.[2]

The problem of purely malicious arson became so prevalent by 1943 that the U.S. Forest Service hired a psychologist who reported that many people set the woods on fire because they craved excitement in "an environment otherwise barren of emotional outlets."

This undoubtedly had some truth to it. Even after Huey Long's massive statewide roads and bridges improvement program, rural people in Louisiana remained an isolated lot, leading lives that also could have stood a little improvement.

Palmer and his men were not the only people having trouble with fire, of course, nor were they the only ones trying to do something about it. In 1949, of the 7,725 fires which destroyed trees in Louisiana, 7,712 were traced to man. Since 1918, the various state foresters had struggled with the Louisiana bureaucracy to get money for fire-fighting equipment, but with limited success. For the most part, until after World War II, private timberland owners were on their own. In 1948, State Forester James Mixon finally secured enough money to buy jeeps, plows, tractors, and, more important, radios, fire towers, and a spotter plane. The latter three items allowed for greater coordination between private and public fire-fighting teams. During extremely dry periods, Palmer would extend the fire-tower watch to twenty-four hours a day by putting his own men in the towers at night after the state men had left for the day.

Palmer was also quick to equip his vehicles with radios and to coordinate their frequencies with the state radios. He made sure

Planting machines being towed in tandem. It looked good but proved impractical. One planter per tractor, however, worked well

hundreds of miles of fire lanes were plowed and maintained each year and constructed an elaborate fire-fighting plan whereby dozens of extra men and hired equipment were available at a moment's notice.

He had good reason for extra concern. For many people in central Louisiana, Palmer and what he represented became the identifiable enemy. By the early 1950s, the Buchanan properties of old had been collectively gathered under the single banner of the Nebo Oil Company. As "Nebo," this sprawling entity grew to become the cause of all ills, not unlike "The Government," "The Reds," or "The Damned Yankees." One local apocryphal complaint in 1969 was that when the astronauts landed on the moon, they found the company had put a fence around it.

The slightest local mishap ascribable to Nebo was countered by the dropping of a match in the woods. In the eight-year period from 1948 to 1955, 1,503 fires broke out, burning a total of 26,892 acres of Nebo land alone.

Methods for setting these blazes ranged from the mundane and the perverse to the truly scientific.

> Boy, there's an art to burning the woods. They'd take these old cotton ropes, and those guys could tie them. They'd take a bunch of these kitchen matches and wrap them around one end of that rope with a rubber band or some twine, and then they'd light the other end and it would just smolder on down till it got to those matches and they'd flare up like that and just set the woods on fire. They could cut that rope just as long as they wanted—make it just like a time bomb.
>
> I know an old boy who was in the enforcement section of the conservation department. And he said he knew one damned old man; he'd been watching him day and night. He knew he was going to burn them woods. So he went out on the road and was gone some time. He come up and blocked him where he couldn't run around him. He said that old man pulled up there in his pickup truck and got out and got up on the hood of it and set there and talked to him for an hour and a half. And he said, "I guess I'd better go." So he moved over and let the old man get by on the road and went on. And he said about thirty minutes after that old man was gone, he looked back and the whole world was on fire. That old man—he knew how long those ropes would smolder.

More primitive methods included simply throwing matches out of car windows or tying gasoline-soaked rags to the tails of hogs and lighting them: "They'd take off through the woods like a bat out of hell, touching off fires right, left, and center. It made the fire all the more uncontrollable since it didn't have a central spot of origin."

Palmer and his colleagues quickly recognized that the source of their problem was largely generational. The older residents—the dyed-in-the-wool country folk—most resented Nebo's repossessing its own land and passed their feelings down along family lines. The solution was for the company to sell itself in as many different ways as possible.

> All of us were trying to turn around the image the company had in that area. It was a one-on-one relationship with the people. We became active with the civic clubs and the

> 4-H and the different projects that were going on. We spent a lot of time visiting John Doe on his front porch and drinking coffee. We had an active program of taking all the children out of school every year and taking them out in the woods and letting them plant trees and showing them what we were doing and why we were doing it. It took a while, you didn't turn it around overnight, but over a period of ten or fifteen years you turned the attitude around.

Thus, the primary weapon was persistence. The more fires were started, the more trees were replanted, sometimes again and again on the same piece of ground. Violence was frequently threatened, but amazingly never occurred, although at least once it was a very near thing.

> We had up north of Jena a fairly good stand of longleaf seedlings and it was being damaged by cattle. So we did undertake to fence that area. And the cattle owners in that area were very aggressive. I remember in particular, we hired a man to be superintendent of the fence-building crew because he had a reputation, and I believe justifiably, as being the steeliest and quickest man with a trigger in the whole area. People were frightened of him. He was a marvelous shot.
>
> They had a mass meeting in Jena one time to go out there and stop the fence building. And there was quite a mob—maybe fifty or sixty people, some with arms—that confronted our man and told him that they wanted to stop that fence building right then. And he said, "Well, I'll tell you. The first guy that fires a shot had better be accurate, because before he can get off another one, there will be two or three of you dead." And they turned tail. The fence was finished.
>
> Then we had the question—we'd hired this man for a specific job; now how do we terminate him? But he was really kind of a reasonable man. Bill Palmer went and talked to him and told him the job was over, and he said, "I know it's over. I hope you're satisfied." Of course we were.

But the biggest problem with livestock and fences usually didn't concern cattle owners. In the early days of Nebo's reforestation during the 1940s and 1950s, there was generally room enough for both plantations and cattle, and Nebo often allowed cattlemen to graze their animals on company land, albeit away from the seedlings. Once the trees grew larger, even this restriction was lifted. Additional compromises and understandings were made: Nebo agreed to burn some of the old grass, under proper supervision and at the proper times, and the cattlemen acknowledged that the fences could be a help in keeping their livestock from wandering out onto the highways and getting killed. It obviously wasn't a perfect marriage and led to a lot of burned fence posts and cut wire, but in the long run it survived.

The same was not true for the hogs. Hogs in the South were legion in number, pork being the main meat staple of the area. They were also not as controllable as cattle: except for telltale markers in their ears, domestic hogs were indistinguishable from their wild counterparts. Lastly, the hope of any peaceful coexistence between grazing hog and growing tree was destroyed by the hogs' fondness for eating seedlings. One hog could wipe out 250 seedlings in a single day, the attraction being the sweet, starchy wood at the base of each young tree. By nibbling at the bark, the hogs successfully girdled the plant, severing its circulatory system and killing it.

Hog owners also proved more difficult to deal with than cattlemen. The general concensus of the Nebo men who worked back in the 1940s and 1950s is that violence was threatened more often over hogs than over any other local bone of contention.

> I had one [hog owner] come to my house one day and threaten me. He just told me, "Now you don't fool with my hogs." These were people that were kin to folks in the West in the early pioneer days. They lived on the range, stayed in the woods, and they wouldn't mind shooting people. It was done pretty regularly in that area. Everywhere I'd go I'd run into somebody and they'd confront me to leave them alone and threats, threats, threats.

An educational program, complete with photographs, was started to show people just how destructive the hogs had become. The locals responded that the company men sprinkled food around the seedlings to incriminate the innocent hogs.

Stanley Seeger's bountiful legacy in 1960

Conventional knowledge had it that hogs adored longleaf, liked slash, and wouldn't eat loblolly. This, in fact, was the determining factor that made Palmer veer away from his earlier slash and longleaf planting and concentrate solely on loblolly. Unfortunately, conventional knowledge proved faulty.

> Mr. W. M. Palmer, Jr., chief forester for the Nebo Oil Co., of La Salle Parish, recently cancelled the company's order for three million seedlings for planting this spring and announced that he will discontinue all planting until some method is devised to control the hogs. The damage to the slash pines has been known for some time, but the attack on the loblolly plantations forced the decision. In the last four seasons the company has planted some 12 million seedlings, and all of them are now in jeopardy.
>
> Here is the story of the damage—the first known instance of hogs destroying large acreages of loblolly pine.
>
> When the company began its planting program in the winter of 1947–48, it used mostly slash pine—longleaf ob-

viously didn't have a chance of getting past the hogs. However, slash was also soon damaged, and in the winter of 1949–50 loblolly was set out on a 478-acre tract of cutover land. The trees were planted by machine at a spacing of 6′ x 8′, or at the rate of 908 trees per acre. Early survival and growth were excellent. In the spring of 1952, some 757 trees per acre were still alive; they averaged 4′ tall.

Then, in March, the hogs moved in! Between March and July, they killed 472 loblolly pines per acre and damaged 90 more. In five months, they reduced the plantation from 757 to 195 undamaged trees per acre.[3]

In the first four years of operation, from 1947 to 1951, Palmer and his crews planted 12,500,000 seedlings of loblolly and slash—not counting many more millions of longleaf—most of which he saw die. During the next four years, to 1955, he planted a mere 1,445,000 young trees.

His radical cutback in planting reflected a major change in strategy. He had encountered from the start, as he knew he would, animosity, taxes, vandalism, arson, livestock damage, poaching, and drought. Drought, he saw, was out of his control. Other barriers, like animosity, he felt he could treat with stubborn but friendly persistence. But some demanded legislative action. Taxes, fire prevention, and hog control were the foremost among these. "We started out pretty much novices as to how you get legislation passed. We thought you'd just run down there with a statute and a good idea and get the legislation passed. We found out that was sadly amiss."

The solution was a time-honored one: the formation of a trade association. The idea had its roots in the founding in 1941 of the North Louisiana Group of Foresters, a local unit of the Society of American Foresters. The unit, organized by Lloyd Blackwell, had among its members Bill Palmer, who joined when he was hired by Seeger and O'Boyle.

In 1946, there was a consensus among members that the reforestation-contract law that Henry Hardtner had pushed through the Louisiana legislature in 1910 was in need of an overhaul. A committee of five, including Bill Palmer, convened to do just that.

> As the committee completed its writing of a revised contract, it became clear to all the members that there would be an almost insurmountable task in trying to get passage of the new program in the Louisiana Legislature without the support and work of a state-wide organization interested in the program, willing to work for its passage, and recognized in the Legislature.[4]

The upshot of this need was the creation in September 1947 of the Louisiana Forestry Association (LFA). Among its charter members were Bill Palmer, John O'Boyle, and Stanley Seeger. O'Boyle was also a member of the first executive committee and drew up the papers of incorporation of the association. In many instances, O'Boyle was to reveal, for much larger stakes, the prowess he had once displayed as a member of his college student council.

The newly formed LFA had its work cut out for it. It couched its prospectus in the most generous of terms, stressing that its goals were to help one and all by "disseminating information," "assisting the Louisiana Forestry Commission," and "serving as a clearinghouse for proposals and practices in production." Almost unnoticed in the list of potential good deeds was the primary reason for the group's existence: "To work for fair and equitable taxes on forest lands and growing timber."

Despite the soft sell, turning this ambition into law became a frustrating labor of years. Bill Palmer, as head of the Forest Taxation Committee, worked long and hard on its behalf, lobbying legislators in session and at home, inviting them to meet with the leadership of the LFA for informational exchanges, trying to iron out all the suspicions and prejudices. Time and time again, the tax bill came up for a vote and was defeated for one reason or another. In 1952, its failure was blamed on a last-minute rewording of the bill's title, which indicated that its passage would "Exempt Growing Timber from Taxation." This was all the more unfortunate since the contents of the bill clearly pointed out that what was being proposed was not an exemption, but rather a two-pronged tax: a set *ad valorem* tax for the land coupled with a severance tax covering the cut timber.

Perseverance, once again, won the day. In 1954, the Swine Impounding Act (designed to control the hog problem) and the tax package (now a statewide constitutional amendment) both passed with flying colors. The LFA, heady with its accomplishments, turned its attention to fire control.

The passage of the tax and hog laws was a watershed event for Nebo.[5] The year 1955 saw a resurgence in planting, with 2,062,500 seedlings, up from none the year before; and in 1956, 5,500,000 more young loblollies were put in the ground. Nebo finally hit its stride in the reforestation business.

The similarity of this story to the earlier success of Henry Hardtner in passing the 1910 tax law is an interesting quirk of history, but Nebo's commitment to politics stopped with its involvement with the LFA. In all other instances, the company showed a marked aversion to politics in any way, shape, or form.

> We never did contribute to any political campaigns, local or otherwise. We had a background of that. We always took a very impartial view. We never supported any candidate, we never opposed any candidate, although frequently people would run on the grounds that if elected they would make us pay, one way or the other. That was mostly campaign rhetoric.

In this, Seeger and his two lieutenants were mirroring over fifty years of family tradition. With the exception of William Buchanan's brief anti-union connection with the Yellow Pine Manufacturers' Association and Will Buchanan's dalliance with the Southern Pine Association in the late 1930s, the company had steered clear of any organization tied to state and national politics.

This in fact became an issue with one of the company's oldest employees. Upon the arrival of the Seegers, and later Heldt and O'Boyle, among the most influential people in La Salle Parish, where Nebo had a large part of its holdings, was a man named Herbert N. Tannehill. Tannehill had arrived in the Jena area as a surveyor for the L&A Railroad near the turn of the century. During the ensuing years, he worked for the company in a variety of capacities, ending up by World War II as a kind of general repre sentative—in an old-time phrase, the "company man."

He had also come to wear two hats. As his prestige had grow within the Buchanan organization, so had it grown among th local people. By the time the Seegers took over control from J. A Buchanan, Tannehill, as a politician, had established a miniatur fiefdom of his own, with powers beyond what the company's ne management deemed healthy.

A story related by a man who referred to Tannehill as "m champion" highlights the type of personal involvement in com munity affairs people like Heldt and O'Boyle were trying t avoid.

> Tannehill [for the company] used to lease property to some of these people. He'd charge some of them [say] one dollar and others two dollars. There was a meeting one time in Good Pine. And he said the old guys come in there and one fellow spoke up and said, "Tannehill, how come you charge me two dollars and some of these other fellows you just charge one dollar?"
>
> Mr. Tannehill said he started to explain it to them, and one fellow, one of the one-dollar men, said, "Mr. Tannehill, let me. I can explain it to that fellow."
>
> Tannehill said, "All right."
>
> And he said, "The way it is, Mr. Tannehill is into politics up to his ears. Me, I just pay the one dollar, but I always vot like Mr. Tannehill wants me to vote!"
>
> That was about the truth about it too.

With the hiring of Bill Palmer in 1946, Tannehill's tenure wit the company became distinctly imperiled. A sharper contrast i characters could hardly be found. Tannehill's casual, good o boy, turn-a-blind-eye form of management clashed headlong wit Palmer's largely humorless, workaholic personality. Before long an issue of principle inevitably cropped up—actually, betwee Heldt and Tannehill—that forced a parting of ways.

There was, however, one additional small, and very human detail:

> When Helen Seeger found out they'd fired Mr. Tannehill, the shit hit the fan. She come over here and went right in his house and told him, "Goddamn, get back over there onto your job. Hell, they ain't about to fire you. No sir."
> But he told her that he had got old and all this new wrinkle in reforestation had come in and he wasn't up to all that.[6]

Helen's reaction was typical. Despite her long absence from the area during her years in Milwaukee, her emotional ties to the company and its employees were strong. Both she and Stanley, especially Stanley, came frequently to Jena to visit the foresters and to walk the woods. Stanley admitted he found a genuine satisfaction in seeing the land productive once again.

Stanley's involvement with Nebo's operations was far more intense than his wife's. In many ways, her affection resembled that of a monarch of old—the company was essentially all hers and she found it amusing to drop by occasionally and watch it at work. But in the long run, it represented just another thing to do—interesting, but not worth a great deal of effort.[7] Stanley was just the opposite. While he left the nuts and bolts to Heldt and O'Boyle, he maintained a keen interest in the growing of trees.

> He'd come over sometimes by himself and he'd put on his old blue jeans and old clothes, and he was ready to go into the woods. He studied forestry. He could talk silvaculture and mensuration and things that foresters talk about with a lot of knowledge.
>
> They had a company house there in Good Pine, had a cook and a maid that kept the house up, and when he was there, that's where he stayed. And he'd invite us over to eat with him. I remember going, just myself—I was twenty-three or twenty-four—and eating with Dr. Seeger, just the two of us. I just talked constantly—I spilled everything I knew. And he didn't tell me much of anything. He was a real fine old gentleman. He knew his business well and was very interested in forestry and what we were doing.
>
> I remember one night we were called out for a fire about ten o'clock. We all poured into that office, getting our equip-

ment out and ready, and they were there. They'd come over to see what was going on, both he and his wife. I don't remember much about her, though. He came most of the time by himself.

But Seeger's interaction with the company as a whole didn't extend very far. After the initial turnover struggles of the early 1940s and the hiring of his son-in-law, his role became an odd combination of both cheerleader and nay-sayer.

> He really was not active in the company after John showed up, and what little he did was on the forestry side. John had most of the discussions with him when we'd decide we ought to buy timberland or buy some leases or get more deeply into the drilling business. Jim Heldt's conversations with him were sort of through the back door. He'd call Heldt in and say, "What do you think about this?" Of course, John and Jim always saw eye to eye.
>
> On a few occasions he would say, "I consider my primary responsibility as being a conservator. My duty is to preserve this estate to pass on to the children, and I do not want to get into highly risky business. I do not want to be in oil, and I do not want to spend a lot of money buying timberland; we've got all we need."
>
> In short, he wanted to try to maintain the status quo. He did not want it to diminish, but he didn't really want to run the risk of trying to expand it much either.

Stanley's other occupation became the William Buchanan Foundation, which he had helped William to create in 1923. It had remained untouched for over twenty years, slowly accumulating interest until Stanley, as one observer put it, began "fussing" with it, paying out a little here and there, keeping his hand in medicine through philanthropy.[8] He also wrote several short articles on industrial health that appeared in medical journals.

For the rest of the time, he traveled, accompanying his restless wife on her seemingly endless trips around the country. A contemporary observed, "I never knew whether this was her method of compensating for what he'd given up [in leaving Milwaukee] or whether she just did it because this is what she wanted to do."

At times, both the pace and his wife's acquisitive nature became more than even Stanley's accommodating personality could bear.

> They had a house in Florida, but Mrs. Seeger was hell-bent to get another in Naples, like all her friends had, and hang the expense. She even went and handpicked one out and said, "Stanley, go buy that house."
>
> Stanley knew it would just be another bother to take care of and that they'd probably be there five or six days every two years. So we went over together to see the guy selling the house who was not the usual real estate person. He was a guy named Sample who was head of the largest advertising agency in Chicago until he retired and got into real estate as a hobby.
>
> So there were these two giants sitting there. One of them wanted to sell the house because he could use the Seegers to sell other houses, and the other had no intention of buying that house. It was one of the funniest scenes you ever saw.

Two months later, in June 1952, both Seegers traveled to New Jersey to attend their son's graduation from Princeton. Afterward, they went to New York, and there, giving in to hypertension that had dogged him for years, Stanley died on Friday, June 20. Struggling to find the proper name of the cause of his death, one family member finally said, "I don't know what you call it—the big thing busted."

At the time of Seeger's death, the Nebo Oil Company had just completed its reorganization. It was not as financially healthy as Stanley might have liked—the reforestation program was still at the mercy of arsonists and hogs—but he accomplished what he set out to do. The legacy of William Buchanan had been secured for future generations.

It had also been remolded to reflect the times. Just as William had mirrored his era's exploitive capitalism, and Will his generation's moral laxity and irresponsibility, so Stanley Seeger brought to Nebo a nation's realization that at least one limited resource should be nurtured. The year he died, Southern pine sawtimber growth exceeded harvest mortality by 22 percent, largely as a result of reforestation programs like Nebo's. And that was to be the tip of the iceberg; also in 1952, scientists finally developed a way to coat pine seeds with bird repellent, thereby ensuring greater success in direct-seeding efforts. Planting trees was rapidly becoming as easy as throwing seeds upon the ground.

Linking Seeger's foresight to similar efforts by hundreds of other men like him renders him no disservice. As an individual, he sacrificed much to honor what he saw as his responsibilities. Given many simpler alternatives, he opted to break a destructive historical pattern that foretold a profitable demise of the family business. His medical colleagues shook their heads at his departure from Milwaukee; fellow landowners were at best skeptical at his plans to reforest so many barren acres; local residents were resentful and mischievous in response to his plans. He paid none of them any heed. It is to his credit that with as little specific knowledge as he possessed, he recognized and pursued what was right.

It was now up to John O'Boyle and Jim Heldt to carry on in that new tradition.

9 / New Blood

John O'Boyle and Jim Heldt had become restless under Stanley Seeger's conservative reign. After the initial excitement of suing the U.S. government for the mineral rights under the Kisatchie Forest and setting up the McKamie-Patten unitization, the two men found themselves with more time on their hands than Nebo business could adequately fill. Attempts to expand that business routinely fell victim to Seeger's veto. So, around 1951, the two of them went into the oil and gas business for themselves on the side. "It was phenomenal. Everything they drilled turned out good. When O'Boyle died in '69, they'd already decided they were successful enough and had stopped doing any more. They'd split the partnership, each taking half of the producing properties."

Oil and gas was really Jim Heldt's main interest, and had been from the beginning. When the Louisiana Forestry Association was started up in 1947, Heldt had very little to do with it. Similarly, he rarely visited the woods operation, and when he did, the foresters were struck by his lack of specific knowledge and curiosity. Oil was a different matter. That pursuit was crammed with facts and figures, an arcane language, lots of paperwork, and was peppered with litigable possibilities. It was, according to all who worked with him, Heldt's preferred cup of tea.

He was not, however, a fast-moving operator, nor a man given to imaginative hunches. That was more John O'Boyle's temperament. "All the things that we went into were John's ideas. John said Jim Heldt had the imagination of a cold-water faucet. I'd say in I.Q., Jim was probably higher than John, but he was a persistent type; he didn't have the intuition, you know, the prophetic ability, to pick the investment opportunities that John had."

Of course, too much intuition radiating from the head of an

organization could have its drawback, and it was here that Jim Heldt's more methodical personality helped balance things out.

> [John's] mind worked so fast and with such general concepts usually, that it was hard to figure out specifically what he wanted done. And even if you did, you were liable to find he had changed his mind several times before you got back to him with what you had done according to the first set of instructions. I really enjoyed the man, but working with him could drive you up the wall. He was never hard on you for having misunderstood, but he just moved so fast it was hard to keep up with him.
>
> Jim Heldt was the opposite extreme. He is as precise and German as his name. You always knew exactly what he wanted you to do, although you might not be able to figure out how it ever could get done. And you knew that when you came back a month later with what you had done, he would have perfect recall of the instructions he had given you. There wasn't going to be any misunderstanding, unless you had blown it.
>
> They made a beautiful team. O'Boyle was very imaginative and knew a million people and was capable of charming all of them, and Heldt could pick up with all the details and make sure that whatever was done, was done with great thoroughness.

Something should be mentioned here about John O'Boyle as the ultimate charming man. Of the dozens of people interviewed concerning his personality, virtually all commented on O'Boyle's dual nature. "John was a very gregarious person in many respects. He had a very attractive, sunny, warm disposition. But with all of that, he was a very private person. He never really discussed his personal affairs with anybody. Even his own children complained and said, 'Dad never told me anything about anything.' "

This aloofness became a trademark of the man and marked a public-side, private-side tug-of-war that continually waged inside him. For all his grace and cheerful disposition, he was capable of

Jim and Jane Heldt, 1947

extreme reserve—the more a situation demanded a genuine emotional involvement, the more John O'Boyle held back. His personal dichotomy became part of what made him special in the eyes of those people who didn't know him well.

> He was a man of perfection; he liked perfection. We girls in the office went over the windowsills and everything else to make sure there was no dust, because Mr. O'Boyle was the type that he took a white glove and took a little swipe. He was that type person. And yet he was a man you enjoyed knowing he was coming down. To have him in the office a little while, to get to know as the top man.

It is a credit to Heldt's personality that he worked so well with O'Boyle. For as long as John O'Boyle was alive, Jim Heldt was emphatically the number-two man. Despite the fact that O'Boyle had felt he couldn't join the company without Jim Heldt in tow, he nevertheless insured that his friend always received a lower salary, a lesser title, and fewer fringe benefits than he did.

> There was a bit of the snob in John. I always had the feeling that he had 75 percent of himself that he could be charming and outgoing with, but that he reserved 25 percent for this other, more ambitious part.
>
> He enjoyed the things that wealth could bring. And he had the smarts, the talent, the personality that he could move easily in that [upper society]. But he was probably a little smugger about it—calculating—than the rest of us.

To his children and to the people who occasionally caught the brunt of the autocratic part of his nature, John's jovial, sunny reputation was both baffling and slightly irritating. "It used to annoy me. During the early years we'd both go down through Louisiana together and visit with people and make contact. . . . I'd go down five years later and all they'd say was, 'How's that nice Mr. O'Boyle?' They all remembered. He made a marvelous impression."

That John O'Boyle was putting forth any kind of pleasant front by late 1952 was a credit to his willpower. Not only had his own liver problem steadily worsened over the years to where he knew he would live a vastly shortened life, but now his wife, Mary, had come down with a virulent form of lymph cancer. For the next nine years, until her death in 1961, she struggled to stay alive between massive sessions of chemotherapy and radiation therapy administered both in New York and Dallas. The psychological toll this double calamity had on the O'Boyle family was to be very far-reaching.

And yet through it all, indeed perhaps spurred on because of it, John's ambitions and zeal flourished, even while his personality became more reclusive and self-absorbed. For the company, Stanley Seeger's passing was like the dropping of a leash. Both John and Jim immediately began to enact many of the projects they had been forced to shelve years earlier, with John focusing on the timberlands and Jim heading up the oil projects. New acreage was purchased, wells drilled, and people hired, although never as much nor as frequently as many on the staff recommended. O'Boyle and Heldt would never be accused of being free-spending and speculative—even unleashed, they were a conservative duo.

Compared to Stanley, however, they were like a gust of wild wind. Most of this activity took place in the oil and gas department. Until Seeger's death, Nebo had been strictly a leasing operation. Oil companies were allowed to come on the land, examine it geologically, drill wells, and, with any luck, extract oil or gas, all in exchange for royalties and lease payments. But Nebo itself was never involved in the actual exploration for oil.

With John's elevation to the presidency and Jim's to the vice-presidency, all that began to change.

> We decided *we* ought to be in the oil business on the producing side, not [just] as a royalty owner. As a royalty owner, you get one-eighth [of the proceeds]. As a producer, you'd get eight-eighths. We decided we could do just as well as anyone else. We kept our drilling operations largely on our own lands, or on lands that were adjacent to our own lands. Since we had about five hundred thousand acres, all in good oil country, we could see very little sense in using some of the money to buy leases when we could drill on our own lands and spend almost every buck drilling.

In order to develop this sound, if restrictive, line of reasoning, they hired their own geologist in 1954. It was his job to find the oil. There were, however, familiar problems from the beginning.

> It was a real problem to get started because they'd kept no records. I had to [establish] some base maps and put the properties on the map to show where they were. I had to go back to Hunt, and I must have spent three months in their warehouse down at Nebo in La Salle Parish just copying the records of wells that Hunt had drilled, both dry holes and producers.

That done, the exploration began. In another parallel to the forestry side of the company, the first few years of the oil department were "pretty skinny." Enough dry holes were drilled into Nebo ground to cause Heldt to refer bitterly to the whole process as "random drilling"—a sharp crack indeed to anyone in the business. The burden was all the heavier since the geologist, Gene Hanes, was working all alone. Styles of management differ, of course, but Hanes must have thought wistfully of the stories of Seeger's support of Palmer in the struggling early days of the forestry program.

> There's two types of wells. You can drill exploratory wells or wildcat wells where you have no adjacent production, and you get about one out of twenty with those at best. In exploratory wells, it's more like fifty-fifty. So you can see how much wildcatting Hanes was doing. You got twenty chances of getting a dry hole and you know you've got twenty trips to Jim Heldt's office to tell him about it. So, why would you? Jim Heldt and John O'Boyle were not oil operators. They were lawyers.

They also didn't believe in overstaffing—in fact, to most of their employees, even adequate staffing appeared an anathema. The early woods crew consisted of Palmer and one assistant up to 1950, at which point two more assistants were added. By the mid-1950s, when operations were going ahead full steam, that number hadn't been added to by much. Oil was no different. Gene Hanes was *it* for quite a while, during which time he fulfilled the functions normally assigned to several men. "The attitude was that we would maintain an absolute minimum of real qualified people to run our operation, and when we needed to have something done that was beyond their capacity or time, we'd hire an expert to do it, and when we'd be through with it, we'd be through with him."

This did not necessarily mean that employees were encouraged to expand within the job. When some of the foresters mentioned they were experienced surveyors, but merely lacked the proper licenses to operate, they claimed O'Boyle, Heldt, and Palmer denied them the opportunity to secure those licenses for fear they might start demanding higher salaries.

Slowly, things in Gene Hanes's department improved. Lessons

were learned, the geology began to reveal its secrets. By the late 1950s, the oil staff had grown a bit. A second geologist came on, a production man was added, "switchers"—men assigned to supervise the field storage tanks, switching the oil flow from one tank to the next as each became full—were hired. Interestingly, the company never physically drilled its own wells—independent contractors were hired for that. From 1954 to 1961, during which time the company changed its name from Nebo Oil to the Bodcaw Company (mostly for public relations and sentimental reasons), its holdings increased from some fifteen producing wells to over twice that number.

Most of these wells were shallow, extending to about four thousand feet. They were located primarily in La Salle Parish, the region H. L. Hunt had opened in the 1930s and 1940s, and along the northern Louisiana–southern Arkansas border in Lafayette Parish and Columbia County, where the McKamie-Patten field had been unitized.

It was in this latter area that Hanes and his crew finally succeeded in their quest for a major field. "The Walker Creek field was discovered in about 1967 or '68. The discovery well was in Lafayette County, but the field was so large that it extended into Columbia County. Bodcaw had a great deal of fee minerals. They'd sold the surface, but reserved the minerals."[1]

The discovery encompassed both Bodcaw minerals and adjacent, non-Bodcaw property. The company response, which under Seeger would have been to hold tight and count its blessings, was instead to join the scramble to purchase the outlying minerals. It was a move that paid off.

> We made a lease play along with a lot of others, but we happened to pick what later turned out to be the fairway—a field that's about nineteen miles long and only about three miles wide. We had some real good leases in there. Before it was all over, Bodcaw owned better than 26 percent of the field. That then put us in the big time.

Not everyone was thrilled with their success. Over the years, Nebo, and later Bodcaw, did not make many friends in the oil business. Once the decision had been made to become oil producers, the company all but locked up its mineral rights to outsiders. As a result, if an independent producer was following a certain line of exploration and happened to hit Bodcaw land, that usually marked the end of his search. Except in very rare instances, the company no longer leased its property. Conversely, if oil was discovered next to Bodcaw land, Bodcaw was the first to start drilling to take advantage of the find. In fact, over 75 percent of the company's producing wells were drilled on the edge of its own property and in the wake of someone else's discovery.

An additional bone of contention was the sharing of research information, specifically something called "electric logs." Each time a well was drilled, a recording was made of the various geological zones through which the well had passed. This information was extremely valuable when it came time to make a geological map of the area or establish the possible location of an oil or gas field. Routinely, the logs were freely traded among the various producers as a sign of friendly cooperation. Routinely, Bodcaw didn't participate. The result was a miniature cold war; just as Bodcaw excluded its competitors, so they united to isolate Bodcaw. Only under internal pressure did Heldt finally concede to a limited exchange of mutually advantageous information.

> There was lots of hostility. Nobody liked Bodcaw or Nebo or their employees. We had battles every time we'd go into anything where they were trying to unitize a field or something like that. We'd have to go in those meetings and they'd almost beat you over the head with sticks. There was lots of animosity. When we finally unitized the Walker Creek field, Bodcaw had 26 percent of the field—a majority. We wanted to be elected field operators [i.e., the one company that would actually run the unitized field] but the other 74 percent banded together and voted against us.

Interestingly, as the image of the oil-producing side of Bodcaw deteriorated, the woodlands group's public relations were looking better and better. Pro-forestry legislation increased, the backwoods diehards began giving in to old age, scientific developments continually added to a tree's chances at survival and growth. Protected from any outside economic pressures by the steady cash input from the company's oil revenues, the Bodcaw forest, by the early 1960s, was becoming a very attractive stand of timber. It was obvious to all concerned that before long, the woodlands division would have to start pulling its own weight.

That dependence of one half of the company on the other had given rise to a friendly rivalry. Bodcaw's oilmen kidded about how the foresters sat around all day and watched trees grow, all on oil-produced money. The foresters responded that they had their work cut out for them making sure the oilmen didn't pollute and destroy the timberlands. In a fashion, both were correct. The foresters, far from sitting around, were nonetheless supported by the oil revenues. In fact, in the early 1960s, when some of the timber was becoming marketable but the market itself was depressed, the decision was made to lay back and wait until prices improved—an option hardly available to a company without an extra source of income.

On the other hand, the presence of that growing forest and the vigilant foresters had a beneficial effect on the oilmen. It made them aware that the land was far more than just a place to punch holes.

> Knock a tree down and you'd have to make a deal with them on that tree. It was a little tough when we first started, especially on the road. You know, moving a rig in. You can't move a rig on an eight-foot road. You've got to have at least fifteen, twenty, twenty-five feet. They wanted to know why we wanted such wide roads. They treated every tree like it was their own little baby. I called Hugh Burnham [one of the foresters] "Pine Knot" and he called me "Salt Water."

"Salt Water" came from the fact that a common by-product of oil-well drilling was a runoff of highly salinated subterranean water. Until legislation forced them to do otherwise, most oil drillers just let the salt water flow, polluting the fields and streams and killing both vegetation and wildlife. Bodcaw lands suffered from no such abuse—the foresters made sure of it. And as the young trees slowly grew up around them, the oilmen showed they could share the foresters' sensitivity to nature, although they might not own up to it. "One time there was a little ol' fire and I put it out and I called Burnham and said, "I'll tell you what. I didn't do that on account of these pine trees. I just thought it was going to get to that oil down there."

The question nonetheless was looming: What was to be done with the timber once it reached a marketable stage?

Two traditional possibilities had been bandied around from the beginning of Seeger's tenure. They could either reestablish the sawmills of old or they could build a paper mill. The first option was the least attractive. Despite some forty years of wrangling between lumber trade associations and governmental groups, not much had changed to improve either the cutthroat competitiveness of the business nor its susceptibility to the market's ups and downs. To place Bodcaw's fifteen-year investment of carefully grown timber back into the hands of the industry that had almost destroyed it in the first place was hardly appealing.

The paper business was a different matter. More than any other single factor, it had pulled the Southern pine industry back from the edge of oblivion and turned it once again into the "woodbasket" of the country. The papermaking system most favored in the South was the sulphate process, to which Southern pine trees were perfectly adapted. Developed in Germany in 1884 and imported into the United States around 1910, the process produced unbleached, or "kraft," paper.[2]

> There had been a few small pulp companies operating in the South for many years, but I suppose that there was not the demand for the type of paper they made—kraft wrapping paper and boxes—until the late twenties and early thirties when more and more packaging was in the form of paper boxes because they were cheaper and better than wooden boxes. As the market for paperboard boxes expanded, it was found that southern pine was an excellent wood to use in making paper by the sulphate process.[3]

The advent of the kraft paper industry brought with it several other benefits. Southern lumbermen, long used to either destroying young timber or ignoring it in their search for older sawlogs, now found a commercial use for it just as the mature stands were being cut out. Also, these same men, as well as the farmers who for years had clear-cut land for agriculture, saw that they didn't have to wait forty years for mature timber to produce revenue—in half that time, they could have a cash crop of pulp timber. The result of this epiphany was a sudden rise in forestry and timber conservation. By 1950, half the wood cut in Louisiana was being shipped to the paper mills. Ten years later, the South was producing 60 percent of all the kraft paper in the country.

None of this had been lost on Bodcaw. Even Stanley Seeger had sought advice about setting up a pulp mill, but had decided it would be best to wait until he could supply the mill's appetite exclusively with his own timber. As things turned out, that wasn't necessary or even advisable—paper mills routinely invite outsiders to supply most of their timber needs, for both economic and public relations reasons.

O'Boyle and Heldt apparently realized this, because just a few years after Dr. Seeger's death, O'Boyle began casting about for a way to get into the papermaking business.

> We started looking around and talking to paper companies—we didn't have any staff at all. We concluded that the best thing for us would be to have a jointly owned venture with somebody who was already in the business, could staff it, market the product. We did some checking about financing a wholly owned mill and were uniformly advised that unless we could show our ability to market the product, there was very little chance we could get financing. Of course, we had no marketing organization at all.
>
> So we started talking to pulp and paper companies that we thought might be interested. I guess during the course of over three or four years, we talked to practically every pulp and paper company in the U.S. Some of them showed no interest at all. A number of them said they didn't want partners, but they'd be glad to buy us out. That had no romance for us.

Finally, three companies were located which showed interest in a cooperative deal. Crown Zellerbach had a huge mill in Bogalusa, Louisiana, and was expanding its business. An official at the company was very enthusiastic and said he would propose the deal at an upcoming board meeting in San Francisco. He was never heard from again. Weeks later, word leaked out he had arrived at the San Francisco headquarters and had fallen into a minor corporate civil war which had demanded all his attention. The deal with Bodcaw fell victim; the interested executive later became president of Crown.

Next in line was a Canadian firm, the Powell River Lumber Company, located in British Columbia. Powell River was interested in Bodcaw's location since the Canadian company supplied several Southern newspapers with newsprint and saw Bodcaw as a way to cut down on their shipping expenses. Unfortunately, just as the deal was about to go through, a third party bought out Powell River.

The third and last potential partner was Ernest Kurth, head of the Southland Paper Company and an East Texas political maneuverer of no small merit. There again, Kurth and Bodcaw got up to the final meeting only to find out that Kurth's paper broker didn't think he could find a market for the paper. In fact, he was right. The market for kraft paper was getting soft, and for a couple of years Bodcaw held off looking for any partners.

It was during this last round of meetings with Kurth in the late 1950s that John O'Boyle's health took a sudden turn for the worse.

> John had a big Mercedes. It was nothing but motor and four wheels. It was a tremendous thing. He was going down to Lufkin to see Ernest and he wanted to drive this car down there because he was wild about it. He was driving along in East Texas going maybe ninety miles per hour and a guy in a Ford passed him. So he thought, "Well, I'll show that guy." So he waited until he got to a good straightaway and he ran that Mercedes up to maybe 120 and went tearing past this Ford and drove along at that speed for two or three miles and then slowed down. In another fifteen or twenty minutes, along came that Ford and passed him again.
>
> So he decided, "Well, I'll really have to show this guy what he's toying with." So he waited until he got to another straightaway and he got it up to 120 or 125 miles per hour

> and went tearing past him. Down the road there was a farmer coming out in a pickup truck. He wasn't used to anybody going that fast and he thought he had plenty of space. Of course the gap closed in a hell of a hurry and it was a near thing. But there was no accident; he did get by.

But he was not unscathed. Upon arriving in Lufkin, he discovered he'd begun to hemorrhage internally. He got on a plane immediately and went to see his doctor in New York.

> This doctor advised him, "You've got a real problem. As you're getting older with this hepatitis, your liver is contracting [with scar tissue]. What happened in this near miss with the car was that your heart started pumping blood very fast and it couldn't get through the liver fast enough. It backed up and ruptured a vessel. Fortunately, this was a minor vessel and we could control it. But I can almost promise you that some time in the next six months or maybe a year, something will cause your heart to pump fast again. You'll rupture a blood vessel that might be a major artery or someplace where we can't reach it, and you're going to die."

The proposed solution to this dilemma was an operation called a portal shunt. In a properly functioning body, blood flows from the intestines, through the portal vein, into the liver, and then out to the vena cava, which is the main collecting vein for the lower part of the body. A portal shunt involves gathering the portal vein and the vena cava side by side and creating a small window connecting the two. The result allows the blood coming from the intestines to flow through both the constricted liver and straight into the vena cava—creating a valuable release valve for the overworked portal vein. The trade-off, of course, is that the blood is no longer processed as completely as it should be. The patient has to make up for that with severe dietary restrictions and by leading a more sedentary life. "The net result [of the operation] made him terribly susceptible to any kind of germ, as well as making him feel lousy. His interest span was short, he was consumed by his own problems. In the intervening period, of course, his wife, Mary, slowly died of cancer and that was a very distracting thing for him."

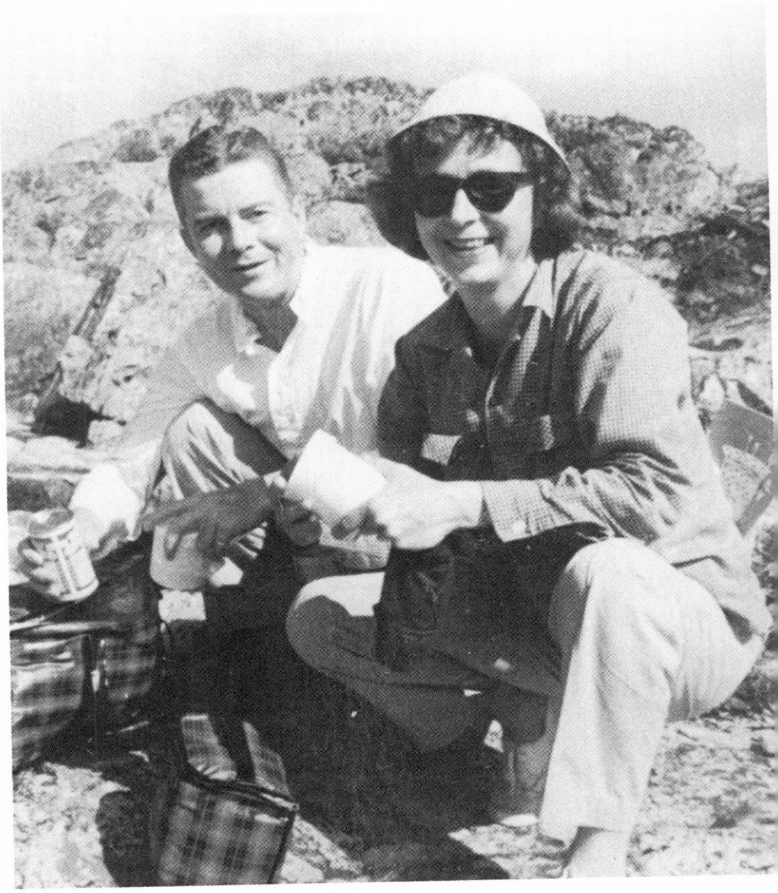

Mary and John O'Boyle at the Huron Mountain Club in Michigan, 1960

But through it all—the loss of his wife in 1961, the sudden responsibility of caring for four children, his own physical decline, and the disappointments in finding a business partner—he remained dedicated to the establishment of a paper mill. In 1955 Nebo, along with the Urania Lumber Company and the Tremont Lumber Company, had hired a man to study potential pulp-mill sites in central Louisiana. His findings indicated that despite a potential problem in locating an adequate water supply, Alexandria would be the best location for a mill. In 1959, with no prospects of a partner in sight, O'Boyle bought over four hundred acres of land just outside Pineville, a town near Alexandria.

In 1964, his persistence paid off. The Food and Agricultur

Organization (FAO) of the United Nations published a routine survey of the world's supply of and demand for paper and paper products. The survey revealed that the demand for paper in Europe was beginning to exceed its supplies of wood pulp, traditionally delivered by the Scandinavian countries. The survey further foretold that in order to satisfy Europe's growing appetite, additional paper mills in western Canada and in the southern United States would have to be called on to help.

John O'Boyle didn't hesitate. He flew to Rome to the FAO headquarters to speak personally with the people who had prepared the survey. While there, he met a former executive of Enso-Gutzeit Osakeyhtiö (a largely government-owned Finnish paper manufacturer and the largest company in Finland) who urged him to contact that company and to propose a partnership. O'Boyle returned home, armed with more data from the FAO people, and spent several months comparing the various Scandinavian paper companies. As it turned out, Enso-Gutzeit was indeed the best prospect. Referred to as the General Motors of Finland because of its size and diversity, it had the expertise and the marketing network that Bodcaw had been seeking in its search among American companies.

In June 1965, O'Boyle and Heldt flew to Finland to meet with Enso-Gutzeit president Pentti Halle and several of his associates. Discussions went so well that Halle suggested bringing in one of Finland's leading makers of paper-manufacturing machines, Oy Tampella A'b. Johann Nykopp, president of Tampella, joined the group the very next day.

> I remember Jim and John told me they were going to Helsinki to have some very preliminary discussions. A couple of days later they called me up and asked me, "Could you come over here tomorrow? Our discussions are moving at a much more accelerated pace than we ever expected and the Finns are interested in trying to work out a contract with us." I did go over and we met with them for a couple of days and worked out a five-and-a-half-page, double-spaced joint-venture agreement—probably the shortest in history for that kind of venture.

After years of pursuing a partnership, Bodcaw struck a deal with the Finns in under a week. The agreement called for the building of a paper mill on the Alexandria site, of which Bodcaw would be a 60 percent owner and the two Finnish companies 20 percent owners each. The plant would be known as Pineville Kraft, a separate entity from the three co-owners. Bodcaw was to guarantee a supply of wood sufficient to the mill's needs, Enso-Gutzeit to take on the marketing of the product, and Tampella to supply the paper-manufacturing equipment. The product would be unbleached kraft linerboard, what most people know as the inner and outer skin of a corrugated cardboard box. The linerboard would be manufactured to European standards, more demanding than American ones, since that's where most of the sales were to take place.

There were several reasons explaining the Finns' enthusiasm for the partnership: As pointed out by the FAO report, Pineville Kraft would help ease European paper-supply problems. The plant would be state-of-the-art new, employing the latest cost-saving technology, and thereby saving money. It would be manned by non-Finnish employees, out from under the control of the very protective, socialistic Finnish government; as a result, it would be a leaner, more economically realistic operation. Tampella could place its machinery in a showcase American plant for the first time, where other potential American buyers could see it at work. And it would be located in the southern United States, where the time it takes a pine tree to mature is half what it would take in the frigid regions of the Scandinavian North, insuring that the paper plant could be forever supplied with wood.

As majority owner of Pineville Kraft, Bodcaw got to call the shots concerning its construction and organization. To oversee this next crucial step, they hired Jim Whelan, who turned out to be truly the best man for the job. Born in the lumber town of Bogalusa, Louisiana, Whelan had spent thirty-three years in the Southern pulp and paper industry, working for a variety of major corporations. He had definite opinions about what he wanted and how to get it, and Heldt and O'Boyle were wise enough to give him free reign.

Bird's-eye view of Pineville Kraft paper mill in Alexandria, Louisiana, August 1968

When Whelan was hired in 1966, the mill site was a bare, hilly field, covered with brush.

> When I came on board, they had plans for a 550-ton plant [that is, a plant capable of producing 550 tons of paper a day]. I said that was too small. Smaller plants use the same number of people, but the production rate is so low it will just eat you up. They had another study made and came up with a 750-ton plant, which was closer to what I wanted. But I had it in my mind how I was going to build some things here and there for a few hundred thousand dollars and get pretty close to 1,000 tons a day. The end of it was that we ultimately made and averaged in one year about 975 tons a day out of that plant.

Whelan was as fortunate to have Heldt and O'Boyle as they were to have him. John O'Boyle was determined that this plant should stick out among its competitors, not only because of its advanced technology, but also because it would look better than any of them. He hired San Antonio architect O'Neil Ford to design an administration building complete with wood paneling, wool carpets, and terrazzo tiles. To this day, it remains the envy of most other paper mills.

Pineville Kraft ran off its first paper on August 12, 1968, and by late that year, after an anticipated series of standard start-up problems, it began producing liner board in earnest. It had cost approximately $52 million to build and employed over 340 people. With its completion, Stanley Seeger's righteous concept had come full circle, for 25 percent of the new mill's timber needs were met by pulpwood culled from Bodcaw land.

Unfortunately, Seeger's son-in-law and principal torch carrier was not healthy enough to attend the opening ceremonies nor to ever see the finished mill. His liver problems had made him a virtual invalid.

> He would stay at home. He wouldn't let anybody come to see him because he knew if they came they'd turn to his health and he didn't want to discuss himself with anybody. He'd come to his office sometimes. He'd come in and close the door, to indicate to people he didn't want to be disturbed.
>
> He became more and more private. For example, he drew up his will, and as nearly as I can tell, he never talked to anybody about it. He never consulted his [second] wife [Nancy], his children—not anybody. He's got one sister he was very close to and I don't think he said anything to her.
>
> People may have gotten the impression he was very self-centered—of course, any ill person ultimately gets this way. When they get sick enough they get terribly obsessed with "When is my next medication due?" and "What are we having for lunch and how is it going to affect me?" Of course, he got that way too.

> It changed him. It really did. He became almost a bit of a hypochondriac about himself. Afraid. He was so anxious to

raise those kids, and he was so afraid that he'd get sick and die tomorrow because he knew that it was very tenuous. So he was always worried about getting a cold and everything. He became a little too concerned with germs and all that. I think it took more of his thought and attention than he should have been giving it.

It may be that he did come to realize the limitations he'd placed upon himself, for in the summer of 1969, he became adamant about attending a meeting in London.

It was really a question of was he stable enough to travel. I think we thought he was. But after he got to London, he became comatose. I don't know if it was dietary excess or just pushing physical overactivity. He was seen by an excellent physician, Roger Williams, who said he needed a liver transplant. That was at a stage when liver transplantation was really in its infancy. The chances of success were modest.

There are many people who would say, "Why not let the guy die?" But John wasn't that kind of person. He would go all out to recognize: "What the hell have I got to lose?"

So he had the transplant, and didn't survive.

John O'Boyle died on Wednesday, July 30, 1969, at the age of fifty-four. He was buried in North Lake, Wisconsin, near his childhood summer home, in a Catholic cemetery next to his wife Mary. For many of the key employees of Bodcaw, a good deal of the company's spirit died with him. Despite his personal complexities, exacerbated by his illness, John O'Boyle was always seen as Bodcaw's guiding light. The perception that his death extinguished that light was to lean heavily—and unfairly—against Jim Heldt.

It was, after all, Jim Heldt's passion for detail that had made most of John O'Boyle's ideas bear fruit. What John planted, Jim watered and cared for, making each man indispensable to the other. By the same token, as parts of a team, each was seen to have his flaws. Many people resented John's acquisitiveness, his occasionally snobbish, patrician demeanor, his competitive drive.

But at his graveside, these flaws melted away; Father Michael Driscoll, a college friend, invoked *Hamlet* in his eulogy:

> Now cracks a noble heart. Good night, sweet prince,
> And flights of angels sing thee to thy rest!

Jim Heldt was now deprived of his counterbalance, and while John's image in death took on a saintly glow, Jim's became burdened with the shortcomings of both men.

> Jim Heldt was a very strong leader, and most of the people spent their time trying to figure out what he wanted—what *he* would like to do rather than what they thought should be done. You didn't go to him with different ideas. All he'd do was cut them down. He wasn't a new-idea man.
>
> Heldt's position was always "No" first. Then, maybe if you pushed him, he might rethink his position. A lot of people walked in fear of Heldt because he was so unyielding. If you went to him with some kind of deal—whether it was oil or timber of whatever—he told you what he'd do. There wasn't any negotiating at all.

These comments are typical of our times. Resentful criticism of management is as common in the 1980s as it was heretical in William Buchanan's day. Jim Heldt was a conservative, unflamboyant, serious, demanding detail man—not unlike, in those respects, the company's highly lauded founder. He was also, according to several employees, a man who went out of his way to help people in a personal crisis, something John O'Boyle pointedly avoided. Many of them, from the executives to the oil switchers, recall feeling more comfortable around Heldt: "He was more of a country-type boy than Mr. O'Boyle."

Also, Heldt made some company stock available to the management team, reflecting the encouragement Stanley Seeger had deemed so important when Heldt and O'Boyle had first come aboard. Ironically, John O'Boyle, who had benefited most from Seeger's largess and had made it a condition to his joining the company, also strenuously opposed making any shares available to any employees to the day he died.

Under Heldt, many of the department heads were made vice-presidents and their salaries increased accordingly.

Most memorable, however, was his helpfulness in troubled times. He contributed to individual employees' medical payments and once even made the company plane available for five months so that an employee could make weekly flights to and from his stricken son's hospital bedside.

None of this was done with any expansive expressions of goodwill. Jim Heldt was all business. But unlike his much hallowed friend John O'Boyle, more people remember him for his restrained acts of kindness. "There are a lot of bosses that come around that you're afraid of, but he wasn't that type, really, once you got to know him. When he first walked in, you got that reserved picture of him—very businesslike. Yet he was a person that would come in and talk with you."

In at least one respect, it was fortunate that Jim Heldt took control of the company when he did, for it was soon to need all his industrious talent. In the early 1970s, the Finns at Enso-Gutzeit were continuing the diversification that had made them so receptive to Bodcaw's proposed partnership. This time, however, they got involved in building a paper mill in Canada.

> They built the plant and it was one of those deals where they started out at one tonnage and then went to another and did not make all the needed changes to balance out the plant. And they were losing about $1 million a month there. So they were taking a whale of a licking. In order for them to be able to take care of the operation in Canada, they needed cash.

To secure that cash, Enso-Gutzeit proposed selling its share of Pineville Kraft to Bodcaw. Heldt was interested, but not at their price. While the two parties performed the ritual dance of negotiation, a third party, Hoerner-Waldorf, slipped in and made a proposal.

That development caused a real flurry; Hoerner-Waldorf was a major paper manufacturer, a competitor of Bodcaw's, and indications were strong that if they were successful in their dealings with the Finns, the management of Bodcaw would be forced to undergo some changes. The crucial catch in the deal was that Enso-Gutzeit was also speaking for Tampella, so the ownership percentage wasn't just Enso's 20 percent, but involved Tampella's 20 percent as well.

Heldt understood that Hoerner-Waldorf's real interest wasn't in gaining control of Bodcaw per se—it primarily wanted an extra supplier of kraft paper. Heldt's proposal, therefore, was that Bodcaw enter into a five-year, five-thousand-tons-a-month supply contract with Hoerner-Waldorf, at very favorable rates to them. In exchange, Bodcaw was to acquire 90.1 percent of the shares, leaving Hoerner-Waldorf in control of the remaining 9.9 percent. Hoerner-Waldorf would have no say in Bodcaw management, and at the end of the five years, the 9.9 percent ownership would be offered to Bodcaw at Hoerner-Waldorf's price.

An agreement was reached on those terms, and around 1973 the Finns forever left the stage. As luck would have it, Hoerner-Waldorf wasn't long in following. About two years later, the linerboard market became glutted and Bodcaw's monthly supply of five thousand tons was giving Hoerner-Waldorf nightmares. Heldt offered to let them out of their contract for a settlement, and after a certain amount of pride swallowing, they agreed. Pineville Kraft became a wholly owned subsidiary of the Bodcaw Company.

One by-product of all this was that Pineville Kraft was forced to take over its own sales. With the departure of the Finns went Enso-Gutzeit's worldwide marketing network, not to mention its sizable fleet of cargo ships. Bodcaw, however, had become disenchanted selling through Enso, and had even begun taking over some of its own American sales. Thus, what might have been a traumatic shock turned into a long-awaited chance at independence. In short order, Pineville Kraft by itself was selling paper throughout Europe, Israel, and the United States.

The other major project of Jim Heldt's presidency, aside from the sale of the company, was the building of a chip-'n-saw mill in Coushatta, Louisiana, in 1973–74. The idea originally came out of Bodcaw's woodlands division, but reflected a trend that many other lumber companies were beginning to follow.

The chip-'n-saw concept makes two uses of a tree. After a log is stripped of its bark, it is squared off along its entire length by four chipper saws, leaving what amounts to a long wooden beam. The beam is then run through conventional saws to produce primarily two-by-four lumber. The advantage of this system is that while lumber is being produced, so chips are amassed for shipment to a pulp mill. In a production scheme that is a far cry from the early days of William Buchanan's sawmills, the whole of every log is put to two different commercial uses. It seemed a perfect way to protect oneself, to a certain degree, from the vagaries of either the lumber or the paper-pulp markets.

That was the theory. Its success hinged on the processed timber being pulpwood, which was considerably cheaper than sawlogs; it was the one particular financial advantage that gave the chip-'n-saws their appeal. In fact, Jim Heldt was enthusiastic enough about what he saw on paper that he had the woodlands division examine the possibilities of setting up several of these mills.

As events proved, it was a good thing they stopped at one. Between the planning stage and the actual day Coushatta opened, two crucial developments took place. The lumber market softened, making lower-quality pulpwood lumber far less salable, and the value of stumpage underwent radical changes. The distinctions between the two types of timber had begun to blur—smaller, younger pulpwood was being upgraded to sawlog status to appeal to the market, with a corresponding hike in its price. Thus, all the financial assumptions on which the mill had been based were thrown off keel.

As a result, the only marginally good thing about the mill became its production of chips, which the foresters had originally considered merely a supplementary source of income. This depressing realization also forced the use of more expensive sawlogs because they, being straighter and larger than pulpwood, yielded more chips.

The end result was that ownership of Coushatta was transferred to Pineville Kraft, and it was kept alive almost entirely because of its use to the pulp mill. Jim Whelan, who had not been thrilled with the idea of the chip-'n-saw mill in the first place, now had the responsibility of running it, despite the fact that he could produce chips more cheaply at Pineville Kraft. Nevertheless, he fought the good fight for five years and the chip-'n-saw mill limped along, mired in its own red ink. The decision to finally close it down altogether was stayed only because International Paper, which was on the brink of buying Bodcaw, wanted it operating.

That one failure notwithstanding, Bodcaw's overall picture looked very good by the late 1970s. It owned some 288,500 acres of pine-growing timberland, almost 29,000 acres of hardwood bottomland, and 18,000 acres of agricultural land.[4] It also held long-term purchase contracts on 90,000 additional acres of pine forest. It owned over a half million acres of mineral rights and owned or had an interest in several hundred producing oil and gas wells. It also owned one of the lowest-cost linerboard facilities in the world,[5] complete with an international sales network. Its operating income in 1975 was $37.3 million; in 1976, $17.4 million; in 1978, $24.3 million; and in 1979, $21 million. Net profits in 1979 were $14.4 million. In January 1979, Bodcaw hired independent evaluators who put a rough total worth of the company and all its holdings at $670 million.

According to Jim Heldt, times had never been busier. Plans were afoot to purchase more land and thereby expand the company's timber base considerably; a second paper-manufacturing machine was being considered for the mill; and there were high hopes of improving both the production and the geology departments on the oil side of the company. As far as Bodcaw's leadership was concerned, the future of the company was promising and bright—until International Paper made its first bid for a takeover.

10 / The Sale

The sale of the Bodcaw Company was the result of many intertwining factors. Age, pride, resentment, inheritance taxes, a thirst for cash, the marketplace, a fear of hostile takeovers, and the coping with parental ghosts played a part. The personalities involved were so divergent, were spurred by so many different interests, and were after so many separate goals that the tale borders on melodrama.

One overriding peculiarity of American business is the notion that it is primarily populated by quick-thinking, hard-driving, well-trained, unerring people whose wisdom is such that the fate of the nation is often best laid in their hands. From Calvin Coolidge's "The business of America is business" to Charles Wilson's "What was good for our country was good for General Motors and vice versa," business has been held as the lifeblood of the nation. Its popularity may rise and fall in tandem with prevailing trends, especially among intellectual circles, but it remains so enmeshed with the image of leadership that even the president of the United States is referred to as the "chief executive."

When it comes to detailing a transaction like the sale of the Bodcaw Company, one finds this view of the business world is shared by its inhabitants. With a few candid exceptions, business people rarely own up to error or defeat or loss of control. While the outcome of every auction dictates the emergence of but one successful purchaser, business people tend to claim victory even while retreating empty-handed. That is their special pride, linked with time-tested human nature.

Thus in the Bodcaw sale, not one of the losers owns up to having failed, at least not without some face-saving rationale. Interviewing most of the participants, one finds a predominantly self-satisfied crowd, happy that while their stated goal may not have been reached, the end result was the best for all. In a fashion, this is true, as will be pointed out. But in another, there is a sadness in these reminiscences, even among the true victors. For what occurred, after all, was the death of a family business and the ending of a successful ninety-year effort to bring about the American Dream.

The "management" of Bodcaw in 1979 was fundamentally in Jim Heldt's hands. Despite his elevating of several middle-echelon people to vice-presidential rank, no one had any doubts that one-man rule still prevailed. There was, however, a shadow cabinet of sorts consisting of the company's board of directors and its legal counsel—a Washington-based lawyer named Bennett Boskey, who had attended law school with Heldt and O'Boyle. Of the five board members, Jim Heldt, Hannah Davis, and Joe Seeger—sister and brother of the late Mary O'Boyle—were major stockholders. William Fuller—a descendant of William Buchanan's banker, W. R. Grim—and Bill Palmer were minimal owners. The last unofficial adviser, and a crucial one, was John Connor, board chairman of Allied Chemical, once Lyndon Johnson's secretary of commerce, and in 1979 co-trustee of the single largest group of Bodcaw stock. John O'Boyle had set up some sixteen family trusts before his death—consisting of his shares, the shares he had inherited from his wife, and a few others he picked up along the way—and had placed them with the United States Trust Company of New York under Connor's watchful eye. John Connor was not only another of O'Boyle's law school classmates, he was also married to O'Boyle's sister Mary.

These people, excluding the usually absent Joe Seeger, served as Jim Heldt's sounding board more than any company-recognized steering committee. Heldt was captain of the ship, and respected as such, but if any questions of policy arose, he usually went to this group to secure its opinions and backing. Apart from being friends of many years' standing, they represented a significant power base; of the company's total of 227,444 shares, they held or directly influenced approximately 130,000—almost 57 percent of the total.

It was they who were first made aware of Jim Heldt's growing

James Heldt

desire to resign the leadership of the company, long before International Paper (IP) ever appeared with an offer to buy Bodcaw.

> Jim Heldt and I talked over a period of years, and with Bennett Boskey, about the future of the company as Jim was approaching normal retirement age. Since he indicated a desire to retire at that time the question was about management's succession. He had a senior lawyer in the company who was able and he had some career people handling various parts of the business who were able, but he felt that he didn't have management succession in sight for a period of some years.

He also had some family members to consider, but they were judged too young and inexperienced or had declared themselves uninterested.

> Helen Davis [Hannah Seeger Davis's daughter, aged twenty-four at the time] is as bright as you ever saw; sharp as a tack. She certainly would have been a possibility. In the O'Boyle family, Mary [John's youngest daughter, twenty-six years old] certainly would have been a real candidate. Bill [John's eldest son] we tried to interest at one time—we had him actually working down here, but then he came in and said, "I don't want any part of this. If I worked here, all I can see is a long line of Ramada Inns." [So] nobody ever came and said, "Now I'm ready to go."

This, in fact, was not entirely true. John's daughter Mary was attending law school with the intention of joining the company, but she was impressed by Jim Heldt's lack of enthusiasm about the idea. There was great concern among the elders about what might happen if one of the younger generation took over Heldt's reins. As one of them put it,

> I've seen so many of these family things disintegrate, not because of incompetence in the family, but because of hostility and jealousy—case after case where they've tried to keep it going, and tried to keep it going and finally had to break it up just because the family members could not get along.

> And when you break it up under those conditions, you are not going to get the top dollar out of it.

Heldt denied that he had any thoughts of selling the company prior to International Paper's first show of interest in 1977, but another member of the unofficial top group admits that given all the above factors, "Our conclusion was that, under the circumstances and in view of the valuable nature of the business, it would be better to look for a purchaser."

Much of this feeling was picked up by others in the company. Some, no doubt relying on hindsight, claim they guessed Heldt was looking for a buyer right after John's death. One engineer became so convinced a sale was imminent that he quit to find another job. Another sensed that from the day O'Boyle and Heldt took over from Seeger, the whole thrust of the company's development was to make it attractive to some buyer.

Heldt claimed none of this was true. To the charge that he never groomed anyone to replace him—an obvious sign that he thought there was no point to it—he said that the men were there, inside the organization, but that they didn't know they were being considered. That is something no one can refute.

But it is an insight to Heldt's management style at the time. Embodying what had become a company obsession, he stood as a paragon to privacy. Most everyone was approached on a need-to-know basis, and as little information as possible was circulated outside his control. This was a long-standing tradition. William Buchanan himself was rarely in the news, and stockholders who had been with the company from the start could brag only of a handful of one-line letters from management advising them of dividend payments and little else. Bodcaw's front door was unadorned with its name; a telephone call to headquarters was answered with a phone number instead of a standard greeting identifying the answerer. When the sale process began, potential purchasers were impressed at the amount of work Heldt conducted all by himself and at the number of letters of confidentiality they were obligated to sign.

> Yeah, he wants to be the center of the universe, no doubt about it. And he used his lawyers and bankers as—he knew

> he needed them, so he had them and then proceeded to give them very little rope to do anything. You rarely see a manager sitting down and spending literally hundreds of hours on a line-by-line, paragraph-by-paragraph, section-by-section negotiation of a definitive merger agreement, and doing a lot of the research himself.

All this quite naturally had its advantages. Not only was everyone kept in the dark, but Heldt became imbued with the aura of a sage—he was all knowing of all things, and no one could prove otherwise. As the tempo of the sale increased and more people became involved, Heldt was the island in a wind-whipped storm—protective of some, a barrier to others. At the end of it all, he could claim, and few could deny, that he had kept everything under control from the start. That, however, is doubtful.

Heldt's apparent lack of a successor was not the only thing that raised doubts over Bodcaw's avowed autonomous future. By the late 1970s, the assets of the company had never looked more attractive. The land, the timber, the mill, the oil and gas holdings were all at a premium—in a shaky economic environment, they represented a tangible, rock-solid investment, especially if the price were right.

The major stockholders were fully aware of this. To several of them, the company had accomplished what it had set out to do. Even Heldt, with his stated plans to buy more land and expand the paper mill, was admitting that the best he could do was just more of the same. Also, no one was getting any younger—Heldt wanted to retire, and several of the other major stockholders were starting to consider what their shares were actually worth. Turnover of Bodcaw stock was very small and not terribly lucrative. One estimate was that each share had an approximate value of three hundred dollars—not much if death and inheritance taxes were ever to claim a part.

Finally, there was an increasing clamor for cash, especially from the younger generation of stockholders. Many of these were financially comfortable through dividend payments and family trusts, but there was a growing frustration among them that they were wealthier on paper than they were in fact. Joe Seeger, Mary and Hannah's younger brother, was of prime concern to Heldt's group. A bachelor in his forties, Joe was known to be unhappy with his lack of liquidity, and as a member of the board and the owner of some twenty-five thousand shares, his discontent alone made them all a bit uneasy.[1]

Thus, whether Heldt had been looking for a buyer or not, IP's arrival on the scene in 1977 was serendipitous indeed.

Certainly it was motivating.

> It took me greatly by surprise and of course I immediately got the board together and told them what had happened. When a company the size of IP decides they're going to make an offer, they'll probably make it no matter what the management wants them to do. We realized that if they made an unfriendly offer, there would probably be a number of stockholders who would sell to them. Not the least of our worries was Joe Seeger.
>
> I was concerned, and I think Bill Palmer was concerned and William Fuller and a couple of others possibly, that if IP went to Joe and said they wanted to buy his stock, Joe might very well have sold it to them. And that would have put us in a god-awful position.

What was playing on Jim Heldt's fears was the recent acquisition by St. Regis of 35 percent of the Southland Paper Company, the same company that had almost merged with Bodcaw on the building of Pineville Kraft. Not only had St. Regis gained effective voting clout in the running of the company, but their large ownership of stock had made Southland unattractive to any other potential buyer. Thus, at a bargain price, they all but controlled Southland Paper. "So when IP came along and said they were going to make an offer, wanted to make an offer, I decided, 'Boy, if they're going to come in here, I'd better start rounding up and trying to get some active competition.' "

Heldt began to do just that, quietly talking to Mobil's Container Corporation of America, Crown Zellerbach, Tenneco's Packaging Corporation of America, the Weyerhaeuser Company, and many others, some of which were purely oil and gas companies.

International Paper's negotiator, Don Brennan

He had some time in which to do this because IP wasn't sure at first if it wanted all of Bodcaw or just Pineville Kraft. Their interest was in expanding and modernizing their paper-mill holdings, and Pineville Kraft fit perfectly into that. But Bodcaw's land fitted neatly into a corner of IP country and represented a tasty and well-maintained morsel. As time passed, Don Brennan, who was bidding for IP, began to increase his appetite. To be fair, Heldt wasn't letting him do otherwise. Realizing that the mill was Bodcaw's crown jewel, he wasn't about to let someone walk off with just it. Estimates for building a Pineville Kraft–type mill in 1979 were five times its original $52 million price tag.

Early in 1978, a little under a year after Brennan's first covetous glances at Pineville Kraft, IP made an offer for the Bodcaw Company of $275 million, which Heldt rejected out of hand. He did not do it scornfully, however. "Even at that figure, I was afraid if they made an unfriendly offer to some of the stockholders, we'd lose some of them." He knew the time had come to do battle.

So did William Buchanan O'Boyle, John O'Boyle's firstborn. Then a man in his late thirties, Bill O'Boyle had led an eclectic life. Having enjoyed a relatively normal and happy childhood, he'd been gradually separated from his increasingly ailing parents by nannies and private boarding schools as he approached his early teens. He opted after college to complete the break by joining the army and enrolling in its Chinese-language school. Following the army, he wandered through several years without any heartfelt goals, dabbling more often than not in the theater, both acting in and backing theatrical productions. By 1977, he'd set most of his personal demons to rest, and while still pursuing a master's degree in drama, he set up an office from which to run his growing business interests.

It was there in the spring of 1978 that he received a letter from Jim Heldt, addressed to all stockholders, advising them that the company had been approached by a potential purchaser.[2]

> At that point, I really sat up and said, "Hey, you know, I'd better look into this before it's too late." I felt that I wanted to take some responsibility myself for making sure that the

Bill O'Boyle

> situation was handled to the maximum advantage of the people in the family. Of course, there is some self-interest in that, because I'm a member of the family too. But I couldn't have lived with myself later if I had just sort of let it all happen and not paid any attention to it.

In the early 1970s, he had made approximately $1 million investing in precious metals. He now used that money to start rounding up people who could advise him about Bodcaw's financial status and worth. One of the first of these was a friend named Vernon Bremberg, then working in New York for the Du Pont Company. As a favor, Bremberg began checking some of the figures Bill was gathering. The process became so engrossing that by May or June 1978 he began being paid as a consultant.[3] It was in that capacity, in July, that he put a roughly estimated value on Bodcaw of between $600 million and $900 million. Since by that time news of IP's early offer of $275 million had been circulated, the two men realized they were facing a potential bonanza. Bill decided he should try to buy the company.

> We were worried that [Heldt] might be considering selling it for $200 million or $300 million. Well, if the company was going to be sold cheaply, you have two options. You can either try to make enough of this thing to get it sold at fair value, or, if everybody wants to sell it cheap, you can buy it. You know, what the heck? You couldn't lose either way.

In the meantime, Heldt had not been idle. Toward September 1978, he had managed to interest Placid Oil, Tenneco, and Mobil, all unbeknownst to each other, to bid for Bodcaw; the unofficial stakes began to hover around $400 million. At about the same time, Bill flew down to Dallas to introduce himself to Heldt and the board as a legitimate bidder. The reception was polite, but unpromising. Heldt was unconvinced that Bill could come up with the money. Heldt's approach up to this point had been to quietly shop among only truly qualified bidders. Bill's presumption to join this group struck Heldt as meddlesome.

Bill started getting nervous that his newfound interest in the company might have been aroused too late. Armed with marginal assessments of Bodcaw's timber and paper-mill values, and backed by the investment banking firm of Lehman Brothers and a handful of merger lawyers and accountants, Bill approached Prudential Insurance for a $400 million loan. Prudential was interested, but unimpressed by the assessments and probably wary of Bill's inexperience. For several months, O'Boyle's team worked on Prudential, trying to add to their credibility by securing asset data from Heldt. Heldt's insistence on confidentiality, coupled with his obvious doubts concerning Bill's chances, began to get under the younger man's skin.

By the end of the year, any possible deal with Prudential became moot. It was obvious the bids were going to exceed $400 million. Bill broke off with the insurance company and reassessed his approach.

> We realized we weren't going to be able to get this organized from the point of view of buying the entire company—we decided we'd better concentrate on one aspect of the company: the oil and gas. I could join up with a major corporate partner. I would go for the oil and gas assets and would be responsible for raising my part of the bid for that; they would go for the timber and the mill and that sort of thing.

Lehman Brothers, who had suggested this tactic, started calling potential partners for Bill. In December 1978, they came up with George Weyerhaeuser.

The Weyerhaeuser Company was very interested. Since the mid-1950s, they'd been slowly expanding their horizons beyond the Northwest, specifically toward the South. Unconsciously paralleling John O'Boyle's activities, they bought a pulp-mill site in Mississippi around the same time John purchased the Pineville site, and in 1969, the year Pineville Kraft came on line, Weyerhaeuser bought the 1.8-million-acre Dierks Forest Products in Arkansas and Oklahoma and built their own paper mill in Oklahoma.[4] "We looked at the Bodcaw linerboard mill as being a very good one and something we were interested in. We were also impressed with the timber stand and the possibilities of expanding our Southern acreage."

It also didn't hurt that acquiring Bodcaw would place Weyerhaeuser right in the midst of IP territory.

George Weyerhaeuser was no stranger to Bodcaw. When John O'Boyle had been looking for a partner to build the paper mill, he had approached the Tacoma-based firm. Similarly, Weyerhaeuser had been on Jim Heldt's list of potential bidders after IP's Don Brennan had made his first pass at Bodcaw in 1977. On that occasion, Weyerhaeuser hadn't responded to Heldt because of the latent restrictions involved. Their impression was that Heldt was arranging a kind of private, closed auction sale and that he wanted only a tax-free stock-swap deal—no cash. However, when news began leaking that the sale price was hovering around $400 million, Weyerhaeuser's interest peaked again; that, the company realized from many years in the timber business, was a bargain figure.

In New York, in late December 1978, Bill O'Boyle was becoming terribly excited. What had begun partly as a guilt-fed inquiry into the worth of his father's old company was building into an acquisitive fever.

> I mean here we were talking about a deal with George Weyerhaeuser. I was involved in the theater before this; as a matter of fact, I was still enrolled in graduate school. I would say to myself, "I really love the theater; why are you leaving the theater—why are you doing this?" [But] by the time it was at $400 million, I was in there working full-time. It's the kind of thing that's worth getting up out of bed and going to work. I mean, it was exciting—it was electrifying. And it turned everybody on. . . . It was almost like a war was on or something.

All during January, O'Boyle and his advisory group exchanged information and data with Weyerhaeuser. Then Heldt announced late that month that all those interested had until February 13, 1979, to submit their final bids.

On the weekend of February 3, Weyerhaeuser flew a timber-cruising crew down to Louisiana to consult with the timber appraisers Bill had hired earlier and to do their own spot check of

George Weyerhaeuser

the Bodcaw lands. The next week, O'Boyle and his entire team of lawyers, investment bankers, and accountants flew to Tacoma to meet with George Weyerhaeuser and his people. For several days, they worked long hours, fashioning an appropriate bid. Weyerhaeuser was both attracted to and a bit wary of Bill. The attraction was there because of the younger man's enthusiasm and the fact that he was making an effort to keep a family business "in the family"—a concept naturally close to George Weyerhaeuser's heart. The wariness stemmed from Bill's lack of experience and his blatant self-interest.

Bill, at this point, couldn't lose. If he and Weyerhaeuser were successful with their bid, he would end up as head of the O'Boyle Oil Company, having gotten Weyerhaeuser to provide most of the cash. If their bid failed, it would be because someone else came in higher, in which case Bill, as a Bodcaw stockholder, again would ultimately benefit. Neither of these points were lost on the Weyerhaeuser people.

The deal was finally struck in the early hours of the morning. Weyerhaeuser was to come up with $400 million and Bill an additional $50 million. Bill's money would be a bank loan from Continental Illinois in Chicago, arranged through Weyerhaeuser contacts. An addendum to the contract was that if the bid failed and Weyerhaeuser wanted to try again, Bill had to be included as a partner, as in the first go-around. "So, we bid $450 million and it knocked everyone's socks off, ours included, coming up with this bid. Everyone was euphoric at this stage; I mean, it was really like a dream world."

Heldt, it turned out, was less impressed. Of the five bidders involved—the others being IP, Placid, Mobil, and Tenneco—Weyerhaeuser was in the middle of the pack; also, it had bid in cash, which at this point was a minus to Heldt. On February 27, Bodcaw announced it had signed an agreement in principle with Mobil Oil to merge with that company for $475 million in tax-free shares.

This early preference of Heldt's for a share transaction seems to have stemmed from the financial status of the handful of majority stock owners. People like Hannah Davis and Heldt himself were in no mood to increase their income tax by selling Bodcaw for cash, although that would have sounded very attractive to the hundreds of stockholders who owned only fifty to one hundred shares each. This prejudice against cash was heightened by section 341 of the Internal Revenue Code which threatened individual holders of 5 percent or more of a company's stock with an ordinary income tax instead of a much more lenient capital gains tax.

Nevertheless, Heldt's acceptance of the Mobil bid is a little curious. Just before the agreement was made, Bodcaw's own outside appraisers put a total market value on the company of about $670 million, including the paper mill, or about $200 million more than what Mobil was offering. One likely explanation is that Heldt was conservatively hedging his bets. By having Mobil's offer in hand, he was guaranteed no less than that amount, and by signing an agreement, he was informing other potential bidders that they had better make their move.

What Heldt was relying on was a Delaware court decision stating that if a company for sale ever received a reasonable offer better than the one it had in hand, it was obligated to consider it. This could be a two-edged sword, of course. If a serious bidder kept being put off because of an endless series of last-minute offers by people who had no intention of actually carrying through, the company for sale might find itself all alone once more. In Bodcaw's case, both scenarios were about to occur.

With the announcement of the Mobil deal, Bill O'Boyle and his team contacted Weyerhaeuser for a second try. This time, the meeting was in San Francisco, George Weyerhaeuser having cut short a trip to Indonesia to attend. Weyerhaeuser was now feeling less charitable toward his young partner. Realizing the Bodcaw merger was going to entail more of a fight than he'd anticipated, he no longer wanted Bill along for the ride. He hired the investment banking firm of Goldman Sachs and tried to get Bill to back out of their earlier agreement. Bill wouldn't budge, realizing this was his last chance to acquire any part of the business his father had spent years building up. The final compromise read that the two partners would be united as before, but that Weyerhaeuser would own part of O'Boyle's interest in the Bodcaw oil and gas as well as all the rest.

Goldman Sachs then made a fateful decision. Arguing that Heldt probably thought he had the best bid he could expect, they contended that Weyerhaeuser should offer a "time-fused" bid of $550 million cash in order to force Heldt's hand. Weyerhaeuser agreed, over Bill's objections. Accordingly, the bid was sent to Heldt on March 8, 1979, with the provision that if he did not accept it by March 13, it would be withdrawn.

Bill was becoming anxious. Having already been reduced to a minor role with Weyerhaeuser, he was now watching his last chance to own a piece of Bodcaw go down the drain.

> A fuse on the bid puts the management in a real bind, you know, because they're kind of forced to either take it or be responsible for losing it and having to explain to their stockholders why they let a $550 million bid go away.
>
> I sort of knew that that wouldn't do any good with Jim. And he toughed it out and said, in effect, "To hell with you; I'm not gonna bow to that kind of pressure." I think it hurt them in the long run because all it did was make Jim mad.

It also caused a near-permanent rift between Heldt and Bill O'Boyle. Heldt, already irritated at what the termed Bill's "muddying of the waters," communicated only with Weyerhaeuser during the burning of the fuse, and ignored Bill's efforts to find out what was happening. As a result, after the March 13 deadline had been allowed to slip by, Bill gave in to an unfortunate outburst of frustration and anger. Writing as a stockholder, he sent Heldt a note accusing him of irresponsibility and threatening a lawsuit. Heldt responded in a terse but proper telegram informing Bill that during the time the fuse was burning on Weyerhaeuser's offer, Mobil indicated it would match Weyerhaeuser's $550 million cash bid as an alternative to its $475 million stock offer. That, as Heldt saw it, took the wind out of Weyerhaeuser's sails.

It is undeniable that Bill's passion got the better of him. As remarkable as his conversion from thespian to businessman had been—and it was an impressive accomplishment—he had not had the experience or the time to develop the necessary tough hide of the beast. Once he saw his hopes ground up between Weyerhaeuser, Goldman Sachs, and Jim Heldt, he let his emotions overrule his wisdom. It caused a division between himself and his father's old partner that he regrets to this day.

Jim Heldt was not entirely without fault. By nature and by training, he was a careful, private man. His preference during the two years it took to sell Bodcaw was to keep as many facts to himself as possible. That might have had something to do with his success, but it also angered and frustrated almost all the other participants. They, however, were in the bidding purely as businessmen. Bill was not, and Heldt could have been more sensitive to this.

In any case, Bill was now out of the bidding. He secured from Heldt a list of stockholders and retired to the sidelines, like a spectator at a horse race. Weyerhaeuser was running entirely on its own.

International Paper, in the meantime, had not been idle. In March, just as Goldman Sachs was playing hardball with Weyerhaeuser's bid, IP was auctioning off General Crude, a petroleum subsidiary, to Mobil, Tenneco, and Southland. Mobil, in the midst of a general buying spree, won on the twenty-ninth of the month with an $800 million offer.[5] In one of several ironies woven throughout this story, IP pocketed Mobil's money and bid $565 million cash or $490 million in tax-free stocks for Bodcaw, thereby displacing Mobil's bid.

Bodcaw barely had time to respond. On April 19, the Weyerhaeuser Company made an offer of $610 million in cash.

Again, rather curiously, Hedlt attempted to bring things to a close. On April 23, he told Mobil, Weyerhaeuser, and IP that they had until May 3 to come up with final bids. Heldt actually may have been motivated by inside information. Interviewed long afterward, the Weyerhaeuser team admitted that at $610 million, they were at their stopping point. That figure would justify the purchase of the land, the mill, and the chance to further invade the South. They admitted that the oil and gas might have been worth bidding more, but they had no firm idea of what Bodcaw's reserve holdings were. It was an area beyond their immediate expertise, and without a partner who was willing to risk putting money on the minerals, Weyerhaeuser was playing it safe.

Mobil Oil's William Tavoulareas, at a hearing before the Senate Judiciary Committee on March 15, 1984

Similarly, Mobil was at its limit. With the General Crude purchase weighing on its books, it, like Weyerhaeuser, was wary of swimming too far into unfamiliar waters.

Heldt's insight was proven correct when the final bids came in on May 3. Weyerhaeuser stayed put with $610 million in cash, with an option to pay out that sum in installment notes. Mobil, in a bizarre move that Bodcaw immediately rejected, offered an unspecified amount of cash that would be higher than Weyerhaeuser's bid. But as conditions, it stipulated that all the other bids had to be in cash only and that the entire process should be prolonged in order that it may have more time to solidify its offer.

IP came on the strongest. It increased its bid to Weyerhaeuser's level, but made it in tax-free stocks, an offer that even Weyerhaeuser admitted was the equivalent of some $700 million in cash.

The issue seemed decided. Bodcaw accepted IP's bid and the deal was submitted in preliminary form to the Securities and Exchange Commission for registration. The government was expected to declare the registration effective on or before July 2.

What Bodcaw and IP hadn't counted on, however, was the combined perseverance of both William Tavoulareas, Mobil's president, and George Weyerhaeuser. Sometime during May or June, Tavoulareas called Weyerhaeuser and proposed a joint bid against IP—a partnership to be divided along the same lines as Weyerhaeuser's first arrangement with Bill O'Boyle. Weyerhaeuser would get the timberlands, the mill, and the farmlands, and Mobil would get the oil and gas. On July 2, almost minutes before the SEC officially responded to the IP-Bodcaw registration, Weyerhaeuser offered $655 million in cash.

The offer was accompanied by certain conditions, one of which was that the merger of Bodcaw and Weyerhaeuser would take place only if the sale of the oil properties from Weyerhaeuser to Mobil directly following that merger occurred without any legal tangles. There was also an item stating that if the Bodcaw board decided against the Weyerhaeuser offer, then Weyerhaeuser would take it upon itself to directly approach the Bodcaw stockholders and try to purchase their shares.

Bodcaw rejected the offer seven days later, stating its continued support of IP's preferred-stock deal. At about the same time, it announced that it was going to hold a meeting on July 31 at which the merger with IP, supported by the full board, would be formally presented to the stockholders for a vote.

The reasons for the rejection reflected the company's standard bias against cash, but in addition there was a newly formed prejudice against Mobil itself. Since the first go-around in February, Mobil had acquired General Crude and had become, along with other oil companies, the target of both Congress and President Carter, who were increasingly irritated at the oil companies' recent fabulous profits and their present acquisitiveness. Bodcaw was fearful that the sale of its oil and gas properties to Mobil might arouse the enthusiasms of the government's antitrust people. Considering Weyerhaeuser's condition that its bid for Bodcaw would be null and void if the associated Weyerhaeuser-Mobil deal collapsed, Bodcaw could hardly be blamed for its lack of interest.

Nevertheless, on July 19, Weyerhaeuser came back with $695 million in cash and instituted a suit against Bodcaw to stop the sale to IP from going through at the July 31 meeting. It also began intensively wooing Bodcaw shareholders, as it had promised it would. One of them, who was vacationing in Michigan at the time, remembered being told by a Weyerhaeuser representative that if he signed his proxy over to them, they would fly a jet up to Michigan to pick it up so they could present it at the stockholder's meeting.

Now that the total difference in bids had climbed to $85 million, the Bodcaw board could no longer justifiably back IP without running the risk of a stockholder suit similar to the landmark Delaware case. It therefore circulated a letter among the shareholders on July 23 that it was withdrawing its prior recommendation to approve the IP merger and was assuming a neutral position. The letter also announced that both IP and Weyerhaeuser would be present at the upcoming meeting to make their pitches.

Just five days before that meeting, Weyerhaeuser further sweetened its pie by adding that as an alternative to a flat cash payment, it would also offer an installment-note option for those shareholders who wished to defer the tax bite. Additionally, it was dropping its condition that a merger could only go through if the Mobil-Weyerhaeuser oil transfer was successful.

It was obvious Weyerhaeuser was worried. Don Brennan of IP and Jim Heldt had been circling each other now for over two years, coming close enough on occasion that twice Brennan thought he had sealed a deal. This time, they had even written a contract and mailed out proxy cards to the Bodcaw shareholders. Weyerhaeuser was beginning to look like a spurned lover trying to break up the wedding.

In addition, Weyerhaeuser was nervous of the black cloud Mobil was carrying over its head. As a result, on July 27, with just four days to go, it released a statement that it would present a resolution on the thirty-first to adjourn the meeting until either Weyerhaeuser or IP was cleared by the Federal Trade Commission to consummate its bid.

That caused one final flurry. On the same day of that statement, Herbert C. Rule III, a Little Rock lawyer with seventy-seven shares, filed suit in New Orleans to also adjourn the meeting, stating the need to "review complex material" as the reason. Whether Rule was acting for Weyerhaeuser or operating independently wasn't revealed, although the coincidence is interesting.

In any case, the effort failed. Over the weekend of the twenty-eighth and twenty-ninth, Judge Morey Sear of the federal district court refused to allow the postponement.

And so the scene was finally set. On the Tuesday morning of July 31, 1979, over 450 people tried to cram into Bodcaw's Dallas offices.

> The program called for the meeting to take place in the boardroom of the Bodcaw Company. It was a fairly modest room—twenty by thirty, maybe more, but three-hundred-odd people tried to get into it. It was out of control, and Heldt took off across the street to see if he could get the ballroom of the Hilton Hotel on an hour's notice. And the whole mob traipsed over there; and it kept getting larger. I suspect a fair number of people at that meeting had no idea of what was going on—they were just folks who wandered in from

the lobby of the hotel. It looked like there was on the order of five hundred or six hundred people, and there were only two hundred eighty stockholders of record, some such number as that.

So what happened was, people got out their Bodcaw certificates which they hadn't seen in years, and husbands and wives, children, and cousins came—people who hadn't seen each other in years. So it was kind of a family reunion.

After Heldt laid out the details of what had led to this meeting, he gave the floor to Don Brennan of IP. Brennan, internally, was on the edge of his seat. Up until a few days ago, he had finally succeeded—the deal was signed, sealed, and almost delivered. Now, as he stood up in a ballroom full of people, he was already feeling the rug being pulled out from under him. This was to have been a mere formality—a ceremonial showing of hands with the full backing of the board. All of a sudden, he was standing alone.

Nonetheless, he came on like one of the family. He sympathized with the gathered shareholders for all the harassment they'd put up with from Weyerhaeuser and stressed that IP had played all the way by the rules that their own Jim Heldt had set up. All the wrinkles had been ironed out to Bodcaw's satisfaction: the deal was for a lot of money, was tax-free, was set in concrete, was not in danger of any obvious antitrust problems, and IP had even gathered the support of all of Bodcaw's customers, who naturally had become nervous at the prospect of losing their contracts. Brennan sat down on a final note, mentioning that if the stockholders gave his contract the nod, it could be in effect as soon as three weeks from that very day.

Bob Schuyler, Weyerhaeuser's senior vice-president of finance and long-range planning, then took the podium. With an easy manner and an uncanny resemblance to actor Alan Alda, he took a folksy, familiar approach. He compared the dynastic backgrounds of both Bodcaw and the Weyerhaeuser Company and mentioned what great friends John O'Boyle and George Weyerhaeuser were, which really wasn't true. He also implied Jim Heldt's original visit to Weyerhaeuser in 1977 was a result of

Weyerhaeuser's vice-president, Robert Schuyler

that bond and was the reason that Weyerhaeuser was in Dallas as a bidder, which was also stretching things a mite. But his main pitch, and it was undeniably appealing, was that they were all listening to the low bidder, Don Brennan, who had lost the earlier backing of the Bodcaw board, say that they should all go with IP.

Schuyler's major ace in the hole was IP's form of payment, which again had been tailored to Heldt's specifications. Brennan had put a bright face on the tax-free stock swap, but even from him it had sounded a little complicated. Schuyler played that up to the hilt. He went to great lengths outlining the complexities of a stock deal—the fluctuations in capital gains, IP's right to redeem its preferred stock in seven years, the fact that the preferred stock was new, "with no existing market," and that, beginning in 1985, IP would be obligated to redeem 7 percent of their stock by lot each year in any case, making a stockholder's long-range tax planning difficult.

Weyerhaeuser, on the other hand, was offering "cash on the barrel head." Alternatively, it was offering installment notes reaching out to the year 2004, bearing an interest rate of 9.3 percent.

Brennan's rebuttal only added fuel to Schuyler's fire. In an attempt to appeal to the cash-hungry in the crowd, he mentioned that the IP offer included a cash option of up to 20 percent of the total price which could be paid without endangering the tax-free aspects of the overall offer—an alternative called "appraisal rights." While he explained the intricacies of how this worked, there was a tangible numbing of brains among the audience. Also, during the question-answer period, there was—ominously, for Brennan—a growing interest in cash.

> This was quite a show. People had no idea what they were coming to. It might have been the first stockholder meeting that anyone had physically attended. You could have sent in your proxy, but all these people came. There were forms to be filled out, and I recall there weren't enough forms to go around. Folks hadn't eaten, so there was a constant trail of people going in and out the doors with hot dogs and sodas.

> People were very upset with each other because they thought something bad was going to happen to them. It was an odd situation.

Matters became so heated concerning the appraisal rights that it became obvious that 20 percent cash might not be enough. IP began to twist and turn, explaining that alternative merger arrangements could supply a larger percentage of cash and still maintain a tax-free stock payment. With that, Schuyler pounced, asking how the audience could conceivably approve a contract that was starting to change before their very eyes. He drummed home his main thesis: allow both Weyerhaeuser and IP to firm up their proposals, have both of them clear the Federal Trade Commission, and then vote. All that can happen is that the final selling price will probably go up.

The argument was compelling. John Connor, representing 23.5 percent of the Bodcaw stock, stood up and moved to vote against the IP merger proposal. Heldt, who had worked so long and so doggedly to maintain the tax-free stock transaction, had to concede he'd been backing a share-majority but a shareholder-minority position. He too rose as a private shareholder and voted against the merger, mentioning that Hannah Davis was in agreement.

The final vote was 1,099 shares for the merger, 182,055 against. As Heldt summed up, "The proposal has been defeated and we are now faced with the necessity of going forward. As you can see from the tone of my voice, voting against that matter was very difficult for me."

He did, however, have the last word. He added that such a meeting would not take place again, that things would move quickly from now on, and that he was not about to wait around for the FTC to pass judgment on both Weyerhaeuser's and IP's proposals.[6] Instead, he was going to hammer out the differences between the two competitors, and with the written consent of 51 percent or better of the Bodcaw stockholders, the board was going to pick the winner. With that, the meeting adjourned. As Brennan was to admit years later, "That was not one of the great days of my life."

Felix Rohatyn of Lazare Frères

The top brass at IP could only agree. At $610 million, they were paying top dollar for the part of Bodcaw they could see and evaluate. The wild card, as it had been for Weyerhaeuser, was the oil and gas properties, which were largely unappraisable. Not only were they an unknown quantity physically, they were also virtually impossible to price—1979 was the year oil values went through the roof. With Mobil's arrival on the scene, however, a general figure began to emerge. As part of the legal shenanigans prior to the July 31 meeting, Weyerhaeuser and Mobil, being publicly held companies, had to make public the approximate totals they were going to bid. Mobil, interested solely in the oil and gas, came in with a figure of $175 million. Thus, while the actual worth of Bodcaw's minerals might still have been a mystery, Mobil had given IP an insight to their potential market value.

Keeping Brennan in charge, IP removed First Boston Corporation, which had been IP's investment banker for years, from its exclusive position and forced it to coexist with newly hired Lazard Frères. Then they approached Placid Oil, H. L. Hunt's company, to arrange a secret partnership, the terms of which were similar to Weyerhaeuser's and Mobil's. All this was done in a matter of days, since Heldt, true to his word, was calling for an auction at his office on August 9.

> Placid was a private company, and their ability to make expeditious decisions was quite good. I had had conversations over the year with the Placid folks, where we had chatted about the idea of maybe doing something together. But it never came to very much. [Now] it became very real. I think Placid viewed Mobil's intrusion into their area of interest to be detrimental, both from a strategic standpoint as well as precluding them from the opportunity to develop the properties that they knew well.
>
> [After] the stockholder's meeting, I remember going back to Dallas to talk the concept out with the Placid folks. We met at Love Field, the airport, and then got back on the plane, flew back to New York, got board authorization to do

it, and went back on a Thursday or Friday to the auction. I remember three trips to Dallas in a week.

The agreement with Placid called for their supplying IP with a maximum of $205 million, bringing IP's war chest up to a total of $815 million. This was versus Weyerhaeuser and Mobil's published total of approximately $775 million.

Heldt in the meantime had conceded to the mood of the stockholder's meeting and arranged for a cash-only auction. He shuttled between the two bidders and quickly drew up duplicate contracts—one with Weyerhaeuser, and another with IP.[7] The only portion left blank in both copies was the selling price.

On Thursday, August 9, George Weyerhaeuser and William Tavoulareas showed up personally at Heldt's office, representing their companies. Don Brennan was there for IP, and Felix Rohatyn stood in for Lazard Frères. Brennan also had two open phone lines to IP's president, Edwin Gee, and its chairman, J. Stanford Smith. This time, IP was covering as many bets as it could.

> The way Heldt set it up, he set a minimum price that both groups would have to meet [$696 million]. It was to be a never-to-be-repeated type of auction where there was technically an upset price and both teams were required to submit bids at least $1 million in excess of that. If the lower bidder decided he wanted to improve his bid, he had fifteen minutes to increase the size, and vice versa."

Both teams were given private offices in opposite wings. In the boardroom were assembled enough of the major stockholders to guarantee the 51 percent minimum vote necessary to lock in the final transaction. Heldt, too, was taking no chances. One observer recalled, "You never saw so many white-faced, highly placed corporate executives scurrying back and forth. They were going in and presenting their bids and coming back and looking worried. It was wonderfully entertaining. And of course everyone was wondering, you know, what was going on."

As was the Weyerhaeuser team. Because of Placid's invisibility, Weyerhaeuser couldn't guess the source of IP's sudden surge of cash, and imagined that IP might be merely stretching its reserves in a desperate move to win. That element of combat, of seeking the other side's weakness and of emerging triumphant, definitely played a part in the bidding, especially with men with such recognizably combative profiles as George Weyerhaeuser and Bill Tavoulareas. But some two hours into the process, the tables were turned. With their $775 million already on the table, Weyerhaeuser and Tavoulareas increased their bid to $800 million and waited. IP came back with $805 million. Weyerhaeuser quit.

> There's no question during the course of this thing, you get caught up in it. You get more convinced the values are there and the mineral values look bigger and bigger. Now at a point that stops, of course. Somebody stops. It would be interesting to know what IP was prepared . . . Well, here was our friend Felix [Rohatyn] on the phone wheeling and dealing with New York, and they were going to go. I don't know. I was making my own judgment. We got to a point where enough was enough.

Heldt took IP's final bid into the boardroom where it was instantly approved. The Bodcaw Company forever left the control of the Buchanan family.

The sale of Bodcaw was called by *Fortune* magazine "one of the biggest private land deals in U.S. history."[8] It was also one of the best-timed. Immediately following that heady summer, prices, especially for timber and lumber, began to fall sharply. Interviewed in April 1984, George Weyerhaeuser admitted, "If you asked me would we like to be managing that property today, my answer would be yes. And at those values, my answer would be no."

IP, which ended up with the property, and Jim Heldt, who benefited from its sale, are the only two who contend the price wasn't inflated, even given the optimism of the times. Insiders at IP, however, admit that as of 1984, the company still hadn't earned back what it spent. That, of course, is hindsight. As Weyerhaeuser's Bob Schuyler put it:

> Who could have seen President Reagan being elected, the Volker change, the monetary policy, the credit crunch, disinflation? They didn't buy bad property—they got hooked on externals. There could have been a different set of circumstances just as easily where they would have been very, very happy with it. They were optimistic—we were all riding the wave.

Part of IP's view of the outcome also concerns a less commercially measurable matter. With their purchase of Bodcaw, they were able not only to complete their paper-mill modernization program, but they were able to keep Weyerhaeuser out of their backyard. These are both very long-range achievements, and for the comfort they provide, they might have been worth the price.

Placid Oil had no such problems. With equal unanimity, people agree that the $188 million price Placid paid IP for the Bodcaw oil and gas properties as part of their arrangement was very decent—some even said a bargain. Unfortunately for Placid, the Hunts soon got into trouble trying to corner the silver market and had to dig deep into their pockets to get out of debt. That action seriously crimped the way Placid might have otherwise profited from the sale, but even so, they did all right, at least until further financial reversals forced them to seek chapter 11 bankruptcy protection in September 1986.

The stockholders of the Bodcaw Company fared very well, and the reasons why are still subject to debate. The central figure in the drama was of course Jim Heldt, the laurel-crowned victor of the entire process. In the eyes of many, it was he who single-handedly manipulated the sale process until it had reached the highest possible point. As one of the Weyerhaeuser team ruefully put it, "It's hard to argue with success."

And yet, as events clearly reveal, Heldt was not always in the driver's seat. By his own admission, if he'd had his own way he would have sold the company for almost $200 million below the final price. Similarly, in February, he had signed preliminary papers for \$475 million with Mobil, a company with whom he admitted he had the best relations at the time. In retrospect, of course, this appears as merely a shrewd conservative move on his part—a way of playing for time.

Bill O'Boyle is eager to leave the past alone and is not interested in rekindling old flames. Erstwhile members of his team have no such concerns. Their contention is that without O'Boyle's efforts, Weyerhaeuser would not have been brought into the bidding process and the Mobil deal with Heldt would not have been upset. But what about IP? It was Don Brennan, after all, who had started the whole process. Was IP just going to stand around and watch a valuable property disappear at a bargain price?

These points are moot. The most plausible interpretation is most likely an amalgamation of views. Jim Heldt, Bill O'Boyle, Weyerhaeuser, Mobil, Placid, and IP were all invaluable parts of the whole, each one playing one or more crucial roles. It is, in fact, the ever changing swirl of their alliances and challenges, of inexperience interacting with jaded self-confidence—rather than the actions of one individual—that brought the story to its lucrative end.

Epilogue

The Bodcaw Company no longer exists. Despite IP's earlier claims that the company would be kept alive as a subsidiary, it was soon absorbed by IP's massive bureaucracy. The Coushatta chip-'n-saw mill still operates—marginally, despite impressive additional expenditures—and Pineville Kraft turns out high-quality linerboard. But the forestlands are unrecognizable.

Bodcaw's decades-long plans to develop a cyclical, ever richer timber crop have been scrapped. Many of those acres, found stripped by Seeger in the 1940s, are denuded once more, victims of IP's global strategies to stay competitive.

The Bodcaw staff have largely scattered or have died; most of the younger members now work either for IP or Placid. Heldt arranged that this might be so, making both companies agree that all benefits, plus years counted toward pension, be the same or better than they were at Bodcaw. Bill Palmer, Helen Seeger, and most of the other people in power who stood firmly by their beliefs in the dark days following the Depression and the war are no longer alive.

Jim Heldt too is dead. After about a year working with IP, smoothing out the transition, he went into the oil and gas business for himself, working out of the original Bodcaw offices in Dallas. Although a millionaire many times over, he still found his greatest pleasure arranging deals and poring over contracts. He died in 1987.

Descendants of the founding families—Buchanans, Browns, Davises, Fergusons, Moores, O'Boyles, Seegers, and many others—mostly live lives of plenty. They've made homes in California and Texas, New York and Arkansas, and a surprising number still inhabit Texarkana. That they benefited from the sale can hardly be disputed: one neutral Texarkanan ruminated that he had never seen so many millionaires crop up so suddenly as he had during that summer of 1979. But surprisingly, the lucrative passing of the Bodcaw Company caused many of its beneficiaries more sadness than glee. An indefinable something had passed out of their lives—something to which they had paid little heed while it was there.

> A lot of people were very sad when the company was sold because it was sort of the end of an era, or the end of something. . . . I don't know. I think the company held the family together in a lot of ways.
>
> Somehow the fact that it was put together and held together through about four generations was important. It seems a shame that that tradition has been stopped.

There is comfort to be taken, however. It is true the land William Buchanan first visited on horseback finally slipped beyond his grasp. It is also true that this is probably as it should be, since those trees were not his to begin with. They died by his hand and were replaced by those who followed him, who were in turn followed by others who cut the trees down. But the appearance of some of that denuded Bodcaw land is misleading. Where before it indicated capitalist greed and waste, now it stands for an ongoing, evolutionary process—a process that William Buchanan inadvertently set in motion. Today, among the grass growing on those seemingly barren acres is a third generation of short and spindly pine trees.

> I was fortunate enough to fly in an airplane in the late forties on a course that took me from East Texas across Louisiana and Mississippi and on in toward Georgia. And in an aircraft looking across those states, you were looking at a vast, open, light brown area that was the same in each of those states. The early virgin forests had been removed. People were running cattle over open lands just trying to keep alive.
>
> But today when you make that same flight, it's just an

ocean of green. It's a good feeling to know that what we did, and were lucky enough to be in on from the start as charter members, was to put the South back on its feet in the forest products industries.

Notes

Chapter 1. The Beginning

1. The phrase is E. B. Long's and covers everything from campaigns and battles to "affairs," occupations, and reconnaissances. E. B. Long with Barbara Long, *The Civil War Day by Day* (Garden City, N.Y.: Doubleday and Co., 1971), 719.

2. There is one report that James Wortham Buchanan was a paymaster in the Confederate army. This is not supported, however, by either the National Archives records in Washington, D.C., or those available locally in Tennessee.

3. By today's standards, this would seem appropriate. His grandfather, William Buchanan—whose name he gave his eldest son—had emigrated to Lancaster, Pennsylvania, fought with Washington's troops as a sergeant during the Revolution, and was an uncle of President James Buchanan.

4. There is one contention that William set out at the invitation of an old friend named Marshall Northcott, who was supposed to have been living in the Forrest City, Arkansas, area at the time. Similarly, it has been said that William's migration was prompted by relatives who had preceded him west. These relatives have been variously identified as being named Moore, Brown, or Buchanan.

5. In chronological order, they are Forrest City, Arkansas; Texarkana, Texas; Buchanan, Texas; Leadville, Colorado; Stamps, Arkansas; and Springhill, Selma, Trout, Good Pine, and Tall Timber, all in Louisiana. While several of these communities, like Forrest City and Texarkana, existed prior to his arrival, their charters were either a few months old or had yet to be written.

6. Bodcaw Lumber Company minutes, book 3, 1924.

7. Considering that truthfulness to the tax collector back in those days was a matter of degree, all these income figures should be viewed with the assumption that they are at best low estimates. Nonetheless, when compared with one another, they do earn a certain statistical merit.

8. Will was to become the eldest child. By the mid-1890s, both of his older sisters had died of "appendicitis," actually probably influenza or a gastrointestinal virus. Will's full name was William J. Buchanan, but he was always referred to as "Will" by the family, "Young Will" by the workers, and "Bill" by many of his Texarkana drinking and gambling buddies.

9. "Bodcaw" comes from the name local Indians gave a nearby creek.

10. In 1890, however, he declared bankruptcy, his bank having issued a railroad bond that went sour. By this date, however, his son's Bodcaw deal had already gone through, so it is not unlikely that J.W. helped William to a certain extent.

11. A less happy source of income may well have been from the estate of Joseph Ferguson, who died in August 1889. It was certainly after this date that William began seriously to accumulate Bodcaw stock.

Chapter 2. The Buildup

1. And a first marriage. There is no family recollection of the twenty-two-year-old woman named Cansada whom Robert listed as his wife in the 1880 Colorado census. One immediate relative suspects that the relationship was less blessed by the laws of convention than Robert let on. In any case, for six years at least, it seems they enjoyed one another's company. It wasn't until late 1885 that he transferred ownership of his house to her, and he still claimed residence there until he left town one year after that.

2. Of course, white farmers didn't have that memory. Instead, they harked back to a countryside that had largely excluded black farmers—a reminiscence that allowed them to pin all their current problems on there being too many black farmers working for too low a price.

3. This is not to imply that Buchanan did not hire locally. By the time a mill was well under way and operating at peak capacity, a majority of its workers were locals. Nonetheless, the phenomenon of the imported crews existed and was resented.

4. Parrott Eason Turner, *Southern Killens,* privately printed (Abilene, Tex., 1982), 37 and 38.

5. Just to reiterate, they were, chronologically: Bodcaw in Stamps; Pine Woods in Springhill; Minden in Minden; Grant in Selma; Trout Creek in Trout; and Good Pine in Good Pine. The last mill, Tall Timber, would be added later in the town of that name. The last three mills were all clustered west of Jena, Louisiana.

6. In 1917, this changed somewhat. The Clayton Act, reflecting President Wilson's attempt to control Big Business, made it illegal for any one individual to be a director in any two or more corporations having a worth in excess of $1 million. As a result, William Buchanan resigned most of his directorships, but held on to his stock. The ease with which he sidestepped the law highlighted its general ineffectiveness.

7. *American Lumberman,* March 5, 1904 (reprint).

8. Taxes, on the other hand, could be a smoke screen to hide the lumberman's own greedy excesses. It is a statistical fact that interest rates on money borrowed to build these mills, and to purchase land and timber, hurt more

than taxes, which were on the whole way below value. It is, however, a modern human reaction to blame taxes for one's failures, even if the claim is disingenuous.

Chapter 3. Day-to-Day Operations

1. That, of course, meant a departure time of 5:00 A.M. Many of these men lived outside of town on their farms, which in turn could be an hour's walk away. Thus, in these worst cases, the work day began at four in the morning and ended at nine at night.

2. The term "flathead" came from the name given a small pine-dwelling grub that infested the trees of the area.

3. Otis Dunbar Richardson, "Fullerton, Louisiana: An American Monument," *Journal of Forest History* 27, no. 4 (Oct. 1983): 195.

4. Stuart Purser, *Applehead* (Gainesville, Fla.: Purser Publications, 1973), 79–80.

5. This may well account for the hostility with which this book was greeted in present-day Jena and Good Pine. While admittedly preachy and holier-than-thou, the book is given high marks by less-defensive old-timers for candor and accuracy in its depiction of the region's violence, brutality, and racism.

6. There were ferries, some of which were large enough to transport railroad cars across the water, but they were hardly the preferred mode of travel.

7. In fact, the L&A Railroad was a curious anomaly. Reputed in 1902 to be the only railroad in the country free of bonded indebtedness, it also paid few if any dividends and was always considered to be on the lean side financially. The common explanation for this is that William, who loved his railroad above all his other properties, lavished expensive attention on it, denying it the opportunity to build any appreciable profit margin.

8. This man was hired during World War I when wages rose abruptly in an effort to match an equivalent sudden rise in costs. After the war, both costs and wages settled down again.

9. Such a contract dictated that a worker be hired only on the condition that he never join a union.

Chapter 4. Mill-Town Life

1. According to an unnamed source quoted in the *Christian Science Monitor* in April 1948, these houses were so named "because you can stand at the front door and shoot a shotgun shell out the back." They were common to most company towns, whether located in the coalfields of the North

or the forests of the South. They were generally small, square, one-story buildings with symmetrically laid out rooms leading off of a central hallway.

2. There were also instances in some of the towns where the company never did provide the black quarters with piped water—it came later as a part of government-sponsored relief during the Depression.

3. There was one other advantage to having a lot of workers instead of a few machines, at least in the eyes of one owner; when that kind of modernization was proposed to him, he dismissed the machinery by saying, "Hell, no. It wouldn't trade at the commissary." Robert Maxwell and Robert Baker, *Sawdust Empire: The Texas Lumber Industry, 1830–1940* (College Station, Tex.: Texas A&M University Press, 1983), 75.

4. Geoffrey Ferrell, "The Brotherhood of Timber Workers and the Southern Lumber Trust, 1910–1914" (Ph.D. diss., University of Texas at Austin, 1982), 201.

5. C. Vann Woodward, *Origins of the New South* (Baton Rouge: Louisiana State University Press, 1971), 159–60.

6. Maya Angelou, *I Know Why the Caged Bird Sings* (New York: Bantam Books, 1980), 40.

7. This was the Pine Street Presbyterian Church, which originally was a member of the Cumberland Presbyterian Church. The Cumberland church, in 1869, segregated its black worshipers into the Colored Cumberland Presbyterian Church. The Texarkana church changed affiliations in Buchanan's time, joining in 1906 the Presbyterian Church in the United States of America, but its segregationist policy was unaffected by the change.

8. This one distinction was best revealed in the charter of a foundation he created just days before his death. One of the first resolutions passed stressed "that Negroes shall not be excluded from the benefits of the William Buchanan Foundation."

9. Purser, *Applehead,* 36.

Chapter 5. The Good Life

1. Pine Woods, though located in Louisiana, owned property in Arkansas, just as Bodcaw owned some in Louisiana.

2. The diagnosis of appendicitis in those days was a catchall for several common disorders, including influenza and a variety of gastrointestinal diseases causing hyperplasia of the appendix wall, resulting in a blockage resembling appendicitis. What doctors misdiagnosed as appendicitis became so widespread that people started calling it "appendi*seed*is," believing its cause was linked to eating seed-bearing fruit.

3. As an impressive example of value appreciation, it should be noted that those shares initially went for one hundred dollars apiece. Now, each of the same fifty shares is worth about fifteen thousand dollars.

4. James E. Coggin, *J. K. Wadley: A Tree God Planted* (Texarkana, Ark.: Southwest Printers and Publishers, n.d.), 30.

5. One of the more widely used catalogs of Wright's architecture is by William Storrer, *The Architecture of Frank Lloyd Wright* (MIT Press, 1974). The Irving house is catalog no. 165.

6. As is the question, Did Buchanan and Wright ever exchange words? One has to wonder why Buchanan, who could have easily afforded Wright's fee, didn't get the architect to actually do the work. Aside from obvious possibilities, such as bad timing for both parties, there is the more intriguing one concerning the personalities and tastes of both men: considering how Buchanan furnished the inside of his house, there would have been ample room for heated disagreement. According to the Wright Foundation correspondence files at Taliesin West in Scottsdale, Arizona, however, the two men never did meet or write to one another.

7. *Texarkana Gazette,* May 23, 1946, p. 1.

8. Coggin, *J. K. Wadley,* 26.

9. One of his children remembers how he used to spit into the fireplace; it was her job to wipe the tobacco-juice splatters off the white tile of the hearth.

10. Conversely, William is constantly praised as being "an educated man." In fact, he may have had no more education than Robert, and certainly had less than James. To this day, the figment of education in a person's makeup is often given more weight than its actual existence.

Chapter 6. The Bell Tolls

1. More happily, his twenty-one-year-old daughter Helen, who had accompanied him on the trip (as did the entire family), met her future husband, Stanley Seeger, on the staff at Mayo.

2. The reason he waited three years to take advantage of his own law was because he didn't want people to say that he had arranged its passage purely for his own benefit. As it turned out, rumors grew anyway.

3. In fact, legend blames the blaze that closed the Minden plant in 1918 on a disguised German agent who had arrived in town complete with accent and mysteriously expensive tools. The man, if he existed in the first place, vanished after the fire.

Chapter 7. Rebirth

1. The house was back in the news when it sold in 1957 as the single largest real estate transaction for a private residence in the city's history to that date.

2. Lloyd Blackwell, interview with author, June 29, 1984. Noted by request.

3. A process involving the matching of soil and environment to the appropriate type of tree to be grown.

4. John Hillis Carnahan, "Texarkana, Arkansas and Texas: A Study in the Relationship of Community and Government" (B.A. thesis, Harvard College, 1951), 2

5. Ibid., 86.

6. It sold for seventy-five thousand dollars two years after Hannah Buchanan's death. John Holman and Leon Kuhn, who made the purchase, hoped to convert it into a combination apartment complex and first-class restaurant. They also had plans for building several service stations on the corners of the property and for developing a string of commercial buildings along Seventh Street. Unfortunately, none of that worked out because the city wouldn't give the two men the needed financial support to make the conversion and yet maintain the outer appearance of the building. In frustration, they finally gave up, had the house torn down, and developed the land commercially from the ground up. The entire block is now a Ford dealership.

7. "Unitizing" a field means that all the interested companies unite to form a single field operator, with proceeds divided on an ownership percentage basis. The savings accrued from the nonduplication of effort and equipment can be considerable.

Chapter 8. Growing Trees

1. Elwood R. Maunder, ed., *Voices from the South: Recollections of Four Foresters* (Santa Cruz, Calif.: Forest History Society, 1977) 49. (The FHS has since moved to 701 Vickers Ave., Durham, N.C. 27701.)

2. Ibid., 50. This situation has its own cyclical irony. Modern forestry practices dictate that a certain amount of controlled burning is beneficial to tree growth—it keeps down highly flammable undergrowth and in the case of very young longleaf actually helps the tree fight disease. An added benefit is that the cattlemen appreciate it for grazing purposes and are more likely to let foresters do the burning at the appropriate time in the season instead of just dropping matches themselves—a public relations plus.

3. Fred A. Peevy and William F. Mann, Jr., "Slash and Loblolly Pine Plantation Destroyed by Hogs," *Forests and People* (1952): 20.

4. Lloyd Blackwell, "The Beginnings of the Louisiana Forestry Association" (Address presented at the 1983 annual meeting of the association in Alexandria, La., on Sept. 15, 1983. Provided courtesy of Mr. Blackwell.)

5. The hog law basically allowed landowners to round up hogs and to pen them. Fines levied against the hog owners were light, however, and there

was no compensation for a landowner's costs in erecting the pens and for feeding the hogs while they were in his custody. But it was better than nothing, and in 1960 both oversights were corrected in an updated hog law.

6. It should be pointed out that Tannehill was not fired. Feeling increasingly hemmed in by the newcomers, he stated his integrity was being questioned by Heldt's request for a documented expense voucher, and he resigned.

7. One of her favorite pastimes was to attend the "blowing in" of an oil well, which often amounted to a spigot being turned on and some black crude splashing into a ditch. Humorously acerbic as usual, when asked during World War II—a period of severe rationing—if she was thrilled at the addition of another well, she answered, "Hell, no. All I want is some gasoline."

8. The Buchanan Foundation never amounted to much. In the late 1950s, after Seeger's death, O'Boyle and Heldt, who considered it a "nuisance," tried to split it down the middle and give half of it to the University of Arkansas Medical School and the other half to Southwestern Medical School in Dallas. Some citizens of Texarkana became incensed. They claimed the foundation was set up to benefit Bowie and Miller counties (in Texas and Arkansas, respectively), and they sued to bring that about. Bodcaw lost the case. A settlement was reached whereby both medical schools would receive at least something, as would the Wadley Hospital which was just then being constructed outside Texarkana. That marked the end of the Buchanan Foundation.

Chapter 9. New Blood

1. In Arkansas and Texas, unlike in Louisiana, mineral rights may be retained in perpetuity. There is therefore no advantage in keeping the land.

2. *Kraft* in German means "strength."

3. Maunder, *Voices from the South,* 141.

4. Most of the farm project resulted from the reclamation of hardwood bottomland. The company primarily raised soybeans. Bodcaw's agricultural division was only marginally profitable.

5. According to International Paper's publicity magazine, *Viewpoints* (Sept.–Oct. 1979): 1–4.

Chapter 10. The Sale

1. Joe, whose actual name was Stanley Seeger, Jr., was rarely seen in the Bodcaw offices and usually communicated with the others through his sister Hannah. He finally left the board on June 5, 1979.

2. Bill inherited eighty-seven shares of the company that were not tied into the trusts his father had established. He was therefore a shareholder in his own right and in a position to make some demands of Bodcaw's leadership.

3. By October, Bremberg had quit Du Pont and was working for O'Boyle full-time.

4. The amount paid for this property came to $325 million, or over $1 billion in 1984 terms. This is interesting, considering that Bodcaw's final selling price, also in 1984 terms, was about the same.

5. As one business journal put it, this period was rife with "takeover fever." One large company after another was out shopping for attractive additions. Several of the firms involved in the Bodcaw sale were simultaneously involved in other major deals.

6. As things turned out, the FTC gave a vague preliminary approval almost immediately—just enough to allow matters to proceed.

7. In addition to cash, both contracts also allowed for installment-note options at 9.3 percent—in other words, what Weyerhaeuser had been offering from the start of the July 31 meeting.

8. *Fortune*, Sept. 10, 1979, 23.

Bibliography

Books, Theses, and Dissertations

Allen, Ruth. *East Texas Lumber Workers: An Economic and Social Picture, 1870–1950*. Austin: University of Texas Press, 1961.

Angelou, Maya. *I Know Why the Caged Bird Sings*. New York: Bantam Books, 1980.

Biographical and Historical Memoirs of South Arkansas. Goodspeed Publishing Co., 1890.

Brown, Nelson C. *A General Introduction to Forestry in the United States*. New York: John Wiley and Sons, 1935.

———. *Lumber: Manufacture, Conditioning, Grading, Distribution, and Use*. New York: John Wiley and Sons, 1953.

———. *The American Lumber Industry*. New York: John Wiley and Sons, 1923.

Brown, Stanley. *H. L. Hunt*. New York: Playboy Press, 1976.

Bryant, Ralph. *Logging: The Principles and General Methods of Operation in the United States*. New York: John Wiley and Sons, 1913.

Cable, George Washington. *The Silent South*. Montclair, N.J.: Patterson Smith, 1969.

Carnahan, John. "Texarkana, Arkansas and Texas: A Study in the Relationship of Community and Government." B.A. thesis, Harvard University, 1951.

Cash, W. J. *The Mind Of The South*. New York: Random House, 1969.

Chandler, Barbara, and J. Howe, eds. *History of Texarkana and Bowie and Miller Counties, Texas-Arkansas*. Texarkana, Tex., 1939.

Clepper, Henry. *Professional Forestry in the United States*. Baltimore: Johns Hopkins University Press, n.d.

Coggin, James. *J. K. Wadley: A Tree God Planted*. Texarkana, Ark.: Southwest Printers and Publishers, n.d.

Commager, Henry Steele, ed. *Documents of American History*. 2 vols. Englewood Cliffs, N.J.: Prentice-Hall, 1973.

Conlin, Joseph, ed. *At the Point of Production: The Local History of the I.W.W.* Westport, Conn.: Greenwood Press, 1981.

Curry, C. C. "The Buchanan Story." 1957. Manuscript.

Defebaugh, James E. *History of the Lumber Industry of America*. American Lumberman, 1906.

Ferrell, Geoffrey. "The Brotherhood of Timber Workers and the Southern Lumber Trust, 1910–1914." Ph.D. diss., University of Texas at Austin, 1982.

Fickle, James. *The New South and the "New Competition": Trade Association Development in the Southern Pine Industry.* Urbana: University of Illinois Press in association with the Forest History Society, 1980.

Hall, Orville. *Economic Problems of Arkansas Sawmills.* Industrial Research and Extension Center, College of Business Administration, University of Arkansas, 1963.

Hayes, Ralph. *Trees and Forests of America.* Bureau of Educational Materials, Statistics, and Research in the College of Education, Louisiana State University, 1945.

Howard, John. *The Negro in the Lumber Industry.* Industrial Research Unit, Department of Industry, Wharton School of Finance and Commerce, University of Pennsylvania, n.d.

Hurt, Harry III. *Texas Rich: The Hunt Dynasty from the Early Oil Days through the Silver Crash.* New York: W. W. Norton and Co., 1981.

Jensen, Vernon, *Lumber And Labor.* New York: Farrar and Rinehart, 1945.

Klorer, John, ed. *The New Louisiana: The Story of the Greatest State of the Nation.* New Orleans: Franklin Printing Co., 1936.

Lewin, Ronald. *The American Magic: Codes, Ciphers, and the Defeat of Japan.* New York: Farrar, Straus, and Giroux, 1982.

Long, E. B. *The Civil War Day by Day: An Almanac, 1860–1895.* Garden City, N.Y.: Doubleday and Co., 1971.

Marquis, Ralph. *Economics of Private Forestry.* New York: McGraw-Hill, 1939.

Maunder, Elwood, ed. *Voices from the South: Recollections of Four Foresters.* Santa Cruz, Calif.: Forest History Society, 1977.

Maxwell, Robert, and Robert Baker. *Sawdust Empire: The Texas Lumber Industry, 1830–1940.* College Station: Texas A&M University Press, 1983.

Merryman, Terry Ann. "Henry E. Hardtner: Reforestation Pioneer." Master's thesis, Louisiana Tech University, 1977.

Morison, Samuel Eliot; Commager, Henry Steele; and Leuchtenburg, William E. *The Growth of the American Republic.* 2 vols. 6th ed. New York: Oxford University Press, 1969.

Morris, Richard and Jeffrey Morris, eds. *Encyclopedia of American History.* 6th ed. New York: Harper and Row, 1982.

Nevins, Allan. *The Emergence of Modern America, 1865–1878.* New York: Macmillan, 1927.

Noble, L. H., and R. B. Everill. *From Forest to Woodworker.* Larchmont, N.Y.: Bruce Publishing Co., 1938.

Palmer, R. R. *A History of the Modern World*. New York: Alfred A. Knopf, 1965.
Purser, Stuart. *Applehead*. Gainesville, Fla.: Purser Publications, 1973.
Robbins, William. *Lumberjacks and Legislators: Political Economy of the U.S. Lumber Industry, 1890–1940*. College Station: Texas A&M University Press, 1982.
Schlesinger, Arthur. *The Rise of the City, 1878–1898*. New York: Macmillan, 1933.
Sindler, Allan. *Huey Long's Louisiana: State Politics, 1920–1952*. Baltimore: Johns Hopkins University Press, 1956.
Stampp, Kenneth M. *The Era of Reconstruction, 1865–1877*. New York: Vintage Books, 1965.
Storrer, William. *The Architecture of Frank Lloyd Wright*. 2d ed. Cambridge, Mass.: MIT Press, 1982.
Tarbell, Ida. *The Nationalizing of Business, 1878–1898*. New York: Macmillan, 1927.
Turner, Parrott Eason. *Southern Killens*. Abilene, Tex., 1982. Privately printed.
Urdang, Lawrence, ed. *The Timetables of American History*. New York: Simon and Schuster, 1981.
U.S. Bureau of the Census. *Historical Statistics of the United States, Colonial Times to 1970*. 2 vols. Washington, D.C.: Government Printing Office, 1975.
Wall, Bennett, et al., eds. *Louisiana: A History*. Arlington Heights, Ill.: Forum Press, 1984.
Ward, Henry. *Opening Memory's Door*. Texarkana, Tex., 1975. Original typescript supplied by author.
Williams, T. Harry. *Huey Long*. New York: Alfred A. Knopf, 1969.
Woodward, C. Vann. *Origins of the New South*. Baton Rouge: Louisiana State University Press, 1971.
———. *The Strange Career of Jim Crow*. 2d ed. New York: Oxford University Press, 1966.
Works Progress Administration. *Louisiana: A Guide to the State*. Hastings House. 1941.

Articles, Pamphlets, and Bulletins

American Lumberman, March 5, 1904. Reprint of material originally published by Alvin John Huss, 1973.
Brandt, Ray. "The History of the Kisatchie National Forest." *Forests and People* 1 (1963).

Bureau of Labor Statistics. *Lumber Wages and Hours of Labor, 1890–1912*. Bulletin no. 77. Washington, D.C.: Government Printing Office, 1913.

———. *Wages and Hours of Labor in the Lumber Industry in the United States: 1923*. Bulletin no. 363. Washington, D.C.: Government Printing Office, 1924.

———. *Wages and Hours of Labor in the Lumber Industry in the United States: 1925*. Bulletin no. 413. Washington, D.C.: Government Printing Office, 1925.

———. *Industrial Accident Statistics to the End of 1927*. Bulletin no. 490. Washington, D.C.: Government Printing Office, 1928.

———. *Wages and Hours of Labor in the Lumber Industry in the United States: 1930*. Bulletin no. 560. Washington, D.C.: Government Printing Office, 1932.

Burns, Anna. "Louisiana's Golden Age of Lumbering." *Louisiana Renaissance* 1, no. 1 (1977).

Cassady, John. "Researchers Study Louisiana's Cutover Pineland Production." *Forests and People* (Oct. 1952).

Chapman, Herman. *Factors Determining Natural Reproduction of Longleaf Pine of Cut-Over Lands in La Salle Parish, Louisiana*. Yale University, School of Forestry, 1926.

Collier, John. "The Southern Pine Story." *Forests and People* 1 (1963).

Corty, Floyd, and Alden Main. *The Louisiana Forest Industry: Its Economic Importance and Growth*. Department of Agricultural Economics and Agribusiness, Louisiana State University, Jan. 1974.

Creel, George. "The Feudal Towns of Texas." *Harper's Weekly*, Jan. 23, 1915.

Croker, Thomas. "The Longleaf Pine Story." *Journal of Forest History* 23, no. 1 (1978).

Delaney, Charles. *A Forest Management Report on the Nebo Oil Co., Inc.* Baton Rouge: Louisiana Forestry Commission, 1956.

Dowdy, Vernon. "The Forests That Oil Built." *Forests and People* 2 (1959).

Fickle, James. "Defence Mobilization in the Southern Pine Industry: The Experience of World War I." *Journal of Forest History* 22, no. 4 (1978).

Horn, Stanley, with Charles Crawford. "Perspectives on Southern Forestry: The *Southern Lumberman*, Industrial Forestry, and Trade Associations." *Journal of Forest History* 21, no. 1 (1977).

Kerr, Ed. "From Timber to Famine and Back Again: The Story of Louisiana's Forest Industries." *Southern Lumberman*, Dec. 15, 1956.

———. "The History of Forestry in Louisiana." Alexandria: Louisiana Forestry Association, 1981.

La Salle Parish Development Board. *La Salle Parish, Resources and Facilities*. Baton Rouge: Department of Public Works, Planning Division, State of Louisiana, n.d.

Louisiana Forestry Association. Minutes. Alexandria, La., 1947–.

Louisiana Forestry Commission. *Forest Landownership in Louisiana*. 3d ed. Baton Rouge, Jan. 1955.
Mann, William. "Pine Best-Suited to Choice Sites in Mid-Louisiana: Loblolly." *Forests and People* 3 (1953).
———. "Rapid Growth of Loblolly Pine." *Forests and People* (Jan. 1952).
Maxwell, Robert. "The Impact of Forestry on the Gulf South." *Journal of Forest History* 17, no. 1 (April 1973).
McWhiney, Grady. "Louisiana Socialists in the Early Twentieth Century: A Study of Rustic Radicalism." *Journal of Forest History* 20, no. 3 (Aug. 1954).
Phillips, Travis. "Louisiana Forests: 1880." *Forests and People* 2 (1955).
"Pineville Kraft, Louisiana's Answer to World Needs." *Forests and People* 1 (1969).
"Report of the Conservation Commission of 1910–1912." Baton Rouge, n.p.
Richardson, Otis. "Fullerton, Louisiana: An American Monument." *Journal of Forest History* 27, no. 4 (Oct. 1983).
Robertson, Charles, and Delos Knight. "The Coming of the Paper Mills." *Forests and People* 1 (1963).
"The Trout–Good Pine High School Reunion, 1921–1948." N.p., 1981.
Tynes, Terry Tuite. "La Salle Parish." Manuscript in Jena Public Library.
Ward, Glen. "History of Stamps, Arkansas." Original typescript, supplied by author.
Williams, Robert. "Cattle and Longleaf Pine Trees . . . Successful Combination." *Forests and People* 3 (1953).

Additional, Nonspecific Periodical Sources

Arkansas Democrat
Arkansas Gazette
Fortune
Four States Press
Jena Times
Lafayette County Democrat
Milwaukee Sentinel
New York Times
Texarkana Gazette
Time
Wall Street Journal
Webster Signal

Illustration Credits

Page 6: William Buchanan. Courtesy of Hannah Davis.

Page 8: Water well, Texarkana, 1874. Courtesy of the Texarkana Historical Museum.

Page 13: Buchanan's mill in Buchanan, Texas. Courtesy of the Texarkana Historical Museum.

Page 22: Robert Buchanan. Courtesy of Robert A. Brown.

Page 24: Large Bodcaw mill, 1902. Courtesy of Robert B. Watz of Southern Arkansas University, who made the copy negative under grants from the Arkansas Endowment for the Humanities and the Magale Foundation.

Page 26: Black workers. Courtesy of W. C. Brown, Jr.

Page 29: Minden Lumber Company. Courtesy of the Library of Congress.

Page 30: Virgin stand of yellow pine, entitled "A Broad View on the C. Childers Survey of One Hundred Acres in Livingston, Texas." Photograph by John D. Gress for the *American Lumberman* during 1907–8, courtesy of Stephen F. Austin State University, Forest History Collections.

Page 39: Shay locomotive. Courtesy of Robert B. Watz of Southern Arkansas University, who made the copy negative under grants from the Arkansas Endowment for the Humanities and the Magale Foundation.

Page 40: Flatheads. Courtesy of Ellis Dawson.

Page 41: Mule skinners. Courtesy of Elsie Seals.

Page 42: Cross-loading. Courtesy of Stephen F. Austin State University, Forest History Collections.

Page 43: Steam crane, photograph taken between Stamps and Minden. Note the two sections of portable rail the crane could place ahead of itself in order to crawl from car to car, piling logs behind it as it went. Courtesy of Doa Keith; copy negative by Robert B. Watz of Southern Arkansas University, working under grants from the Arkansas Endowment for the Humanities and the Magale Foundation.

Page 44: Timber crop. Courtesy of Stephen F. Austin State University, Forest History Collections, Thompson albums number 426.

Page 47: The log carriage, here at the Thompson and Tucker Lumber Company in Willard, Texas, 1907–8. Courtesy of Stephen F. Austin State University, Forest History Collections, Thompson albums number 58.

Pages 56–57: The Trout Creek Lumber Company. Courtesy of W. C. Brown, Jr.

Page 67: Bodcaw commissary. Courtesy of Robert B. Watz of Southern Arkansas University, who made the copy negative under grants from the Arkansas Endowment for the Humanities and the Magale Foundation.

Page 68: Trout Creek commissary. Courtesy of Elsie Seals.

Page 73: Young workers. Courtesy of Elsie Seals.

Page 82: A Sunday outing. Courtesy of Mildred Andrews.

Page 92: William Buchanan and Mary Seeger. Courtesy of Mary O'Boyle II.

Page 101: Grassy Lake. Photograph by Archer H. Mayor.

Page 104: E. P. Irving home. Photograph by Paul Carnahan.

Page 105: William Buchanan home. Courtesy of Wilbur Smith.

Page 120: Will Buchanan. Courtesy of Hannah Davis.

Page 122: James Buchanan. Courtesy of the Texarkana Historical Museum.

Page 124: J. A. Buchanan's mansion. The group standing before it, and on it, is unidentified. Courtesy of the Texarkana Historical Museum.

Page 125: Trio on railroad car. Courtesy of Mildred Andrews.

Page 128: State National Bank. Courtesy of the Texarkana Historical Museum.

Page 133: H. L. Hunt and companions. Courtesy of the Hunt Family Archives.

Page 137: Buchanan matriarchy. Courtesy of Mary O'Boyle II.

Page 138: The Seegers. Courtesy of Hannah Davis.

Page 139: The Seegers' Milwaukee mansion. Courtesy of Hannah Davis.

Page 143: John O'Boyle. Courtesy of Mary O'Boyle II.

Page 148: Jim Heldt. Courtesy of Mary O'Boyle II.

Page 149: Harvard Law Review. Phil Graham of Washington Post fame is holding the baton. Courtesy of Mary O'Boyle II.

Page 159: William Palmer. Courtesy of International Paper Company.

Page 160: Hand-planting with dibble. Courtesy of F. O. McDonald

Page 163: New trees. Courtesy of Hugh Burnham.

Page 166: Planting machines. From left to right: Meredith Corley, Otis Coon, and James Rozier. Courtesy of F. O. McDonald

Page 170: Seeger's legacy. Courtesy of F. O. McDonald.

Page 181: The Heldts. Courtesy of Mary O'Boyle II.

Page 192: The O'Boyles. Courtesy of Mary O'Boyle II.

Page 195: Pineville Kraft paper mill. Photograph by Tommy Kohara of the *Alexandria Daily Town Talk*. Courtesy of International Paper Company.

Page 205: James Heldt. Courtesy of International Paper Company.

Page 210: Don Brennan. Courtesy of Morgan Stanley.

Page 212: Bill O'Boyle. Photograph by Roy Blakeley.

Page 216: George Weyerhaeuser. Courtesy of the Weyerhaeuser Company.

Page 221: William Tavoulareas. Photograph by Terry Ashe. Courtesy of *Time Magazine*.

Page 226: Robert Schuyler. Courtesy of the Weyerhaeuser Company.

Page 229: Felix Rohatyn. Photograph by Bachrach. Courtesy of Lazare Frères.

Index